The New
Soup Bible

The New
Soup Bible

Another 200 wonderful recipes to inspire the emotions, excite the taste buds, warm the body and comfort the soul

Consultant Editor: Anne Sheasby

Published by World Publications Group, Inc.
140 Laurel Street
East Bridgewater, MA 02333
www.wrldpub.net

Produced by Anness Publishing Ltd
Hermes House, 88–89 Blackfriars Road, London SE1 8HA;
tel. 020 7401 2077; fax 020 7633 9499

www.hermeshouse.com; www.annesspublishing.com

If you like the images in this book and would like to investigate using them for publishing, promotions or advertising,
please visit our website www.practicalpictures.com for more information.

Publisher: Joanna Lorenz
Editorial Director: Judith Simons
Project Editors: Felicity Forster and Molly Perham
Editorial Reader: Rosanna Fairhead
Designer: Nigel Partridge

ETHICAL TRADING POLICY
Because of our ongoing ecological investment programme, you, as our customer, can have the pleasure and reassurance
of knowing that a tree is being cultivated on your behalf to naturally replace the materials used to make the book you are
holding. For further information about this scheme, go to www.annesspublishing.com/trees

ISBN10: 1-57215-136-6, ISBN13: 9781572151369
Printed and bound in China

NOTES
Bracketed terms are intended for American readers.

For all recipes, quantities are given in both metric and imperial measures and,
where appropriate, in standard cups and spoons. Follow one set, but not a mixture,
because they are not interchangeable.
Standard spoon and cup measures are level. 1 tsp = 5ml, 1 tbsp = 15ml, 1 cup = 250ml/8fl oz.
Australian standard tablespoons are 20ml. Australian readers should use 3 tsp in place
of 1 tbsp for measuring small quantities of gelatine, flour, salt, etc.

The nutritional analysis given for each recipe is calculated per portion
(i.e. serving or item), unless otherwise stated. If the recipe gives a range,
such as Serves 4–6, then the nutritional analysis will be for the smaller portion size,
i.e. 6 servings. Measurements for sodium do not include salt added to taste.

Medium (US large) eggs are used unless otherwise stated.

CONTENTS

INTRODUCTION

Soups are very versatile and can be made using many different ingredients. One of the great things about soup is that you can put a selection of fresh, raw and sometimes cooked ingredients into a pan with some well-flavoured stock, let the mixture bubble away for a short while, and within no time at all you have created a delicious, flavourful, home-made soup with very little effort.

Many soups are quick and easy to make and simply combine a few key ingredients with added flavourings, such as herbs or spices, whereas other soups – perhaps those ideal for a special occasion or a more substantial meal – may require a little more preparation.

Below: Tom Yam Gung with Tofu is a famous Thai speciality.

Some soups make ideal starters to a meal, and they are always a popular choice, while others are substantial enough to be meals in themselves, served with plenty of fresh crusty bread as an accompaniment. There are light and refreshing soups that are chilled, ideal for summer dining *al fresco*, and rich and creamy soups, perfect for meals shared with family and friends. Whichever kind you choose, it is well worth the effort to create fresh and flavourful soups in your own kitchen.

An essential ingredient in most soups is a good well-flavoured stock, preferably home-made. Stock (bouillon) cubes and stock powder save time, but it is hard to beat the flavour and quality of home-made stocks, and they are relatively easy and inexpensive to make.

Above: Meatballs in Pasta Soup with Basil makes a substantial main course.

Once you have a good basic stock, whether it is vegetable, fish, meat or chicken stock, there is a huge range of soups that you can create in your kitchen. However, remember that your stock will only be as good as the quality of ingredients used to make it – you cannot produce a good, tasty stock from old, limp, past-their-best vegetables! If you are really short of time, you could choose one of the chilled fresh stock products available from some supermarkets and delicatessens.

Very little specialist equipment is needed to make soups, although you will find that a food processor or blender is invaluable and will save time and effort when you want to purée soup mixtures before serving – although pressing the soup through a sieve (strainer) or using a hand-held blender are perfectly good alternatives. You will probably already have in your kitchen a good-quality, heavy-based pan, a sharp knife and chopping board, and a vegetable peeler.

The addition of an attractive garnish, perhaps a sprinkling of chopped fresh herbs, some vegetables cut in julienne strips, or a swirl of cream added at the last minute, will enhance even the simplest of soups. Soups may be served on their own or topped with a few crunchy croûtons or grilled croûtes.

Soups feature in every cuisine around the world – whether they are called gumbos, potages, broth, chowders or consommées. Now that once-unfamiliar ingredients are readily available in specialist food shops and many supermarkets, there is absolutely no reason why you cannot make these in your own home.

In summer, choose from light and refreshing soups such as French Vichyssoise, Chilled Avocado with Cumin from Spain, or Mexican Chilled Coconut Soup. Smooth vegetable soups include Irish Parsnip Soup, Caribbean Peanut and Potato Soup, or velvety Pumpkin Soup with Rice from Morocco. Chunky vegetable, legume, pasta and noodle soups are ideal winter warmers. You could try classic Russian Borscht with *Kvas* and Soured Cream, Tuscan Bean Soup or North African Spiced Soup. Pasta and noodle soups range from Borlotti Bean and Pasta Soup and Avgolemono with Pasta to more exotic choices, such as Malaysian Prawn Laksa and Udon Noodles with Egg Broth and Ginger.

Soups made with chicken, meat, fish or shellfish are full of nourishment and make a complete meal served with

Below: Corn and Red Chilli Chowder is for those who enjoy hot and spicy food.

Above: Soda bread is traditionally served with this Irish Country Soup.

slices or chunks of fresh crusty bread or bread rolls, served warm or cold. Here the choice is wide and varied – from traditional Irish Country Soup and Lobster Bisque to the more unusual and exotic Smoked Haddock Chowder, Vermouth Soup with Seared Scallops, Rocket Oil and Caviar, or Scallop and Jerusalem Artichoke Soup.

Each recipe in this book has easy-to-follow step-by-step instructions and a beautiful colour photograph to show the finished dish. Few dishes give more all-round pleasure than a good home-made soup, and in this wonderful collection of recipes the world of soups is yours to explore.

VEGETABLES

Using vegetables offers the cook an infinite number of culinary possibilities, including creating a wide range of delicious and flavourful soups. The choice of vegetables is immense, and the growing demand for organic produce has led to pesticide-free vegetables becoming widely available. Vegetables are an essential component of a healthy diet and have countless nutritional benefits. They are at their most nutritious when freshly picked.

Carrots

The best carrots are not restricted to the cold winter months – summer welcomes the slender, sweet new crop, often sold with their feathery tops. Look for firm, smooth carrots – the smaller they are, the sweeter they taste. Carrots should be prepared just before use to preserve their valuable nutrients. They are delicious in Carrot and Orange Soup, as well as being an important ingredient in many other soups and in home-made stock. Raw carrots, cut into thin julienne strips, make an unusual and attractive garnish.

Beetroot

Beetroot is the key ingredient in the classic Russian Borscht. It also combines well with other flavours, for example in Beetroot Soup with Mascarpone Brioche, which is a light and refreshing choice, or the more substantial Fragrant Beetroot and Vegetable Soup with Spiced Lamb Kubbeh. If cooking beetroot whole, wash carefully in order not to damage the skin or the nutrients and colour will leach out. Trim the stalks to about 2.5cm (1in) above the root. Small beetroots are sweeter and more tender than the larger ones.

Below: Celeriac is bumpy with a patchy brown/white skin.

Celeriac

Strictly speaking, celeriac is a root vegetable, as it is the root of certain kinds of celery. It has a similar but less pronounced flavour than celery, but when cooked it is more akin to potatoes. It is used in soups such as Celeriac Soup with Cabbage, Bacon and Herbs.

Swedes

The globe-shaped swede (rutabaga) has pale orange-coloured flesh with a delicate sweet flavour. Trim off the thick peel, then treat in the same way as other root vegetables. For soups, swede is usually peeled and diced, then cooked with other vegetables and stock until tender. It may be finely chopped and used in chunky vegetable soups, or cooked with stock and other ingredients, then puréed to create a smooth soup.

Right: Carrots give soup a sweet flavour, and add colour too.

Left: Beetroot's deep ruby-red colour adds a vibrant hue to soups. It is a classic ingredient of the Russian soup Borscht.

Above: Parsnips are best used in the winter months and make good, hearty, warming soups.

Parsnips

These winter root vegetables have a sweet, creamy flavour and are a delicious element in many soups. Parsnips are best purchased after the first frost of the year, as the cold converts their starches into sugar, enhancing their sweetness. Scrub well before use and peel only if the skin is tough. Avoid large roots, which can be rather woody.

Turnips

Turnips have many health-giving qualities, and small turnips with their green tops intact are especially nutritious. Their crisp, ivory flesh, which is enclosed in white, green and pink-tinged skin, has a pleasant, slightly peppery flavour, the intensity of which depends on their size and the time of harvesting. Turnips add a lovely flavour and substance to vegetable-based soups, for example Russian Spinach and Root Vegetable Soup.

Jerusalem artichokes

This small, knobbly tuber has a sweet, nutty flavour. Peeling can be fiddly, although scrubbing and trimming is usually sufficient. Store in the refrigerator for up to one week. Use in the same way as potatoes – they make good, creamy soups.

Potatoes

There are thousands of potato varieties, and many lend themselves to particular cooking methods. Main crop potatoes, such as Estima and Maris Piper, and sweet potatoes (preferably the orange-fleshed variety which have a better flavour than the cream-fleshed type) are ideal for using in soups. Potatoes are also good (especially when mashed or puréed) as a thickener for some soups. Discard any potatoes with green patches. Vitamins and minerals are stored in, or just beneath, the skin, so it is best to use potatoes unpeeled.

Buying and storing root vegetables

Seek out bright, firm, unwrinkled root vegetables and tubers, which do not have soft patches. When possible, choose organically grown produce, and buy in small quantities to ensure freshness. Store root vegetables in a cool, dark place.

Broccoli

This nutritious vegetable should be a regular part of everyone's diet. Two types are commonly available: purple-sprouting, which has fine, leafy stems and a delicate head, and calabrese, the more substantial green variety with a tightly budded top

Above: Trim the stalks from broccoli and divide it into florets. The stems of young broccoli can be sliced and used, too.

and thick stalk. Choose broccoli that has bright, compact florets. Yellowing florets, a limp woody stalk and a pungent smell are an indication of overmaturity. Broccoli adds flavour and texture as well as a lovely colour to soups. Once cooked, it is often puréed to create an attractive green-coloured soup. It is a versatile vegetable and combines well in soups with other ingredients.

Cauliflower

The cream-coloured compact florets, or curds, should be encased in large, bright green leaves. There are also varieties with purple or green florets. Raw or cooked cauliflower has a mild flavour and is delicious when combined with other ingredients to make tasty soups such as Curried Cauliflower Soup or Cream of Cauliflower.

Cabbage

There are several different varieties of cabbage, and one of the best to use in soups is Savoy, which has substantial, crinkly leaves with a strong flavour. Firm red and white cabbages are also good for soups as they retain their texture.

Left: Cauliflower can be used either raw or cooked.

Spinach

This dark green leaf is a superb source of cancer-fighting antioxidants. It contains about four times more beta carotene than broccoli. It is also rich in fibre, which can help to lower harmful levels of LDL cholesterol in the body, reducing the risk of heart disease and stroke. Spinach does contain iron but not in such a rich supply as was once thought. It also contains oxalic acid, which inhibits the absorption of iron and calcium in the body. However, eating spinach with a vitamin C-rich food will increase absorption. Spinach also contains vitamins C and B6, calcium, potassium, folate, thiamine and zinc. Spinach and other leafy green vegetables are ideal shredded and added to soups or cooked in them and then puréed to create flavourful, nutritious dishes with a lovely deep green colour, ideal for swirling cream into just before serving.

Pumpkins

These are native to America, where they are traditionally eaten at Thanksgiving. Small pumpkins have sweeter, less fibrous flesh than the larger ones. Pumpkin can be used in smooth soups such as Pumpkin Soup with Rice. Squash, such as the butternut variety, makes an alternative to pumpkin – Roasted Garlic and Butternut Squash Soup with Tomato Salsa will waken up the taste buds.

Right: Making soup is a good way of using up a glut of courgettes in the autumn.

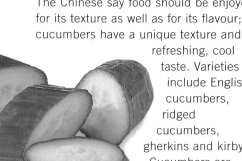

Below: Fresh, crisp cucumbers are excellent in chilled soups.

Above: Corn works particularly well in creamy fish-based soups.

Courgettes

The most widely available summer squash, courgettes (zucchini) have most flavour when they are small and young. Standard courgettes, as well as baby courgettes, may be used on their own or with other ingredients, such as mint and yogurt, to create delicious soups. They are a key ingredient in Greek Aubergine and Courgette Soup, served with tzatziki.

Cucumbers

The Chinese say food should be enjoyed for its texture as well as for its flavour; cucumbers have a unique texture and refreshing, cool taste. Varieties include English cucumbers, ridged cucumbers, gherkins and kirbys. Cucumbers are ideal for chilled soups such as Cucumber and Yogurt Soup with Salsa and Chilled Cucumber and Prawn Soup.

Corn

There are several varieties of corn – the kind we eat on the cobs is sweetcorn (corn). Baby corn cobs are picked when immature and are cooked and eaten whole. Corn and baby corn, as well as canned or frozen sweetcorn kernels, are all used in creative soup recipes such as Corn and Potato Chowder or Corn and Red Chilli Chowder.

Fennel

Florence fennel is closely related to the herb and spice of the same name. The short, fat bulbs have a similar texture to celery and are topped wtih edible feathery fronds. Fennel has a mild aniseed flavour, which is most potent when eaten raw. Cooking tempers the flavour, giving it a delicious sweetness. Fennel marries wonderfully with fish in Bourride of Red Mullet and Fennel.

Tomatoes

There are dozens of varieties to choose from, which vary in colour, shape and size. The egg-shaped plum tomato is perfect for many types of cooking, including soups, as it has a rich flavour and a high proportion of flesh to seeds – but it must be used when fully ripe. Too often, store-bought tomatoes are bland and tasteless because they have been picked too young. Vine-ripened and cherry tomatoes, together with large beefsteak tomatoes, have good flavour and are also good for soups. Sun-dried tomatoes add a rich intensity to soups. Genetically engineered tomatoes are now sold in some countries; check the label. If tomatoes are cooked with their skins on, you will find that the soup may need puréeing and straining to remove skins and seeds.

Peeling and seeding tomatoes

Tomato seeds can give soups a bitter flavour. Removing them and the tomato skins will also give a smoother result, which is preferable for many soups.

1 Immerse the tomato in boiling water and leave for about 30 seconds – the base of each tomato can be slashed to make peeling easier.

2 Lift out the tomato with a slotted spoon, rinse in cold water to cool slightly, and then peel off the skin.

3 Cut the tomato in half, then scoop out the seeds with a teaspoon and remove the hard core. Dice or coarsely chop the flesh according to the recipe.

Buying and storing tomatoes

When buying tomatoes, look for deep-red fruit with a firm, yielding flesh. Tomatoes that are grown and sold locally will have the best flavour. Farmers' markets are a good place to buy vegetables, or you could grow your own. To improve the flavour of a slightly hard tomato, leave it to ripen fully at room temperature. It is best to avoid refrigeration because this stops the ripening process and adversely affects the taste and texture of the tomato.

Peppers

In spite of their name, (bell) peppers have nothing to do with the spice pepper used as a seasoning. They are actually members of the capsicum family and are called sweet peppers, bell peppers and even bull-nose peppers. The colour of the pepper tells you something about its flavour. Green peppers are the least mature and have a fresh "raw" flavour. Red peppers are ripened green peppers and are distinctly sweeter. Yellow/orange peppers taste more or less like red peppers, although perhaps slightly less sweet. Peppers add a lovely flavour and colour to soups such as Gazpacho or Chilled Tomato and Sweet Pepper Soup.

Right: Peppers add wonderful colours to soups – red, green, yellow and orange.

Above: Puréed avocados make soups really creamy.

Chillies

Native to America, this member of the capsicum family is extensively used in many cuisines, including Mexican, Indian, Thai, South American and African. There are more than 200 different varieties, and they add a fiery spiciness to soups.

Avocados

Strictly a fruit rather than a vegetable, the avocado has been known by many names – butter pear and alligator pear to name but two. There are four varieties: Hass, the purple-black small bumpy avocado, the Ettinger and Fuerte, which are pear-shaped and have smooth green skin, and the Nabal, which is rounder in shape. The black-coloured Hass has golden-yellow flesh, while green avocados have pale green to yellow flesh. Avocados can be used to make tempting soups such as Avocado and Lime Soup with a Green Chilli Salsa.

Right: Aubergine is delicious in minestrone soups.

Aubergines

The dark-purple, glossy-skinned aubergine (eggplant) is the most familiar variety, although it is the small, ivory-white egg-shaped variety that has inspired its American name. There is also the bright-green pea aubergine that is used in Asian cooking, and a pale-purple Chinese aubergine. Creamy Aubergine Soup with Mozzarella and Gremolata is a delicious soup that will impress your dinner party guests.

Celery

Celery has a sharp and savoury flavour, which makes it excellent for soups and stocks. The tangy, astringent flavour and crunchy texture of celery contrasts well with the other ingredients. Most supermarkets sell both green and white celery (when celery grows naturally the stalks are green; banking up earth against the shoots makes it pale and white). Look for celery with fresh-looking leaves, and avoid any that have outer stalks missing.

Onions

Every cuisine in the world includes onions in one form or another. They are an essential flavouring, offering a range of taste sensations, from the sweet and juicy red onion and powerfully pungent white onion to the light and fresh spring onion (scallion). Pearl onions and shallots are the babies of the family. Shallots and leeks can be used in place of onions in many recipes, while spring onions may be used as a flavouring or garnish.

Buying and storing onions

When buying, choose onions that have dry, papery skins and are heavy for their size. They will keep for 1–2 months in a cool, dark place.

Garlic

An ingredient that everyone who does any cooking at all will need, garlic is a bulb that is available in many varieties. Their papery skins can be white, pink or purple. Colour makes no difference to taste, but the attraction of the large purple bulbs is that they make a beautiful display in the kitchen. As a general rule, the smaller the garlic bulb, the stronger it is likely to be. If stored in a cool, dry place and not in the refrigerator, garlic will keep for up to eight weeks.

Leeks

Like onions and garlic, leeks have a long history and are versatile, having their own distinct, subtle flavour. They are less pungent than onions, but are still therapeutically beneficial. Excellent in soups, leeks add delicious flavour and texture to many recipes. A classic combination of leeks and potatoes produces the popular soup Vichyssoise, which can be served hot or cold as a light starter. Commercially grown leeks are usually about 25cm (10in) long, but you may occasionally see baby leeks, which are very mild and tender and can also be used in soups. Try winter soups such as Chicken, Leek and Celery Soup or Irish Leek and Blue Cheese Soup.

Above: Garlic is used in meat and vegetable soups.

Above: Spring onions, shallots and onions add essential flavour to soups.

Above: Shiitake mushrooms are popular in Japanese soups.

Mushrooms

The most common cultivated variety of mushroom is actually one type in various stages of maturity. The button (white) mushroom is the youngest and has, as its name suggests, a tight, white, button-like cap. It has a mild flavour. Cap mushrooms are slightly more mature and larger in size, while the flat field (portabello) mushroom is the largest and has dark, open gills. Flat mushrooms have the most prominent flavour. Mushrooms are a useful ingredient in many soups, and add flavour and texture, as well as colour (especially the brown cap/chestnut [cremini] or field mushrooms). Fresh and dried wild mushrooms also add delicious taste to some soup recipes, such as Wild Mushroom with Soft Polenta.

Several varieties of wild mushroom are now available in supermarkets, for example oyster and shiitake. Oyster mushrooms are ear-shaped fungi that grow on rotting wood. Cap, gills and stem are all the same colour, which can be greyish brown, pink or yellow. They are now widely cultivated, although they are generally thought of as wild mushrooms. Delicious in both flavour and texture,

they are softer than button (white) mushrooms when cooked but seem more substantial, having more of a "bite" to them.

Shiitake mushrooms are Japanese fungi from the variety of tree mushrooms (called *take* in Japan, the *shii* being the hardwood tree from which they are harvested). They have a meaty, slightly acid flavour and a distinct slippery texture. Try them in Shiitake Mushroom Laksa.

Buying and storing mushrooms

Buy mushrooms that smell and look fresh. Avoid ones with damp, slimy patches and any that are discoloured. Store in a paper bag in the refrigerator for up to 4 days. Wipe mushrooms with damp kitchen paper before use but never wash or soak them.

Rocket

Usually thought of as a salad vegetable, rocket is actually a herb with a strong peppery taste that adds flavour and colour to soups such as Leek, Potato and Rocket Soup.

Sorrel

Another salad vegetable that is a herb, sorrel has a refreshing, sharp flavour. In soups it is good mixed with other herbs and green leaves, as in Sorrel, Spinach and Dill Soup. Salad leaves are best when they are very fresh, and do not keep well. Avoid leaves that are wilted or discoloured. Store in the refrigerator for 3–4 days.

Above: Rocket gives soups a strong, peppery flavour.

Above: Fresh sorrel mixes well with other herbs.

Cleaning leeks

Leeks need meticulous cleaning to remove any grit and earth that may hide between the layers of leaves. This method will ensure that the very last tiny piece of grit will be washed away.

1 Trim off the root, them trim the top of the green part and discard. Remove any tough or damaged outer leaves.

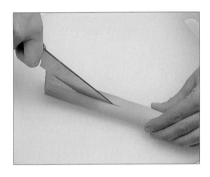

2 Slash the green part of the leek into quarters and rinse the entire leek well under cold running water, separating the layers to remove any hidden dirt or grit. Slice or leave whole, depending on the recipe.

LEGUMES

Pulses, lentils and peas provide the cook with a diverse range of flavours and textures, and they are a great addition to soups. They have long been a staple food in the Middle East, South America, India and the Mediterranean. Low in fat and high in complex carbohydrates, vitamins and minerals, legumes are also an important source of protein for vegetarians, matching animal-based sources when eaten with cereals.

PULSES

The edible seeds from plants belonging to the legume family, pulses are packed with protein, vitamins, minerals and fibre, and are low in fat. For the cook, their ability to absorb the flavours of other foods means that pulses can be used as the base for an infinite number of dishes, and many are ideal in soups.

Red kidney beans

These are dark red-brown kidney-shaped beans that keep their shape and colour when cooked. They are excellent in soups as well as many other dishes. Raw kidney beans contain a substance that cannot be digested and which may cause food poisoning if the toxins are not extracted. It is therefore essential that you fast-boil red kidney beans for 15 minutes before use.

Above: Dried broad beans can be used when fresh ones are not in season.

Broad beans

Usually eaten in their fresh form, broad (fava) beans change in colour from green to brown when dried, making them difficult to recognize. The outer skin can be very tough and chewy, and some people prefer to remove it after cooking. Broad beans add delicious flavour to soups – try Broad Bean, Minestrone or Catalan Potato Broad Bean Soup.

Cannellini beans

These small, white, kidney-shaped beans – sometimes called white kidney beans – have a soft, creamy texture when cooked and are popular in Italian cooking. They can be used in place of haricot (navy) beans and make a tasty addition to soups such as Pasta, Bean and Vegetable Soup.

Chickpeas

Also known as garbanzo beans, robust and hearty chickpeas have a delicious nutty flavour and creamy texture. They need lengthy cooking and are much

Left: Cannellini beans give soups a velvety and creamy texture, as well as extra fibre.

Cooking kidney beans

Most types of beans, with the exception of aduki beans and mung beans, require soaking for 5–6 hours or overnight and then boiling rapidly for 10–15 minutes to remove any harmful toxins. This is particularly important for kidney beans, which can cause serious food poisoning if not treated in this way.

1 Put the beans in a sieve (strainer) or colander and wash them well under cold running water.

2 Place the washed beans in a large bowl that allows plenty of room for expansion. Cover with cold water and leave to soak overnight or for 8–12 hours, then drain and rinse.

3 Place the beans in a large pan and cover with fresh cold water. Bring to the boil and boil rapidly for 10–15 minutes, then reduce the heat and simmer for 1–1½ hours until tender.

4 Drain and use as required.

used in Middle Eastern cooking, including soups such as Chickpea and Lentil Soup with Honey Buns and North African Spiced Soup.

Soya beans

These small, oval beans contain all the nutritional properties of animal products but without the disadvantages. They are extremely dense and need to be soaked for up to 12 hours before cooking. They combine well with robust ingredients such as garlic, herbs and spices, and they make a healthy addition to soups. Soya beans are also used to make tofu, tempeh, textured vegetable protein (TVP), flour and the different versions of soy sauce. Tofu is widely used in Asian soups – try Thai Hot and Sweet Vegetable and Tofu Soup, which uses tofu as an ingredient.

Buying and storing beans

Below: Chickpeas add heartiness to soups.

Right: Soya beans vary in colour from creamy-yellow through brown to black.

Look for plump, shiny beans with unbroken skins. Beans toughen with age so, although they will keep for up to a year in a cool, dry place, it is best to buy them in small quantities from stores with a regular turnover of stock. Avoid any beans that look dusty or dirty or smell musty, and store them in an airtight container in a cool, dark and dry place.

LENTILS AND PEAS

These are among our oldest foods. Lentils are hard even when fresh, so they are always sold dried. Unlike other pulses, they do not need soaking before being cooked.

Red lentils

Bright orange-coloured red split lentils, sometimes known as Egyptian lentils, are the most familiar variety. They cook in just 20 minutes, disintegrating into a thick purée. They are ideal for thickening soups. Try creative recipes such as Thai-style Lentil and Coconut Soup, or Spiced Lentil Soup with Parsley Cream.

Puy lentils

These tiny, dark blue-green lentils are superior in taste and texture to other varieties and are great added to soups.

Green and brown lentils

Sometimes referred to as continental lentils, these pulses

Above, from top: Red lentils and puy lentils make excellent thickeners for soup.

retain their disc shape when cooked. They take longer to cook than split lentils – about 40–45 minutes – and are ideal for adding to warming soups.

Peas

Dried peas come from the field pea, not the garden pea, which is eaten fresh. Unlike lentils, peas are soft when young and require drying. They are available whole or split; the latter have a sweeter flavour and cook more quickly. Like split lentils, split peas do not hold their shape when cooked, making them perfect for soups. They take about 45 minutes to cook. Dried peas require soaking overnight before use.

Buying and storing lentils and peas

Although lentils and peas can be kept for up to a year, they toughen with time. Buy from stores with a fast turnover of stock and store in airtight containers in a cool, dark place.

MEAT AND POULTRY

Packed with high-quality protein, meat is an excellent food and is used in a variety of soup recipes. Careful rearing means leaner animals and hence healthier cuts of meat, making it perfectly possible to follow current dietary advice while still enjoying meat and poultry. Nowadays we are spoilt for choice with all the types and cuts of meat available. Most butchers and many supermarkets with fresh meat counters are only too happy to advise you on the best cuts of meat to use for all your recipes, including soups.

Chicken

The stock from cooking chicken makes an ideal basis for many delicious soups. If you can, choose corn-fed, free-range or organic birds for the best flavour. Cuts used in soups include breasts, legs and thighs. Boneless thighs or breasts are a good buy.

Duck

There isn't much meat on a duck, so buy big rather than small birds or choose duck breasts. Although leaner than it used to be, duck is still a fatty meat, so remove as much of the fat as possible before cooking. Duck goes well with oranges, and Duck Broth with Orange Spiced Dumplings is a delicious recipe. Lean duck can be used instead of chicken in some soups.

Below, from left: Corn-fed, free-range and organic chickens give the best flavour for chicken stocks.

Turkey

A turkey isn't just for Christmas – today's smaller birds are perfect for soups. Try recipes such as Chinese Chicken and Chilli Soup, or Chicken, Leek and Celery Soup, using turkey in place of chicken.

Bacon

Used in soups to add flavour, bacon can be bought sliced, in lardons (thin strips or dice), or in a piece. It is available smoked or unsmoked (green), and in different cuts – back (lean) or streaky (fatty). Bacon is a key ingredient in Irish Kidney and Bacon Soup, and Bacon Broth.

Pancetta

Pancetta is belly of pork that is cured with salt and spices, and it is eaten either raw in very thin slices, or cut more thickly and used in cooking. It can be substituted for bacon in soup recipes. Try it in the delicious Bacon and Chickpea Soup with Tortilla Chips.

Above: Bacon and pancetta can be used interchangeably.

Beef, lamb and pork

Some soup recipes call for the addition of beef, lamb or pork. These not only bring flavour to a dish, but also make a valuable contribution in terms of nutrition, since they are a source of high-quality protein. When making soup, the best cuts of beef, lamb and pork to choose are steak, chops or fillet, although other cuts such as pork belly, neck of lamb and minced beef, lamb or pork are also used, so be guided by the recipe or ask your butcher for advice. Meat bones are also used for making stocks.

Kidneys

Lamb, pork and ox (beef) kidney may all be used in soups. Ox kidney has the strongest flavour.

FISH

Fish is one of the quickest and easiest foods to cook, and makes an ideal ingredient for soups. As well as being delicious to eat, it is also very nutritious and a great source of easily digestible protein as well as other important nutrients such as B vitamins. White fish such as skinless cod, haddock and monkfish are naturally low in fat. Oily fish such as salmon, trout and mackerel are rich in omega-3 fats, which are beneficial to health, and we are actively encouraged to eat oily fish at least once a week. Oily fish are also a good source of all the B vitamins as well as vitamins A and D.

TYPES OF FISH

We have access to a wide range of fresh sea fish, as well as river and lake fish, some caught from our local shores and others imported from further afield. Although some fish is seasonal, many varieties are available all year round from good fishmongers, supermarkets and town markets.

Both white fish, such as haddock, cod, monkfish and mullet, and oily fish, such as mackerel and salmon, are used as an ingredient in creative soup recipes. Smoked fish such as smoked haddock or smoked cod are also used to create flavourful soups.

Whichever type of fish you are using as an ingredient in your soup, it is always best to buy firm, fresh fish.

Below: Cod blends well with cream or milk to make delicious fish chowders.

Round sea fish

This is a large group of fish that includes cod, haddock, whiting and mackerel, as well as more exotic varieties such as John Dory (or porgy), red mullet or snapper and parrot fish. These fish have a rounded body shape with eyes at each side of the head, and swim with the dorsal fin uppermost. These fish are normally sold whole or in fillets, cutlets or steaks.

Flat sea fish

Plaice, dabs, turbot, sole and skate are common examples of flat sea fish. Flat fish swim on their sides and have both eyes on top of their head. They usually have a white (blind) side and a darker upper surface, which is coloured to camouflage them within their local habitat. Flat fish are usually sold whole or filleted.

Freshwater fish

Freshwater fish may live in freshwater rivers or lakes and include varieties such as salmon, trout and pike. They are usually sold whole or in fillets, steaks or cutlets.

Above: Trout makes a tasty alternative to the more usual clam chowder.

Smoked fish

Fish is usually smoked by one of two methods: hot smoke or cold smoke. Typical examples of smoked fish include haddock, cod, salmon, mackerel, trout and kippers (smoked herrings).

Below: Smoked haddock is sold whole, as fillets (shown here) or thinly sliced.

SHELLFISH

We are fortunate to have a good selection of fresh and frozen shellfish available all year round, either shellfish caught off our local shores, or varieties caught further afield and imported. Many shellfish and crustaceans have wonderfully exotic names and almost all shellfish is considered edible, from clams to razor-shells, sea snails and small scallops. Shellfish is at its best when eaten fresh and in season. Frozen shellfish is also available and is a good substitute if fresh is not available.

SHRIMPS AND PRAWNS

There are many varieties of shrimps and prawns, which are known collectively as shrimp in the United States. The smallest are tiny pink or brown shrimp. Next in size come the pink prawns with a delicate flavour. Then there are the larger variety of prawn, which turn bright red when they are cooked. They are highly prized for their fine, strong flavour. Best, and most expensive of all, are large succulent king prawns (jumbo shrimp) which have a superb flavour and texture. Similar to these is the cicala, which resembles a small, flat lobster. Shrimp and prawns can be used in a variety of different tasty soups such as Prawn and Egg-knot Soup, and Wonton and Prawn Tail Soup.

Buying shrimps and prawns

Shrimps and prawns should have bright shells that feel firm; if they look limp or smell of ammonia, do not buy them.

CRUSTACEANS AND MOLLUSCS

Crustaceans range from crabs and lobsters to bright orange crawfish. Squid and cuttlefish are molluscs – their shells are located inside their bodies.

Crab

There are dozens of varieties of crab, ranging from the large common crab to tiny shore crabs that are good only for making soup. All kinds of crabmeat, both fresh and canned, can be used in creative soup recipes. Try recipes such as Crab, Coconut and Coriander Soup, or Chinese Crab and Corn Soup.

Scallops

Scallops are available almost all year round, but are best in winter when the roes are full and firm. Always try to buy them with their delicious coral, although this is not always possible. You can buy them shelled, which saves the effort of cleaning them. But if you clean them yourself, the beard and all dark coloured parts must be removed before

Below: The common or brown crab contains plenty of tasty meat.

Peeling and deveining raw prawns

Raw prawns and large shrimps are often peeled before cooking. Raw prawns must have their intestinal tracts removed before cooking, a process called "deveining". It is not necessary to devein shrimps.

1 Pull off the head and legs from each prawn or shrimp, then carefully peel off the body shell. Leave on the tail "fan" if you wish.

2 To remove the intestinal vein from prawns, make a shallow incision down the centre of the curved back of the prawn using a small sharp knife, cutting all the way from the tail to the head.

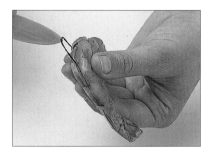

3 Pick out the thin black vein that runs the length of the prawn with the tip of the knife and discard.

Cleaning and preparing squid

Before you start, rinse the squid under cold running water.

1 Holding the body firmly in one hand, grasp the tentacles at the base with the other, and gently but firmly pull the head away from the body. As you do this the soft yellowish entrails will come away.

2 Use a sharp knife to cut off the tentacles from the head of the squid. Reserve the tentacles but discard the hard beak in the middle. Remove and reserve the ink sac, then discard the head.

3 Peel the membrane away from the body. Pull out the "quill". Wash the body under cold running water. Cut the body, flaps and tentacles to the required size.

they are cooked and eaten. Frozen scallops have little or no taste. Scallops are an ingredient in exotic soups such as Seafood Chowder, Vermouth Soup with Seared Scallops, and Scallop and Jerusalem Artichoke Soup.

Lobsters

These are the ultimate luxury seafood. Their flesh has a delicious flavour and makes wonderful soups. Lobsters must be bought live or freshly boiled. Try the luxurious, velvety Lobster Bisque topped with double (heavy) cream to really appreciate this superior seafood.

Squid and cuttlefish

These molluscs are indistinguishable in taste, but cuttlefish have a larger head and a wider body with stubbier tentacles. Once the bone has been removed, cuttlefish are very tender. The shell of a squid is nothing more than a long, thin, transparent quill. Both squid and cuttlefish have ten tentacles. Squid is more commonly used in soup recipes. Small squid and cuttlefish should be cooked briefly, just until they turn opaque, or they will become rubbery and tough. Larger specimens need long, slow cooking to make them tender, making them ideal for use in some soups. Try delicious Coconut and Seafood Soup.

Mussels

These shellfish have a smooth texture and sweet flavour. Both whole and shelled mussels may be used in soups, and they also make an attractive garnish, cooked and served in their open shells. Try flavourful soups such as Saffron-flavoured Mussel Soup.

Right: Queen scallops are smaller and cheaper than the larger king scallops, but have the same flavour.

Clams

There are many different types of clam, ranging from the tiny smooth-shelled variety to long, thin razor shells and the large Venus clams with beautiful ridged shells. All have a sweet flavour and a slightly chewy texture. Because they vary so much in size, it is best to ask the fishmonger how many clams you will need for a particular soup or be guided by the recipe. Try tempting recipes such as Clam Chowder or Chilli Clam Broth.

Buying and storing shellfish

When buying fresh shellfish such as scallops, mussels, clams and oysters, look for those with tightly closed shells. They are still alive when sold fresh, and any sign of an open shell may indicate that they are far from fresh. A sharp tap on the shell may persuade the shellfish to close up, but otherwise, avoid it. When buying cooked shellfish such as crab, lobster and prawns (shrimp), make sure the shells are intact. They should feel quite heavy and have a fresh, agreeable smell.

Once purchased, keep fresh shellfish chilled, and store in the refrigerator, covered with a damp cloth, until it is ready to use. As a general rule, fresh shellfish, as well as frozen (defrosted) shellfish, is best eaten on the day you purchase it or used within 24 hours – your fishmonger will be able to advise you more on the length of time recommended for storing shellfish.

PASTA AND NOODLES

The wide range of fresh and dried pasta available to us today ensures that you have plenty of choice when it comes to selecting which pasta to cook. Pasta is a nutritious food and plays an important part in a healthy, well-balanced diet. It is low in fat and provides a good source of carbohydrate. Pasta, especially small shapes such as stellette or pastina, is ideal for use in soups and is an important ingredient in recipes such as Pasta, Bean and Vegetable Soup.

SOUP PASTA

These tiny shapes, of which there are hundreds of different varieties, are mostly made from plain durum wheat pasta, although you may find them made with egg and even flavoured with carrot or spinach.

Types of soup pasta

Teeny-weeny pasta shapes are called pastina in Italian, and there are literally hundreds of different ones to choose from. In Italy they are always served in broths and clear soups, and are regarded almost as nursery food because they are so often served for children's meals.

Shapes of pastina vary enormously, and seem to get more and more fanciful as the market demands. The smallest and most plain

pasta per minestre (pasta for soups) is like tiny grains. Some look like rice and are in fact called risi or risoni, while others are more like barley and are called orzi. Fregola, from Sardinia, looks like couscous, and has a similar nutty texture and flavour. Semi di melone is like melon seeds, as its name suggests, while acini de pepe or peperini is named after peppercorns, which it resembles in shape and size if not in colour. Coralline, grattini and occhi are three more very popular tiny pasta shapes.

The next size up are the ones that are most popular with children. These include alfabeti and alfabetini (alphabet shapes), stelline and stellette (stars), rotellini (tiny wagon wheels) and anellini, which can be tiny rings, sometimes with ridges that make them look very pretty, or larger hoops. Ditali are similar to anellini but slightly thicker, while tubettini are thicker still.

Another category of pasta per minestre consists of slightly larger shapes, more like miniature versions of familiar types of short pasta. Their

names end in "ine", "ette" or "etti", denoting that they are the diminutive forms. These include conchigliette (little shells), farfalline and farfallette (little bows), funghetti (little mushrooms), lumachine (little snails), quadretti and quadrettini (little squares), orecchiettini (little ears), renette (like baby penne) and tubetti (little tubes). The size of these varies: the smaller ones are for use in clear broths, while the larger ones are more often used in making thicker soups.

Buying and storing soup pasta

The quality of pasta varies tremendously – choose good-quality Italian brands made from 100 per cent durum wheat, and buy fresh pasta from an Italian delicatessen rather than pre-packed fresh pasta from the supermarket.

Dried pasta will keep almost indefinitely in the store cupboard, but if you keep it in a storage jar, it is a good idea to use it all up before adding any from a new packet.

Fresh pasta is usually sold loose and is best cooked the same day, but can be kept in the refrigerator for a day or two. Fresh pasta from a supermarket is likely to be packed in plastic packs and bags and will keep for 3–4 days in the refrigerator. Fresh pasta freezes well and should be cooked from frozen. Convenient packs of supermarket pasta have the advantage of being easy to store in the freezer.

Left: Tiny soup pasta is available in hundreds of different shapes.

NOODLES

The fast food of the East, noodles can be made from wheat flour, rice, mung bean flour or buckwheat flour. Noodles can be used in a variety of flavourful soup recipes. Try some tasty soups such as Soba Noodles in Hot Soup with Tempura, Thai Cellophane Noodle Soup, Chiang Mai Noodle Soup, or Tokyo-style Ramen Noodles in Soup.

Wheat noodles

These are available in two types: plain and egg. Plain noodles are made from strong flour and water; they can be flat or round and come in various thicknesses. Egg noodles are more common than the wheat variety, and are sold both fresh and dried. The Chinese types are available in various thicknesses. Very fine egg noodles, which resemble vermicelli, are usually sold in individual coils. More substantial wholewheat egg noodles are widely available from larger supermarkets.

Udon and ramen are types of Japanese noodles. Udon noodles are thick and can be round or flat. They are available fresh, pre-cooked or dried. Wholewheat udon noodles have a more robust flavour. Ramen egg noodles are sold in coils and in Japan are often cooked and served with an accompanying broth.

Above:
Egg noodles add flavour and texture to Chinese soups.

Rice noodles

These very fine, delicate noodles are made from rice and are opaque-white in colour. Like wheat noodles, they come in various widths, from the very thin strands known as rice vermicelli, which are popular in Thailand and southern China, to the thicker rice sticks, which are used more in Vietnam and Malaysia.

Cellophane noodles

Made from mung beans, cellophane noodles are translucent and do not need to be boiled; they are simply soaked in boiling water for 10–15 minutes. They have a fantastic texture, which they retain when cooked, never becoming soggy.

Buckwheat noodles

Soba are the best-known type of buckwheat noodles. They are a much darker colour than wheat noodles – almost brownish-grey. In Japan they are traditionally used in soups.

Below: Cellophane noodles do not need to be boiled.

Left: Rice noodles form the basis of many Asian soup recipes.

Buying and storing noodles

Dried noodles are readily available in supermarkets. Packets of fresh noodles are found in the chiller cabinets of Asian stores and some supermarkets. They must be stored in the refrigerator or freezer. Dried noodles will keep for many months in an airtight container in a cool, dry place.

HERBS AND SPICES

Herbs, the aromatic and fragrant plants that we use to add flavour and colour to our dishes, have been cultivated all over the world for centuries. The majority of herbs are familiar as culinary herbs, but many are also good for medicinal and cosmetic purposes. In cookery, herbs are chosen mainly for their flavouring and seasoning properties as well as adding colour and texture to dishes. Herbs, both fresh and dried, add delicious flavour and aroma to a whole variety of dishes, including many hot and chilled soups.

HERBS

Herbs can make a significant difference to the flavour and aroma of a soup, and they can enliven the simplest of dishes.

Basil

This delicate aromatic herb is widely used in Italian and Thai cooking. The leaves bruise easily, so they are best used whole or torn, rather than cut with a knife.

Bay

These dark-green, glossy leaves are best left to dry for a few days before use. They have a robust, spicy flavour and are an essential ingredient in home-made stocks and for a bouquet garni.

Coriander

Warm and spicy, coriander (cilantro) looks similar to flat leaf parsley but its taste is completely different.

Dill

The mild yet distinctive, aniseed flavour of dill makes a good addition to soups, for example in Sorrel, Spinach and Dill Soup.

Kaffir lime leaves

These glossy green leaves are commonly used in Asian cuisines, lending a citrus flavour to soups. They are available fresh from Asian stores, or dried from large supermarkets.

Mint

Mint, a popular herb, has deep green leaves with an unmistakable strong and tangy scent and flavour. It is used in soup recipes such as Iced Melon Soup with Sorbet.

Oregano

This is a wild variety of marjoram with a robust flavour. It goes well with tomato-based soups.

Parsley

There are two types of parsley: flat leaf and curly. Both taste relatively similar, but the flat leaf variety is preferable in cooked dishes. Parsley is an excellent source of vitamin C, iron and calcium.

Above: Tarragon goes well with chicken and shellfish.

Above: Indian-style soups use spicy coriander.

Tarragon

This small, perennial plant bears slim green leaves, and its distinctive taste is said to be a cross between aniseed and mint. It marries well with chicken and shellfish in soups.

Thyme

This robustly flavoured aromatic herb is good in tomato-based soups, as well as soups containing lentils and beans. It is also an essential ingredient in a classic bouquet garni.

Buying and storing herbs

Fresh herbs are widely available, sold loose, in packets or growing in pots. Place stems in a jar half-filled with water and cover with a plastic bag. Sealed with an elastic band, the herbs should keep for about a week.

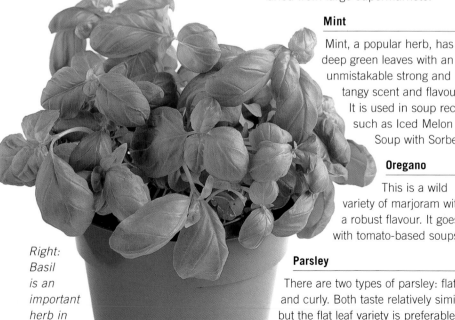

Right: Basil is an important herb in Italian cooking.

SPICES

Highly revered for thousands of years, spices – the seeds, fruit, pods, bark and buds of plants – add flavour, colour and interest to the most unassuming of ingredients, while the evocative aroma of spices stimulates the appetite. Spices add delicious flavour to many soup recipes.

Chillies

Chillies are available fresh as well as in dried, powdered and flaked form. Dried chillies tend to be hotter than fresh, and this is certainly true of chilli flakes, which contain both the seeds and the flesh. The best pure chilli powders do not contain added ingredients, such as onion and garlic. All types of chilli may be used in a variety of soup recipes.

Coriander

Alongside cumin, ground coriander is a key ingredient in Indian curry powders and garam masala, and in northern Europe the ivory-coloured seeds are used as a pickling spice. Coriander seeds have a sweet, earthy, burnt-orange flavour that is more pronounced than the fresh leaves. The ready-ground powder rapidly loses its flavour and aroma, so it is best to buy whole seeds, which are easily ground in a mortar using a pestle, or in a coffee grinder. Before grinding, lightly dry-roast the seeds in a frying pan to enhance their flavour. Coriander adds delicious flavour and warmth to soups.

Cumin

Cumin is a familiar component of Indian, Mexican, North African and Middle Eastern cooking and is added to soups to give a delicious flavour and aroma. The seeds have a robust aroma and slightly bitter taste, which is tempered by dry-roasting. Black cumin seeds are milder and sweeter. Ground cumin can be harsh, so it is best to buy the whole seeds and grind them just before use to be sure of a fresh flavour.

Ginger

Fresh root ginger is spicy, peppery and fragrant, and adds a hot, yet refreshing, flavour to soups such as the Japanese Miso Broth with Spring Onions and Tofu. When buying ginger, look for firm, thin-skinned and unblemished roots and avoid withered, woody-looking roots as these are likely to be dry and fibrous.

Left: Lemon grass stalks are essential in many Asian soup recipes.

Left: Cumin adds taste and aroma.

Lemon grass

This long fibrous stalk has a fragrant citrus aroma and flavour when cut. It is familiar in South-east Asian cooking and may be used as an ingredient in soups from this region. To use, remove the tough, woody outer layers, trim the root, then cut off the lower 5cm (2in) and slice or pound in a mortar using a pestle. Bottled chopped lemon grass and lemon grass purée are also available.

Pepper

Undoubtedly the oldest, most widely used spice in the world, pepper is a versatile seasoning and is invaluable for soups, because it not only adds flavour of its own to a dish, but also brings out the flavour of the other ingredients.

Saffron

The world's most expensive spice is made from the dried stigmas of *Crocus salivus*. Only a tiny amount of this bright orange spice is needed to add a wonderful colour and delicate flavour to fish and shellfish soups.

Salt

It is usually best to leave the seasoning of stocks and soups until the last minute, just before serving. Add salt a little bit at a time, until you have the seasoned flavour you require.

Buying and storing spices

Always buy spices in small quantities from a store with a regular turnover. Store in airtight jars in a cool place.

Above: Pink, black and white peppercorns bring out the flavour of your chosen soup ingredients.

OTHER FLAVOURINGS

There are many other flavourings that are used to add depth to soups – for example, olive oil, flavoured oils and vinegars, alcohol, chilli sauce, pesto and soy sauce, as well as more exotic flavourings such as dashi or fish sauce. Many add that important final touch or richness to a soup, contributing an important element to the overall character. Listed below are some of the flavourings used in this book.

Oils and vinegars

Flavoured oils and vinegars are brilliant for splashing into finished soups to pack an extra punch. Consider chilli oil for a super-fiery flavour in a spicy soup, or basil or rocket oil to enliven a fish or Mediterranean-style soup. Infuse virgin olive oil with chillies, roasted whole garlic cloves, whole spices, woody herbs or citrus peel instead of buying flavoured oil. Flavour and colour oil with soft aromatic herbs such as basil. Vinegar adds bite to some soups, so look out for the many types available, including wine vinegars, balsamic vinegar, sherry vinegar and fruit-flavoured vinegars, such as raspberry.

Left: Balsamic vinegar is used in Italian soups.

Alcohol

Add to soups in moderation. The golden rule is to simmer the soup for a few minutes to cook off the strong alcohol, leaving the flavour. White wine, Pernod and vermouth work very well with creamy fish soups.

Flavoured creams

These provide a wonderful way to introduce contrasting flavour to a finished soup. Crème fraîche or whipped double (heavy) cream can be transformed by adding a purée of fresh herbs, grilled (bell) peppers or sun-dried tomatoes. Infused saffron and pesto can also be added.

Flavoured butters

Flavoured butters can be spread on warm bread to accompany a soup, or added to each bowl just before serving. Flavourings range from herbs and spices to shellfish.

Coconut milk

Buy this in cans or long-life cartons, or make it yourself at home. Put 225g/8oz/ 2²/₃ cups desiccated (dry unsweetened shredded) coconut into a food processor, add 450ml/³/₄ pint/ scant 2 cups boiling water and process for about 30 seconds. Leave to cool slightly, then transfer to a sieve (strainer) lined with muslin (cheesecloth) placed over a bowl and gather the ends of the cloth. Twist to extract the liquid.

Left: Raspberry vinegar adds colour.

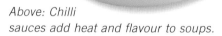

Above: Chilli sauces add heat and flavour to soups.

Pesto and pistou

Pesto and pistou are closely related, the latter hailing from southern France, where it is stirred into a rich vegetable soup. Both are made by mixing crushed garlic, basil and olive oil, and pesto also contains pine nuts and Parmesan cheese. Stir into soup to add flavour and colour.

Chilli sauce

For those who like very hot food, chilli sauce can be offered at the table, or a dash can be added to flavour soups during cooking or to individual servings of soup.

Soy sauce

Made from fermented soya beans, soy sauce is one of Asia's most important contributions to the global pantry. There are three types of Chinese soy sauce on the market: light, dark and regular. As a rule, light soy sauce is used for soups. It is the initial extraction, like the first pressing of virgin olive oil. It has the most delicate flavour and is light brown in colour with a "beany" fragrance.

There are several different types of Japanese soy sauce, too. Usukuchi soy sauce is light in colour and tastes less salty than the Chinese light soy. Tamari is dark and thick with a strong flavour, and is even less salty than the light type. Shoyu is a full-flavoured sauce that is aged for up to two years. In between, there is the very popular Kikkoman, a brand name for the equivalent of the Chinese regular soy sauce – neither too weak nor too strong.

The Indonesian kecap manis is thick and black, with a powerful aroma but a surprisingly sweet taste.

Soy sauce is used as a flavouring in Japanese soups such as Clear Soup with Seafood Sticks, and Sapporo-style Ramen Noodles in Soup.

Fish sauce

Fish sauce is an essential seasoning for Thai and Vietnamese cooking, in the same way that soy sauce is important to the Chinese and the Japanese. In Vietnam it is often made using shrimp, but in Thailand the sauce is more often made using salted, fermented fish.

All types of fish sauce have a pungent flavour and aroma and are very salty. Thai *nam pla* has a slightly stronger flavour and aroma than the Vietnamese or Chinese versions. The colour of fish sauce can vary considerably; lighter-coloured sauces are considered to be better than darker versions. Fish sauce is used as a seasoning in some soup recipes such as Coconut and Seafood Soup, and Thai Pumpkin and Coconut Soup.

Shrimp paste

Known in Malaysia as *blachan*, this is an essential ingredient in many South-east Asian dishes, including soups. It is made from tiny shrimps that have been salted, dried, pounded and then left to ferment in the hot humid conditions until the aroma is very pungent. The colour of the paste can be anything from oyster pink to purplish brown, depending upon the type of shrimp and the precise process used. It is compressed and sold in block form or packed in tiny tubs or jars. The moment you unwrap it, the smell of rotten fish is quite overpowering, but this vanishes during cooking. Shrimp paste adds depth and pungency to a soup, for example in Balinese Vegetable Soup, a popular dish served on beans.

Miso

Many Japanese start the day with a bowl of miso soup for breakfast. Miso is one of the oldest traditional ingredients. Boiled *daizu* (soya beans) are crushed, then mixed with a culture called *koji*, which is made with wheat and rice, barley or beans. The fermented mixture is allowed to mature for up to three years. Numerous kinds and brands of miso are available in supermarkets. They are categorized into three basic grades according to strength of flavour and colour: shiro-miso (white, light and made with rice). aka-miso (red, medium and made with barley), and kuro-miso (black, strong and made with soya beans). Miso is quite salty and has a strong fermented bean flavour. Try it in Miso Broth with Spring Onions and Tofu.

Mirin

This amber-coloured, heavily sweetened sake is used only in cooking. It is one of Japan's ancient sake and is made from *shochu* (distilled sake). There is a synthetically made, cheap mirin-like liquid available called mirin-fuhmi (mirin flavouring), as opposed to hon-mirin (real mirin). Hon-mirin has an alcohol content of 14 per cent, whereas mirin-fuhmi is only 1 per cent. Both are available in bottles of 300ml/$\frac{1}{2}$ pint/1$\frac{1}{4}$ cups or 600ml/1 pint/2$\frac{1}{2}$ cups from Asian stores and good supermarkets. Mirin has a syrupy texture and adds a mild sweetness to soups.

Left: Thai fish sauce adds a strong, salty flavour to soups.

EQUIPMENT AND TECHNIQUES

One advantage of making your own soups is that you won't need any specialist equipment to try a wide range of tasty recipes. You will need basic equipment such as good knives and a chopping board or two, as well as a good-quality heavy-based pan and utensils such as wooden spoons etc. One additional piece of equipment that is very useful in soup-making is a food processor or blender, to enable you to purée cooked soups, if you wish. However, if you don't have one of these, many of the soups that require puréeing can simply be hand-pressed to make them smooth.

Heavy-based pan

For making soups you should choose a good-quality heavy-based pan. A good pan that conducts and holds heat well allows the vegetables to cook for longer before browning, so that they can be softened without changing colour. If you are health-conscious, choose a good-quality non-stick pan, and

Right: There are many different types of vegetable peeler.

Below: Using a balloon whisk.

you may be able to slightly reduce the amount of butter or oil used to sauté the vegetables.

Vegetable peelers

The quickest way to peel vegetables is to use a swivel peeler. For example, trim off the top and end of a carrot, then hold the carrot in one hand and run the peeler away from you down its length, turning the carrot as you work. Use a julienne peeler to cut vegetables such as carrots and courgettes into thin julienne strips. Use julienne strips of vegetables in recipes or as an attractive garnish for chilled or cooked hot soups.

Wooden spoon

Use a wooden spoon to stir soups. This will not damage the base of the pan (important if the pan is non-stick). However, wood absorbs flavours, so wash and dry the spoon well after use, and don't leave the spoon in the soup while it is cooking.

Below: Using a wooden mushroom or champignon.

Chopping an onion

Use a small knife to trim the root end of the onion and remove the skin with the tough layer underneath. Cut the onion in half. Place the cut side down on a chopping board and use a large sharp knife to slice down through the onion without cutting through its root. Slice horizontally through the onion. Finally, cut down across all the original cuts and the onion will fall apart into fine dice.

Whisk

A balloon whisk is useful when making some soups, for quickly incorporating ingredients such as eggs and cream, which could curdle, or flour mixtures that can form lumps. Steady the pan or bowl with one hand and, holding the whisk in the other hand, make quick flicking movements.

Wooden mushroom

A wooden mushroom (or champignon), which looks like a large, flat toadstool, is useful for pressing ingredients through a fine sieve (strainer) to give a smooth purée. The back of a large spoon or ladle can also be used.

Blender

A hand-held blender is brilliant, as it allows you to blend the soup directly in the pan. Controlling the speed is easy, to give the required consistency. Be careful when using a hand-held blender in a non-stick pan, and be sure not to let the blender touch the base or sides of the pan because it will cause damage to the surface.

Chopping fresh herbs

Rinse and thoroughly dry the herbs and remove the leaves from the stalks, if necessary (this is essential when chopping herbs such as rosemary, which has very tough, woody stalks. Place the herbs on a chopping board and, using a knife or other sharp tool, cut the herbs into small pieces (as finely or as coarsely as you wish), holding the tip of the blade against the chopping board and rocking the blade back and forth.

Alternatively, you can use a mezzaluna ("half-moon" in Italian). This is a curved crescent-shaped blade attached to two handles, which rocks back and forth over the herbs to chop them. It is good for chopping a lot of herbs at once.

Above: Aubergine Soup with Mozzarella and Gremolata, made smooth and creamy using a food processor or blender.

Mouli-legume

A more traditional method is to use a mouli-legume, a cooking instrument from France that is a cross between a sieve (strainer) and a food mill. It sits over a bowl and has a blade to press the food through two fine sieves. The blade is turned by hand to push the soup through the sieves, leaving all the fibres and solids behind. A mouli-legume can grind food quickly into a coarse or fine texture.

Electric food processor and blender

The most common items of equipment for puréeing soups are food processors and free-standing blenders. Both types of machine are quick and efficient, but the food processor does not produce as smooth a result as a conventional blender, and for some recipes the soup will need to be strained afterwards. Food processors can also be used for finely chopping and slicing vegetables for salsas and garnishes.

Below: Using a mouli-legume.

Below: Using a hand-held blender.

Below: Using a food processor.

MAKING STOCKS

Fresh stocks are indispensable for creating good home-made soups. They add a depth of flavour that plain water just cannot achieve. Although many supermarkets now sell tubs of fresh stock, these may be expensive, especially if you need large quantities. Making your own is surprisingly easy and much more economical, particularly if you can use leftovers.

Home-made stocks aren't just cheaper, they are also a lot tastier, and they are much more nutritious too, precisely because they are made with fresh, natural ingredients. You can, of course, use stock (bouillon) cubes, granules or bouillon powder, but be sure to check the seasoning as these tend to be particularly high in salt.

Use the appropriate stock for the soup you are making. Onion soup, for example, is improved with a good beef stock. Be careful to use a vegetable stock, though, if you are catering for vegetarians. Recipes are given here for vegetable stock, fish stock, chicken stock, meat stock and basic stocks for Chinese and Japanese cooking.

Freezing stock

A good idea for keen and regular soup makers is to freeze portions of concentrated home-made stock in plastic freezer bags, or ice-cube trays, so you always have a supply at your disposal whenever you need some. Frozen stock can be stored in the freezer for up to three months (fish stock for up to 2 months). Ensure that you label each stock carefully for easy identification later.

Vegetable stock

Use this versatile stock as the basis for all vegetarian soups. It may also be used for meat, poultry or fish soups.

MAKES 2.5 LITRES/4½ PINTS/10 CUPS

INGREDIENTS
  2 leeks, roughly chopped
  3 celery sticks, roughly chopped
  1 large onion, unpeeled, roughly chopped
  2 pieces fresh root ginger, chopped
  1 yellow (bell) pepper, chopped
  1 parsnip, chopped
  mushroom stalks
  tomato peelings
  45ml/3 tbsp light soy sauce
  3 bay leaves
  a bunch of parsley stalks
  3 sprigs of fresh thyme
  1 sprig of fresh rosemary
  10ml/2 tsp salt
  freshly ground black pepper
  3.5 litres/6 pints/15 cups cold water

1 Put all the ingredients into a stockpot or large pan. Bring slowly to the boil, then lower the heat and simmer for 30 minutes, stirring from time to time.

2 Allow to cool. Strain, then discard the vegetables. The stock is ready to use.

Fish stock

Fish stock is much quicker to make than poultry or meat stock. Ask your fishmonger for heads, bones and trimmings from white fish. Lobster or crab shell pieces (taken after boiling lobster or crab and scooping out the meat) can also be used in place of fish trimmings to make a tasty fish stock, together with the other flavourings listed.

MAKES 1 LITRE/1¾ PINTS/4 CUPS

INGREDIENTS
  675g/1½lb heads, bones and trimmings from white fish
  1 onion, sliced
  2 celery sticks with leaves, chopped
  1 carrot, sliced
  ½ lemon, sliced (optional)
  1 bay leaf
  a few sprigs of fresh parsley
  6 black peppercorns
  1.35 litres/2¼ pints/6 cups cold water
  150ml/¼ pint/⅔ cup dry white wine

1 Rinse the fish heads, bones and trimmings well under cold running water. Put in a stockpot or large pan with the vegetables and lemon, if using, the herbs, peppercorns, water and wine. Bring to the boil, skimming the surface frequently, then reduce the heat and simmer for 25 minutes.

2 Strain the stock without pressing down on the ingredients in the sieve (strainer). If not using immediately, leave to cool and then refrigerate. Use within 2 days.

Chicken stock

A good home-made poultry stock is invaluable in the kitchen. If poultry giblets are available, add them (except the livers) with the wings. Once made, chicken stock can be kept in an airtight container in the refrigerator for 3–4 days, or frozen for longer storage (up to 3 months).

MAKES ABOUT 2.5 LITRES/4½ PINTS/
10 CUPS

INGREDIENTS
    1.2–1.3kg/2½–3lb chicken or turkey
      (wings, backs and necks)
    2 onions, unpeeled, quartered
    1 tbsp olive oil
    4 litres/7 pints/16 cups
      cold water
    2 carrots, roughly chopped
    2 celery sticks, with leaves if
      possible, roughly chopped
    a small handful of parsley stalks
    a few sprigs of fresh thyme or
      5ml/1 tsp dried
    1 or 2 bay leaves
    10 black peppercorns,
      lightly crushed

1 Combine the poultry wings, backs and necks in a stockpot or large pan with the onion quarters and the oil.

2 Cook over a moderate heat, stirring occasionally, until the poultry and onions are lightly and evenly browned.

Right: Moroccan Chicken Soup with Charmoula Butter uses a good-quality home-made stock for a rich flavour.

3 Add the water and stir well to mix in the sediment on the bottom of the pan. Bring to the boil and skim off any impurities as they rise to the surface of the stock.

4 Add the chopped carrots and celery, fresh parsley, thyme, bay leaf and black peppercorns. Partly cover the stockpot and simmer the stock for 3 hours.

5 Strain the stock through a sieve (strainer) into a bowl. Discard the chicken bones and the vegetables. Leave the stock to cool, then chill in the refrigerator for an hour.

6 When cold, carefully remove the layer of fat that will have set on the surface. The stock is now ready to use in your chosen soup recipe.

Meat stock

The most delicious meat soups rely on a good home-made stock for success. A stock (bouillon) cube will do if you have no time to make your own, but fresh home-made stock will give a much better flavour and basis for soups, so it's well worth spending a little time making your own. Once it is made, meat stock can be kept in the refrigerator for up to 4 days, or frozen for up to 3 months.

MAKES ABOUT 2 LITRES/3½ PINTS/8 CUPS

INGREDIENTS
    1.8kg/4lb beef bones, such as
      shin, leg, neck and shank, or
      veal or lamb bones, cut into
      6cm/2½in pieces
    2 onions, unpeeled, quartered
    2 carrots, roughly chopped
    2 celery sticks, with leaves if
      possible, roughly chopped
    2 tomatoes, coarsely chopped
    4.5 litres/7½ pints/18¾ cups
      cold water
    a handful of parsley stalks
    few sprigs of fresh thyme or
      5ml/1 tsp dried
    2 bay leaves
    10 black peppercorns, lightly crushed

3 Transfer the bones and roasted vegetables to a stockpot or large pan. Spoon off the fat from the roasting pan. Add a little of the water to the roasting pan or casserole and bring to the boil on top of the stove, stirring well to scrape up any browned bits. Pour this liquid into the stockpot.

4 Add the remaining water to the pot. Bring just to the boil, skimming frequently to remove all the foam from the surface. Add the parsley, thyme, bay leaves and peppercorns.

5 Partly cover the stockpot and simmer the beef stock for 4–6 hours. The bones and vegetables should always be covered with enough liquid, so top up with a little boiling water from time to time if necessary.

6 Strain the stock through a colander, then skim as much fat as possible from the surface. If possible, cool the stock and then refrigerate it; the fat will rise to the top and set in a layer that can be removed easily.

Stock for Chinese cooking

This stock is an excellent basis for soup-making, and is ideal for Asian soups. Refrigerate the stock when cool – it will keep for up to 4 days. Alternatively, it can be frozen in small containers for up to 3 months and defrosted when required.

MAKES 2.5 LITRES/4½ PINTS/11 CUPS

INGREDIENTS
    675g/1½lb chicken portions
    675g/1½lb pork spareribs
    3.75 litres/6½ pints/15 cups
      cold water
    3–4 pieces fresh root ginger,
      unpeeled, crushed
    3–4 spring onions (scallions),
      each tied into a knot
    45–60ml/3–4 tbsp Chinese rice wine
      or dry sherry

Below: Braised Cabbage Soup with Beef and Horseradish Cream.

1 Preheat the oven to 230°C/450°F/ Gas 8. Put the bones in a roasting pan or casserole dish and roast, turning occasionally, for 30 minutes, until they start to brown.

2 Add the onions, carrots, celery and tomatoes and baste with the fat in the pan. Roast for a further 20–30 minutes until the bones are well browned. Stir and baste occasionally.

Above: Kombu seaweed is used in Japanese stocks.

1 Use a sharp knife to trim off any excess fat from the chicken and spareribs, then chop them into small pieces.

3 Bring the stock to the boil and skim off the froth. Reduce the heat and simmer over a gentle heat, uncovered, for 2–3 hours.

Stock for Japanese cooking

Dashi is the stock that gives the characteristically Japanese flavour to many dishes. Known as Ichiban-dashi, it is used for delicately flavoured dishes, including soups. Of course instant stock is available in all Japanese supermarkets, either in granule form, in concentrate or even in a tea-bag style. Follow the instructions on the packet.

MAKES ABOUT 800ML/1⅓ PINTS/3½ CUPS

INGREDIENTS
   10g/¼oz dried kombu seaweed
   10–15g/¼–½oz dried bonito flakes

2 Place the chicken and sparerib pieces into a stockpot or large pan with the cold water. Add the crushed fresh root ginger and the spring onions tied in knots.

4 Strain the stock, discarding the pork, chicken, ginger and spring onion knots. Add the Chinese rice wine or dry sherry and return to the boil. Simmer for 2–3 minutes.

1 Wipe the kombu seaweed with a damp cloth and cut two slits in it with scissors, so that it flavours the stock effectively.

2 Soak the kombu in 900ml/1½ pints/ 3¾ cups cold water for 30–60 minutes.

3 Heat the kombu in its soaking water in a pan over a moderate heat. Just before the water boils, remove the seaweed. Add the bonito flakes and bring to the boil over a high heat, then remove the pan from the heat.

4 Leave the stock until all the bonito flakes have sunk to the bottom of the pan. Line a sieve (strainer) with kitchen paper or muslin (cheesecloth) and place it over a large mixing bowl, then gently strain the stock. Use as required or cool and refrigerate for up to 2 days.

Left: A Chinese-style soup made with home-made Chinese stock.

THICKENING SOUPS

Many soups do not need any thickening ingredients added, as the puréed soup is thick enough. Vegetables such as potatoes, onions and carrots, once cooked and puréed in a soup, will often help to thicken the soup sufficiently. If your soup does need thickening, try one of the methods below.

Beurre manié

This smooth flour and butter paste is used to thicken soups at the end of the cooking time. Equal quantities of plain flour and butter are kneaded together, then a small knob of the paste is added to the soup and whisked until it is fully incorporated before adding the next. The soup is brought to the boil and simmered for about 1 minute, until thickened and to avoid a raw flour flavour. A similarly useful paste can be made using flour and cream.

Cream

Double (heavy) cream can be used to thicken a fine soup. It is added towards the end of cooking, then the soup is brought to the boil and simmered gently for a few minutes until the soup is slightly reduced and thickened.

Ground almonds

Ground almonds can be used as a thickener in soups, and they add extra flavour as well as texture to the soup. The delicate flavour of almonds blends particularly well with fish- and chicken-based soups. However, ground almonds

Below: Making beurre manié.

Above: Adding ground almonds.

do not thicken soup in the same way that ingredients such as flour and cornflour (cornstarch) do, to make a thick, smooth soup. Instead they add body, texture, flavour and richness.

Cornflour or arrowroot

These fine flours are mixed with a little cold water (about double the volume of the dry ingredient) to make a smooth, thick, but runny paste. Stir the paste into the hot soup and simmer, stirring, until thickened. Cornflour (cornstarch) takes about 3 minutes to thicken completely and lose its raw flavour. Arrowroot achieves maximum thickness on boiling and tends to become slightly thinner if it is allowed to simmer for any length of time, so this is usually

Below: Mixing cornflour with water.

Above: Adding breadcrumbs.

avoided. Cornflour gives an opaque result, but arrowroot becomes clear when it boils, so it is useful for thickening clear liquids and soups.

Breadcrumbs

The more rustic approach is to use fresh white breadcrumbs to thicken soup. They can be toasted in oil before being stirred into a simmering soup, or added directly to a finished dish.

Eggs

Beaten eggs, egg yolks, or a mixture of eggs and a little cream can be used to enrich and slightly thicken a smooth soup. Whisk into the hot soup, but do not allow it to boil once they are added or it will curdle.

Below: Whisking in beaten eggs.

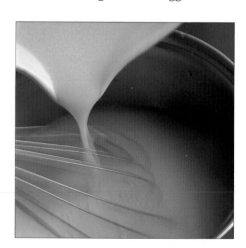

GARNISHES

Garnishes should look attractive, be edible, complement the flavour of the soup and add that final finishing touch. Some typical ones include sprinkling the soup with chopped herbs or stirring them into it just before serving, or topping thick, rich soups with a fresh herb sprig or two for an attractive garnish. Croûtons, made from either plain or flavoured bread, add appeal and crunch to many soups. Below are some typical garnishes, as well as a few tips for some more unusual ones.

Swirled cream

A swirl of cream is the classic finish for many soups, such as a smooth tomato soup and Vichyssoise. This garnish gives a professional finish to your soup, although the technique is simplicity itself.

1 Transfer the cream into a jug with a good pouring lip. Pour a swirl on to the surface of each bowl of soup.

2 Draw the tip of a fine skewer quickly backwards and forwards through the cream to create a delicate pattern. Serve the soup immediately.

Above: Frying croûtes in oil.

Herbs

Adding a handful of chopped fresh herbs to a bowl of soup just before serving can make a good soup look great. A bundle of chives makes a dainty garnish. Cut 5–6 chives to about 6cm/2½in long and tie them in a bundle using another length of chive.

Fried croûtons

This classic garnish adds texture as well as flavour to soups. To make croûtons, cut bread into small cubes and fry in a little oil. Toss the bread continuously so that the cubes are golden all over, then drain on kitchen paper.

Grilled croûtes

Topped with grilled cheese, croûtes not only look good, but taste great in all sorts of soups. To make them, toast small slices of baguette on both sides. If you like, you can rub the toast with a cut clove of garlic, then top with grated Cheddar or Parmesan, a crumbled blue cheese, such as Stilton, or a slice of goat's (chèvre) cheese. Grill (broil) briefly until the cheese is beginning to melt.

Crisp-fried shallots

Finely sliced shallots make a quick garnish for smooth lentil and vegetable soups. Cut them crossways into rings, then shallow fry in hot oil until crisp.

Above: Making vegetable julienne.

Crisps

Try shop-bought thick-cut crisps (US potato chips) or tortilla chips; alternatively, make your own vegetable crisps (chips). Wafer-thin slices of fresh raw beetroot (beet), pumpkin and parsnip can all be deep-fried in hot oil for a few moments to produce delicious and unusual crisps.

Vegetable julienne

An effective way of preparing ingredients for adding a splash of colour to soup is to cut them into julienne strips. Shreds of spring onions (scallions) or red and green chillies make great garnishes.

Below: Diced tomatoes, onions and coriander make an attractive garnish.

LIGHT AND REFRESHING SOUPS

What could be a nicer way of starting a meal on a warm summer

evening than a bowl of refreshing soup, served al fresco with

a bottle of chilled white wine? In this section there are

traditional favourites, such as French Vichyssoise and Spanish

Gazpacho, as well as more unusual soups, such as Chilled

Garlic and Almond Soup with Grapes, and Spiced Mango Soup

with Yogurt. Or for an international flavour, try Japanese

Miso Broth with Spring Onions and Tofu.

VICHYSSOISE

THIS CLASSIC, CHILLED SUMMER SOUP WAS FIRST CREATED IN THE 1920S BY LOUIS DIAT, CHEF AT THE NEW YORK RITZ-CARLTON. HE NAMED IT AFTER VICHY, NEAR HIS HOME IN FRANCE.

3 Stir in the stock or water, 5ml/1 tsp salt and pepper to taste. Bring to the boil, then reduce the heat and partly cover the pan. Simmer for 15 minutes, or until the potatoes are soft.

4 Cool, then process the soup until smooth in a blender or food processor. Strain the soup into a bowl and stir in the cream. Taste and adjust the seasoning and add a little iced water if the consistency of the soup seems too thick.

5 Chill the soup for at least 4 hours or until very cold. Taste the chilled soup for seasoning and add a squeeze of lemon juice, if required. Pour the soup into bowls and sprinkle with chopped chives. Serve immediately.

SERVES 4–6

INGREDIENTS
  50g/2oz/¼ cup unsalted butter
  450g/1lb leeks, white parts only,
    thinly sliced
  3 large shallots, sliced
  250g/9oz floury potatoes (such as
    King Edward or Maris Piper), peeled
    and cut into chunks
  1 litre/1¾ pints/4 cups light chicken
    stock or water
  300ml/½ pint/1¼ cups double
    (heavy) cream
  iced water (optional)
  a little lemon juice (optional)
  salt and ground black pepper
  chopped fresh chives,
    to garnish

1 Melt the butter in a heavy-based pan and cook the leeks and shallots gently, covered, for 15–20 minutes, until soft but not browned.

2 Add the potatoes and cook, uncovered, for a few minutes.

VARIATIONS
• **Potage Bonne Femme** For this hot leek and potato soup, use 1 chopped onion instead of the shallots and 450g/1lb potatoes. Halve the quantity of double (heavy) cream and reheat the puréed soup, adding a little milk if the soup seems very thick. Deep-fried shredded leek may be used to garnish the soup, instead of chopped fresh chives.
• **Chilled Leek and Sorrel or Watercress Soup** Add about 50g/2oz/1 cup shredded sorrel to the soup at the end of cooking. Finish and chill as in the main recipe, then serve the soup garnished with a little pile of finely shredded sorrel. The same quantity of watercress can be used in the same way.

Energy 547Kcal/2260kJ; Protein 4.6g; Carbohydrate 17.7g, of which sugars 6.8g; Fat 51.4g, of which saturates 31.7g; Cholesterol 129mg; Calcium 79mg; Fibre 3.6g; Sodium 103mg.

CUCUMBER AND SALMON SOUP WITH SALSA

CHARRED SALMON BRINGS A HINT OF HEAT TO THE REFRESHING FLAVOURS OF THIS CHILLED SOUP.
GOOD-LOOKING AND BEAUTIFULLY LIGHT, IT MAKES THE PERFECT OPENER FOR AN AL FRESCO MEAL.

SERVES 4

INGREDIENTS
 3 medium cucumbers
 300ml/½ pint/1¼ cups Greek
  (US strained plain) yogurt
 250ml/8fl oz/1 cup vegetable
  stock, chilled
 120ml/4fl oz/½ cup crème fraîche
 15ml/1 tbsp chopped fresh chervil
 15ml/1 tbsp chopped fresh chives
 15ml/1 tbsp chopped fresh
  flat leaf parsley
 1 small fresh red chilli, seeded and
  very finely chopped
 a little oil, for brushing
 225g/8oz salmon fillet, skinned and
  cut into eight thin slices
 salt and ground black pepper
 fresh chervil or chives, to garnish

4 Brush a griddle or frying pan with oil and heat until very hot. Add the salmon slices and sear them for 1–2 minutes, then turn over carefully and sear the other side until tender and charred.

5 Ladle the chilled soup into soup bowls. Top each portion with two slices of salmon, then pile a portion of salsa in the centre. Garnish with the chervil or chives and serve.

1 Peel two of the cucumbers and halve them lengthways. Scoop out and discard the seeds, then roughly chop the flesh. Purée the chopped flesh in a food processor or blender.

2 Add the yogurt, stock, crème fraîche, chervil, chives and seasoning, and process until smooth. Pour the mixture into a bowl, cover and chill.

3 Peel, halve and seed the remaining cucumber. Cut the flesh into small neat dice. Mix with the chopped parsley and chilli in a bowl. Cover the salsa and chill until required.

Per portion: Energy 314Kcal/1299kJ; Protein 17.8g; Carbohydrate 3.9g, of which sugars 3.7g; Fat 26.1g, of which saturates 13.1g; Cholesterol 62mg; Calcium 183mg; Fibre 1.2g; Sodium 92mg.

CHILLED GARLIC <u>AND</u> ALMOND SOUP <u>WITH</u> GRAPES

THIS CREAMY CHILLED SUMMER SOUP IS BASED ON AN ANCIENT MOORISH RECIPE FROM ANDALUSIA IN SOUTHERN SPAIN. ALMONDS AND PINE NUTS ARE TYPICAL INGREDIENTS OF THIS REGION.

SERVES 6

INGREDIENTS

75g/3oz/¾ cup blanched almonds
50g/2oz/½ cup pine nuts
6 large garlic cloves, peeled
200g/7oz good-quality day-old bread, crusts removed
900ml–1 litre/1½–1¾ pints/3¾–4 cups still mineral water, chilled
120ml/4fl oz/½ cup extra virgin olive oil, plus extra to serve
15ml/1 tbsp sherry vinegar
30–45ml/2–3 tbsp dry sherry
250g/9oz grapes, peeled, halved and seeded
salt and ground white pepper
ice cubes and chopped fresh chives, to garnish

1 Roast the almonds and pine nuts together in a dry pan over a moderate heat until they are very lightly browned. Cool, then grind to a powder.

2 Blanch the garlic in boiling water for 3 minutes. Drain and rinse.

3 Soak the bread in 300ml/½ pint/ 1¼ cups of the water for 10 minutes, then squeeze dry. Process the garlic, bread, nuts and 5ml/1 tsp salt in a food processor or blender until they form a paste.

4 Gradually blend in the olive oil and sherry vinegar, followed by sufficient water to make a smooth soup with a creamy consistency.

5 Stir in 30ml/2 tbsp of the sherry. Adjust the seasoning and add more dry sherry to taste. Chill for at least 3 hours, then adjust the seasoning again and stir in a little more chilled water if the soup has thickened. Reserve a few grapes for the garnish and stir the remainder into the soup.

6 Ladle the soup into bowls (glass bowls look particularly good) and garnish with ice cubes, the reserved grapes and chopped fresh chives. Serve with additional extra virgin olive oil to drizzle over the soup to taste just before it is eaten.

COOK'S TIPS
• Toasting the nuts slightly accentuates their flavour, but you can omit this step if you prefer a paler soup.
• Blanching the garlic softens its flavour.

Energy 380Kcal/1582kJ; Protein 7g; Carbohydrate 26.1g, of which sugars 8.4g; Fat 27.3g, of which saturates 3g; Cholesterol 0mg; Calcium 83mg; Fibre 2.2g; Sodium 150mg.

GAZPACHO WITH AVOCADO SALSA

TOMATOES, CUCUMBER AND PEPPERS FORM THE BASIS OF THIS CLASSIC CHILLED SOUP. ADD A SPOONFUL OF CHUNKY, FRESH AVOCADO SALSA AND A SCATTERING OF CROÛTONS, AND SERVE FOR A LIGHT LUNCH OR SIMPLE SUPPER ON A WARM SUMMER DAY.

SERVES 4

INGREDIENTS

  2 slices day-old white bread, cubed
  600ml/1 pint/2½ cups chilled water
  1kg/2¼lb fresh tomatoes
  1 cucumber
  1 red (bell) pepper, halved, seeded
    and chopped
  1 fresh green chilli, seeded
    and chopped
  2 garlic cloves, chopped
  30ml/2 tbsp extra virgin olive oil
  juice of 1 lime and 1 lemon
  a few drops of Tabasco sauce
  salt and ground black pepper
  8 ice cubes, to garnish
  a handful of basil leaves, to garnish
For the croûtons
  2 slices day-old bread,
    crusts removed
  1 garlic clove, halved
  15ml/1 tbsp olive oil
For the avocado salsa
  1 ripe avocado
  5ml/1 tsp lemon juice
  2.5cm/1in piece cucumber, diced
  ½ red chilli, seeded and
    finely chopped

1 Place the bread in a large bowl and pour over 150ml/¼pint/⅔ cup of the water. Leave to soak for 5 minutes.

2 Meanwhile, place the tomatoes in a bowl and cover with boiling water. Leave for 30 seconds, then peel off the skin, remove the seeds and finely chop the flesh.

3 Thinly peel the cucumber, cut it in half lengthways and scoop out the seeds with a teaspoon. Discard the inner part and chop the flesh.

4 Place the bread, tomatoes, cucumber, red pepper, chilli, garlic, olive oil, citrus juices and Tabasco in a food processor or blender with the remaining 450ml/¾ pint/scant 2 cups chilled water and blend until well combined but still chunky. Season to taste and chill for 2–3 hours.

5 To make the croûtons, rub the slices of bread with the garlic clove. Cut the bread into cubes and place in a plastic bag with the olive oil. Seal the bag and shake until the bread cubes are coated with the oil.

6 Heat a large non-stick frying pan and fry the croûtons over a medium heat until crisp and golden.

7 Just before serving, make the avocado salsa. Halve the avocado, remove the stone (pit), then peel and dice. Toss the avocado in the lemon juice to prevent it from browning, then place it in a serving bowl and add the cucumber and chilli. Mix well.

8 Ladle the soup into four chilled bowls and add a couple of ice cubes to each. Top each portion with a good spoonful of avocado salsa. Garnish with the basil and sprinkle the croûtons over the top of the salsa.

Energy 278Kcal/1166kJ; Protein 6.4g; Carbohydrate 32.2g, of which sugars 12.1g; Fat 14.6g, of which saturates 2.6g; Cholesterol 0mg; Calcium 80mg; Fibre 5.1g; Sodium 209mg.

CHILLED TOMATO <u>AND</u> SWEET PEPPER SOUP

A RECIPE INSPIRED BY THE SPANISH GAZPACHO, WHERE RAW INGREDIENTS ARE COMBINED TO MAKE A CHILLED SOUP. IN THIS RECIPE THE INGREDIENTS ARE COOKED FIRST AND THEN CHILLED.

SERVES 4

INGREDIENTS

2 red (bell) peppers, halved
45ml/3 tbsp olive oil
1 onion, finely chopped
2 garlic cloves, crushed
675g/1½lb ripe, well-flavoured
  tomatoes
150ml/¼ pint/⅔ cup red wine
600ml/1 pint/2½ cups vegetable stock
salt and ground black pepper
chopped fresh chives, to garnish
For the croûtons
2 slices day-old white bread,
  crusts removed
60ml/4 tbsp olive oil

COOK'S TIP
Any juice that accumulates in the pan after grilling (broiling) the peppers, or in the bowl, should be stirred into the soup. It will add a delectable flavour.

1 Cut each pepper half into quarters and seed. Place skin-side up on a grill (broiler) rack and cook until the skins have charred. Transfer to a bowl and cover with a plate.

2 Heat the oil in a large pan. Add the onion and garlic, and cook until soft. Meanwhile, remove the skin from the peppers and roughly chop them. Cut the tomatoes into chunks.

3 Add the peppers and tomatoes to the pan, then cover and cook gently for 10 minutes. Add the red wine and cook for a further 5 minutes, then add the stock and salt and pepper, and simmer for 20 minutes.

4 To make the croûtons, cut the bread into cubes. Heat the oil in a small frying pan, add the bread and fry until golden. Drain on paper towels, cool, then store in an airtight box.

5 Process the soup in a blender or food processor until smooth. Pour into a clean glass or ceramic bowl and leave to cool thoroughly before chilling for at least 3 hours. When the soup is cold, season to taste.

6 Serve the soup in bowls, topped with the croûtons and garnished with chopped chives.

Energy 292Kcal/1216kJ; Protein 3.4g; Carbohydrate 18.8g, of which sugars 11.8g; Fat 20.4g, of which saturates 3g; Cholesterol 0mg; Calcium 40mg; Fibre 3.5g; Sodium 92mg.

CHILLED TOMATO AND BASIL-FLOWER SOUP

THIS IS A REALLY FRESH-TASTING SOUP, PACKED WITH THE COMPLEMENTARY FLAVOURS OF TOMATO AND BASIL, AND TOPPED WITH PRETTY PINK AND PURPLE SWEET BASIL FLOWERS.

SERVES 4

INGREDIENTS
15ml/1 tbsp olive oil
1 onion, finely chopped
1 garlic clove, crushed
600ml/1 pint/2½ cups
  vegetable stock
900g/2lb tomatoes, roughly chopped
20 fresh basil leaves
a few drops of balsamic vinegar
juice of ½ lemon
150ml/¼ pint/⅔ cup natural
  (plain) yogurt
granulated sugar and salt, to taste
For the garnish
30ml/2 tbsp natural (plain) yogurt
8 small basil leaves
10ml/2 tsp basil flowers, all green
  parts removed

COOK'S TIP
Basil flowers may be small but they certainly have a beautifully aromatic flavour and are surprisingly sweet. They can be used fresh in all sorts of ways by being added with basil leaves to tomato salads or pizza toppings, sprinkled on pastas, or used as flavourings in tomato juice. To remove the flowers from the stem, simply pull – they will come away easily. Purple-leaved basil has a pretty mauve flower, which is delicious too.

1 Heat the oil in a pan and add the finely chopped onion and garlic. Fry the onion and garlic in the oil for 2–3 minutes until soft and transparent, stirring occasionally.

2 Add 300ml/½ pint/1¼ cups of the vegetable stock and the chopped tomatoes to the pan. Bring to the boil, then lower the heat and simmer the mixture for 15 minutes. Stir it occasionally to prevent it from sticking to the base of the pan.

3 Allow the mixture to cool slightly, then transfer it to a food processor and process until smooth. Press through a sieve placed over a bowl to remove the tomato skins and seeds.

4 Return the mixture to the food processor and add the remainder of the stock, half the basil leaves, the vinegar, lemon juice and yogurt. Season with sugar and salt to taste. Process until smooth. Pour into a bowl and chill.

5 Just before serving, finely shred the remaining basil leaves and add them to the soup. Pour the chilled soup into individual bowls. Garnish with yogurt topped with a few small basil leaves and a sprinkling of basil flowers.

Energy 89Kcal/377kJ; Protein 3.7g; Carbohydrate 11g, of which sugars 10.6g; Fat 3.8g, of which saturates 0.8g; Cholesterol 1mg; Calcium 91mg; Fibre 2.5g; Sodium 52mg.

CHILLED AVOCADO SOUP <u>WITH</u> CUMIN

ANDALUSIA IS HOME TO BOTH AVOCADOS AND GAZPACHO, SO IT IS NOT SURPRISING THAT THIS CHILLED AVOCADO SOUP, WHICH IS ALSO KNOWN AS GREEN GAZPACHO, WAS INVENTED THERE. IN SPAIN, THIS DELICIOUSLY MILD, CREAMY SOUP IS KNOWN AS SOPA DE AGUACATE.

SERVES 4

INGREDIENTS

3 ripe avocados
1 bunch spring onions (scallions),
   white parts only, trimmed and
   roughly chopped
2 garlic cloves, chopped
juice of 1 lemon
1.5ml/¼ tsp ground cumin
1.5ml/¼ tsp paprika
450ml/¾ pint/scant 2 cups fresh
   chicken stock, cooled and all
   fat skimmed off
300ml/½ pint/1¼ cups iced water
salt and ground black pepper
roughly chopped fresh flat leaf
   parsley, to garnish

1 Starting half a day ahead, put the flesh of one avocado in a food processor or blender. Add the spring onions, garlic and lemon juice and purée until smooth. Add the second avocado and purée, then the third, with the spices and seasoning. Purée until smooth.

2 Gradually add the chicken stock. Pour the soup into a metal bowl and chill.

3 To serve, stir in the iced water, then season to taste with plenty of salt and black pepper. Garnish with chopped parsley and serve immediately.

Energy 242Kcal/1001kJ; Protein 2.8g; Carbohydrate 3g, of which sugars 1.3g; Fat 24.2g, of which saturates 5.2g; Cholesterol 0mg; Calcium 22mg; Fibre 4.6g; Sodium 9mg.

BEETROOT SOUP <u>WITH</u> MASCARPONE BRIOCHE

ALTHOUGH IT SOUNDS QUITE COMPLEX, THIS SOUP IS ACTUALLY RIDICULOUSLY EASY TO MAKE.
THE SWEET, EARTHY FLAVOUR OF FRESH, COOKED BEETROOT IS COMBINED WITH ZESTY ORANGE
AND TART CRANBERRY JUICE.

SERVES 4

INGREDIENTS

    350g/12oz cooked beetroot (beet),
      roughly chopped
    grated rind and juice of 1 orange
    600ml/1 pint/2½ cups unsweetened
      cranberry juice
    450ml/¾ pint/scant 2 cups Greek
      (US strained plain) yogurt
    a little Tabasco sauce
    4 slices brioche
    60ml/4 tbsp mascarpone
    salt and ground black pepper
    fresh mint sprigs and cooked
      cranberries, to garnish

2 Press the purée through a sieve (strainer) into a clean bowl. Stir in the remaining cranberry juice and the Tabasco sauce. Season with salt and black pepper to taste. Chill the soup in the refrigerator for at least 2 hours.

3 Preheat the grill (broiler). Using a large pastry cutter, stamp a round out of each slice of brioche.

COOK'S TIP
If the combination of cranberry and orange is a little tart, add a pinch or two of caster (superfine) sugar to the soup, according to taste.

4 Arrange the brioche rounds on a grill (broiler) rack and toast until golden. Ladle the soup into bowls and top each with brioche and mascarpone. Garnish with mint and cranberries.

1 Purée the beetroot with the orange rind and juice, half the cranberry juice and the yogurt in a food processor or blender until smooth.

Energy 404Kcal/1695kJ; Protein 13.5g; Carbohydrate 53.5g, of which sugars 17.2g; Fat 16.6g, of which saturates 7.2g; Cholesterol 13mg; Calcium 237mg; Fibre 1.7g; Sodium 264mg.

ICED MELON SOUP <u>WITH</u> SORBET

USE DIFFERENT MELONS FOR THE COOL SOUP AND ICE SORBET TO CREATE A SUBTLE CONTRAST IN FLAVOUR AND COLOUR. TRY A COMBINATION OF CHARENTAIS, OGEN OR CANTALOUPE.

SERVES 6–8

INGREDIENTS
   2.25kg/5–5¼lb very ripe melon
   45ml/3 tbsp orange juice
   30ml/2 tbsp lemon juice
   mint leaves, to garnish
For the sorbet (sherbet)
   25g/1oz/2 tbsp granulated
     sugar
   120ml/4fl oz/½ cup water
   2.25kg/5–5¼lb very ripe melon
   juice of 2 limes
   30ml/2 tbsp chopped fresh mint

1 To make the melon and mint sorbet, put the sugar and water into a pan and heat gently until the sugar dissolves. Bring to the boil and simmer for 4–5 minutes, then remove from the heat and leave to cool.

2 Halve the melon. Scrape out the seeds, then scoop out the flesh. Purée in a food processor or blender with the cooled syrup and lime juice.

3 Stir in the mint and pour the melon mixture into an ice-cream maker. Churn, following the manufacturer's instructions, or until the sorbet is smooth and firm. Alternatively, pour the mixture into a suitable container and freeze until icy around the edges. Transfer to a food processor or blender and process until smooth.

4 Repeat the freezing and processing two or three times or until the mixture is smooth and holding its shape, then freeze until firm.

5 To make the chilled melon soup, prepare the melon as in step 2 and purée it in a food processor or blender. Pour the purée into a bowl and stir in the orange and lemon juice. Place the soup in the refrigerator for 30–40 minutes, but do not chill it for too long as this will dull its flavour.

6 Ladle the soup into bowls and add a large scoop of the melon and mint sorbet to each. Garnish with mint leaves and serve at once.

SPICED MANGO SOUP <u>WITH</u> YOGURT

THIS DELICIOUS, LIGHT SOUP COMES FROM CHUTNEY MARY'S, AN ANGLO-INDIAN RESTAURANT IN LONDON. IT IS BEST WHEN SERVED LIGHTLY CHILLED.

SERVES 4

INGREDIENTS

2 ripe mangoes
15ml/1 tbsp gram flour
120ml/4fl oz/½ cup natural (plain)
  yogurt
900ml/1½ pints/3¾ cups cold water
2.5ml/½ tsp grated fresh root ginger
2 red chillies, seeded and finely
  chopped
30ml/2 tbsp olive oil
2.5ml/½ tsp mustard seeds
2.5ml/½ tsp cumin seeds
8 curry leaves
salt and ground black pepper
fresh mint leaves, shredded,
  to garnish
natural yogurt, to serve

1 Peel the mangoes, remove the stones and cut the flesh into chunks. Purée in a food processor or blender until smooth.

2 Pour into a pan and stir in the gram flour, yogurt, water, ginger and chillies. Bring to the boil, stirring occasionally. Simmer for 4–5 minutes until thickened slightly, then set aside off the heat.

3 Heat the oil in a frying pan. Add the mustard seeds and cook for a few seconds until they begin to pop, then add the cumin seeds.

4 Add the curry leaves and then cook for 5 minutes. Stir the spice mixture into the soup, return it to the heat and cook for 10 minutes.

5 Press through a mouli-legume or a sieve (strainer), if you like, then season to taste. Leave the soup to cool completely, then chill for at least 1 hour.

6 Ladle the soup into bowls, and top each with a dollop of yogurt. Garnish with shredded mint leaves and serve.

Energy 121Kcal/508kJ; Protein 2.8g; Carbohydrate 14.7g, of which sugars 12.7g; Fat 6.2g, of which saturates 1g; Cholesterol 0mg; Calcium 73mg; Fibre 2.4g; Sodium 28mg.

ICED TOMATO <u>AND</u> VODKA SOUP

THIS FRESH-FLAVOURED SOUP PACKS A PUNCH LIKE A FROZEN BLOODY MARY. IT IS DELICIOUS SERVED AS AN IMPRESSIVE FIRST COURSE FOR A SUMMER'S DINNER PARTY WITH SUN-DRIED TOMATO BREAD.

SERVES 4

INGREDIENTS
    450g/1lb ripe, well-flavoured
      tomatoes, halved or
      roughly chopped
    600ml/1 pint/2½ cups jellied beef
      stock or consommé
    1 small red onion, halved
    2 celery sticks, cut into large pieces
    1 garlic clove, roughly chopped
    15ml/1 tbsp tomato purée (paste)
    10ml/2 tsp lemon juice
    10ml/2 tsp Worcestershire sauce
    a handful of small fresh basil leaves
    30ml/2 tbsp vodka
    salt and ground black pepper
    crushed ice, 4 small celery sticks and
      sun-dried tomato bread, to serve

1 Put the halved or chopped tomatoes, jellied stock or consommé, onion and celery in a blender or food processor. Add the garlic, then spoon in the tomato purée. Pulse until all the vegetables are finely chopped, then process to a smooth paste.

2 Press the mixture through a sieve (strainer) into a large bowl and stir in the lemon juice, Worcestershire sauce, basil leaves and vodka.

3 Add salt and pepper to taste. Cover and chill. Serve the soup with a little crushed ice and place a celery stick in each bowl.

COOK'S TIPS
• Canned beef consommé is ideal for this recipe, but vegetable stock, for vegetarians, will work well too.
• If you or your guests are fond of celery, you can stand more celery sticks in a jug (pitcher) of iced water on the table for people to help themselves. The celery sticks can be used as additional edible stirrers and taste delicious after being dipped into the soup.
• Making your own sun-dried tomato bread is easy and is bound to impress your guests. If you don't have time, however, look out for tomato-flavoured ciabatta or focaccia.

Energy 46Kcal/194kJ; Protein 1.3g; Carbohydrate 5.5g, of which sugars 5.2g; Fat 0.4g, of which saturates 0.1g; Cholesterol 0mg; Calcium 22mg; Fibre 1.6g; Sodium 44mg.

CHILLED COCONUT SOUP

REFRESHING, COOLING AND NOT TOO FILLING, THIS SOUP IS THE PERFECT ANTIDOTE TO HOT WEATHER. EXCELLENT FOR SERVING AFTER AN APPETIZER, IT WILL REFRESH THE PALATE.

SERVES 6

INGREDIENTS

1.2 litres/2 pints/5 cups milk
225g/8oz/2⅔ cups desiccated (dry unsweetened shredded) coconut
400ml/14fl oz/1⅔ cups coconut milk
400ml/14fl oz/1⅔ cups chicken stock
200ml/7fl oz/scant 1 cup double (heavy) cream
2.5ml/½ tsp salt
2.5ml/½ tsp ground white pepper
5ml/1 tsp caster (superfine) sugar
small bunch of fresh coriander (cilantro)

1 Pour the milk into a large pan. Bring it to the boil, stir in the coconut, lower the heat and allow to simmer for 30 minutes. Spoon the mixture into a food processor and process until smooth. This may take a while – up to 5 minutes – so pause frequently and scrape down the sides of the bowl.

2 Rinse the pan to remove any coconut that remains, pour in the processed mixture and add the coconut milk. Stir in the chicken stock (home-made, if possible, which gives a better flavour than a stock [bouillon] cube), cream, salt, pepper and sugar. Bring to the boil, stirring occasionally, then lower the heat and cook for 10 minutes.

3 Reserve a few coriander leaves to garnish, then chop the rest finely and stir into the soup. Pour the soup into a large bowl, let it cool, then cover and put into the refrigerator until chilled. Just before serving, taste the soup and adjust the seasoning, as chilling will alter the taste. Serve in chilled bowls, garnished with the coriander leaves.

Energy 499Kcal/2068kJ; Protein 9.6g; Carbohydrate 15.6g, of which sugars 15.6g; Fat 44.8g, of which saturates 33.4g; Cholesterol 58mg; Calcium 284mg; Fibre 5.1g; Sodium 341mg.

MISO BROTH <u>WITH</u> SPRING ONIONS <u>AND</u> TOFU

THE JAPANESE EAT MISO BROTH, A SIMPLE BUT HIGHLY NUTRITIOUS SOUP, ALMOST EVERY DAY — IT IS STANDARD BREAKFAST FARE AND IT IS EATEN WITH RICE OR NOODLES LATER IN THE DAY.

SERVES 4

INGREDIENTS

- 1 bunch of spring onions (scallions) or 5 baby leeks
- 15g/½oz fresh coriander (cilantro)
- 3 thin slices fresh root ginger
- 2 star anise
- 1 small dried red chilli
- 1.2 litres/2 pints/5 cups dashi stock or vegetable stock
- 225g/8oz pak choi (bok choy) or other Asian greens, thickly sliced
- 200g/7oz firm tofu, cut into 2.5cm/1in cubes
- 60ml/4 tbsp red miso
- 30–45ml/2–3 tbsp Japanese soy sauce (shoyu)
- 1 fresh red chilli, seeded and shredded (optional)

1 Cut the coarse green tops off the spring onions or baby leeks and slice the rest of the spring onions or leeks finely on the diagonal. Place the coarse green tops in a large pan with the coriander stalks, fresh root ginger, star anise, dried chilli and dashi or vegetable stock.

2 Heat the mixture gently until boiling, then lower the heat and simmer for 10 minutes. Strain, return to the pan and reheat until simmering. Add the green portion of the sliced spring onions or leeks to the soup with the pak choi or greens and tofu. Cook for 2 minutes.

3 Mix 45ml/3 tbsp of the miso with a little of the hot soup in a bowl, then stir it into the soup. Taste the soup and add more miso with soy sauce to taste.

4 Coarsely chop the coriander leaves and stir most of them into the soup with the white part of the spring onions or leeks. Cook for 1 minute, then ladle the soup into warmed serving bowls. Sprinkle with the remaining coriander and the fresh red chilli, if using, and serve at once.

COOK'S TIP
Dashi is available powdered in Asian and Chinese stores. Alternatively, make your own by gently simmering 10–15cm/ 4–6in kombu seaweed in 1.2 litres/ 2 pints/5 cups water for 10 minutes. Do not boil vigorously as this makes the dashi bitter. Remove the kombu, then add 15g/½oz dried bonito flakes and bring to the boil. Strain immediately through a fine sieve (strainer).

Energy 60Kcal/252kJ; Protein 5.5g; Carbohydrate 4.4g, of which sugars 4.1g; Fat 2.3g, of which saturates 0.3g; Cholesterol 0mg; Calcium 294mg; Fibre 1.6g; Sodium 453mg.

HOT AND SWEET VEGETABLE AND TOFU SOUP

THIS SOOTHING, NUTRITIOUS SOUP TAKES ONLY MINUTES TO MAKE AS THE SPINACH AND SILKEN TOFU ARE SIMPLY PLACED IN BOWLS AND COVERED WITH THE FLAVOURED HOT STOCK.

SERVES 4

INGREDIENTS
    1.2 litres/2 pints/5 cups
        vegetable stock
    5–10ml/1–2 tsp Thai red
        curry paste
    2 kaffir lime leaves, torn
    40g/1½oz/3 tbsp palm sugar or light
        muscovado (brown) sugar
    30ml/2 tbsp soy sauce
    juice of 1 lime
    1 carrot, cut into thin batons
    50g/2oz baby spinach leaves, any
        coarse stalks removed
    225g/8oz block silken tofu, diced

1 Heat the stock in a large pan, then add the red curry paste. Stir constantly over a medium heat until the paste has dissolved. Add the lime leaves, sugar and soy sauce and bring to the boil.

2 Add the lime juice and carrot to the pan. Reduce the heat and simmer for 5–10 minutes. Place the spinach and tofu in four individual serving bowls and pour the hot stock on top to serve.

Energy 105Kcal/439kJ; Protein 5.3g; Carbohydrate 13.2g, of which sugars 12.8g; Fat 3.8g, of which saturates 0.5g; Cholesterol 0mg; Calcium 320mg; Fibre 0.7g; Sodium 559mg.

Thai Hot and Sour Soup

This light and invigorating soup, with its finely balanced combination of flavours, is best served at the beginning of a meal to stimulate the appetite.

SERVES 4

INGREDIENTS
2 carrots
900ml/1½ pints/3¾ cups
   vegetable stock
2 Thai chillies, seeded and
   finely sliced
2 lemon grass stalks, outer leaves
   removed and each stalk cut into
   3 pieces
4 kaffir lime leaves
2 garlic cloves, finely chopped
4 spring onions (scallions),
   finely sliced
5ml/1 tsp sugar
juice of 1 lime
45ml/3 tbsp chopped fresh
   coriander (cilantro)
salt
130g/4½oz/1 cup Japanese
   tofu, sliced

1 To make carrot flowers, cut each carrot in half crossways, then cut four v-shaped channels lengthways. Slice into thin rounds and set aside.

2 Pour the stock into a large pan. Reserve 2.5ml/½ tsp of the chillies and add the rest to the pan with the lemon grass, lime leaves, garlic and half the spring onions. Bring to the boil, reduce the heat and simmer for 20 minutes.

3 Strain the stock and discard the flavourings. Return the stock to the pan, add the reserved chillies and spring onions, the sugar, lime juice, coriander and salt to taste.

4 Simmer over a gentle heat for 5 minutes, then add the carrot flowers and the tofu, and cook for a further 2 minutes until the carrot is just tender. Ladle into bowls and serve hot.

Energy 40Kcal/169kJ; Protein 3.3g; Carbohydrate 3.4g, of which sugars 3.1g; Fat 1.6g, of which saturates 0.2g; Cholesterol 0mg; Calcium 197mg; Fibre 1.2g; Sodium 11mg.

TOM YAM GUNG <u>WITH</u> TOFU

ONE OF THE MOST REFRESHING AND HEALTHY SOUPS, THIS FRAGRANT DISH IS A FAMOUS THAI SPECIALITY, AND WOULD MAKE AN IDEAL LIGHT LUNCH OR SUPPER.

SERVES 4

INGREDIENTS

   30ml/2 tbsp groundnut (peanut) oil
   300g/11oz firm tofu, cut into small
     bite-size pieces
   1.2 litres/2 pints/5 cups good
     vegetable stock
   15ml/1 tbsp Thai chilli jam (nam
     pick pow)
   grated rind of 1 kaffir lime
   1 shallot, finely sliced
   1 garlic clove, peeled and
     finely chopped
   2 kaffir lime leaves, shredded
   3 red chillies, seeded and shredded
   1 lemon grass stalk, finely chopped
   6 shiitake mushrooms, thinly sliced
   4 spring onions (scallions), shredded
   45ml/3 tbsp Thai fish sauce
     (nam pla)
   45ml/3 tbsp lime juice
   5ml/1 tsp caster (superfine) sugar
   45ml/3 tbsp chopped fresh coriander
     (cilantro) leaves
   salt and ground black pepper

2 Add the stock, chilli jam, kaffir lime rind, shallot, garlic, lime leaves, two-thirds of the chillies and the lemon grass to the pan. Bring to the boil and simmer for 20 minutes.

3 Strain the stock into a clean pan. Stir in the remaining chilli, the shiitake mushrooms, spring onions, fish sauce, lime juice and sugar. Simmer for 3 minutes. Add the fried tofu and heat through for 1 minute. Mix in the chopped coriander and season to taste. Serve at once in warmed bowls.

1 Heat the oil in a wok and fry the tofu for 4–5 minutes until golden, turning occasionally to brown on all sides. Use a slotted spoon to remove the tofu and set aside. Tip the oil from the wok into a large, heavy-based pan.

COOK'S TIP
Kaffir lime leaves have a distinct citrus flavour. Fresh leaves can be bought from Asian shops, and some supermarkets sell them dried. Thai fish sauce (nam pla) and chilli jam (nam pick pow) are available from some supermarkets.

Energy 122Kcal/506kJ; Protein 7.1g; Carbohydrate 3.6g, of which sugars 2.9g; Fat 8.9g, of which saturates 1.5g; Cholesterol 0mg; Calcium 395mg; Fibre 0.7g; Sodium 273mg.

PEAR AND ROQUEFORT SOUP WITH CARAMELIZED PEARS

LIKE MOST FRUIT-BASED SOUPS, THIS IS SERVED IN SMALL PORTIONS. IT MAKES AN UNUSUAL AND SEASONAL APPETIZER FOR AN AUTUMN DINNER PARTY.

3 Cool the soup slightly and purée it in a food processor until smooth, then pass it through a fine sieve (strainer). Return the soup to the pan.

4 To make the caramelized pears, melt the butter in a frying pan and add the pears. Cook for 8–10 minutes, turning occasionally, until golden.

5 Reheat the soup gently, then ladle into small, shallow bowls and add a few caramelized pear wedges to each portion. Garnish with tiny sprigs of watercress and serve at once.

VARIATION
Any blue cheese with a strong flavour could be used in place of Roquefort, for example Stilton or Gorgonzola.

SERVES 4

INGREDIENTS
    30ml/2 tbsp sunflower oil
    1 onion, chopped
    3 pears, peeled, cored and
        chopped into 1cm/½in chunks
    400ml/14fl oz/1⅔ cups
        vegetable stock
    2.5ml/½ tsp paprika
    juice of ½ lemon
    175g/6oz Roquefort cheese
    salt and ground black pepper
    watercress sprigs, to garnish
For the caramelized pears
    50g/2oz/¼ cup butter
    2 pears, halved, cored and cut
        into wedges

1 Heat the oil in a pan. Add the onion and cook for 4–5 minutes until soft.

2 Add the pears and stock. Bring to the boil and cook for 8–10 minutes, until the pears are soft. Stir in the paprika, lemon juice, cheese and seasoning.

Energy 381Kcal/1579kJ; Protein 10.1g; Carbohydrate 21.8g, of which sugars 20.9g; Fat 28.7g, of which saturates 15.6g; Cholesterol 59mg; Calcium 246mg; Fibre 4.7g; Sodium 616mg.

AVOCADO AND LIME SOUP WITH A GREEN CHILLI SALSA

INSPIRED BY GUACAMOLE, THE POPULAR AVOCADO DIP, THIS CREAMY SOUP RELIES ON GOOD-QUALITY RIPE AVOCADOS FOR ITS FLAVOUR AND COLOUR.

SERVES 4

INGREDIENTS

3 ripe avocados
juice of 1½ limes
1 garlic clove, crushed
handful of ice cubes
400ml/14fl oz/1⅔ cups vegetable
    stock, chilled
400ml/14fl oz/1⅔ cups milk, chilled
150ml/¼ pint/⅔ cup soured
    cream, chilled
few drops of Tabasco sauce
salt and ground black pepper
fresh coriander (cilantro) leaves,
    to garnish
extra virgin olive oil, to serve
For the salsa
4 tomatoes, peeled, seeded and
    finely diced
2 spring onions (scallions), finely
    chopped
1 green chilli, seeded and finely
    chopped
15ml/1 tbsp chopped fresh
    coriander leaves
juice of ½ lime

1 Prepare the salsa first. Mix all the ingredients together and season well. Chill in the refrigerator until required.

2 Halve the avocados and remove the stones (pits). Scoop the flesh out of the avocado skins using a spoon or melon baller and place in a food processor or blender. Add the lime juice, garlic, ice cubes and 150ml/¼ pint/⅔ cup of the chilled vegetable stock.

3 Process the soup until smooth. Pour into a large bowl and stir in the remaining vegetable stock, chilled milk, soured cream and Tabasco sauce. Season to taste.

COOK'S TIPS
• It is easy to remove the stone (pit) from an avocado. Halve the avocado and simply tap the stone firmly with the edge of a large knife. Twist the knife gently and the stone will pop out.
• This soup may discolour if left standing for too long, but the flavour will not be spoilt. Give the soup a quick whisk just before serving.

4 Ladle the soup into bowls or glasses and spoon a little salsa on top. Add a splash of olive oil to each portion and garnish with fresh coriander leaves. Serve immediately.

Energy 353Kcal/1463kJ; Protein 7.3g; Carbohydrate 11.1g, of which sugars 9.6g; Fat 31.2g, of which saturates 10.5g; Cholesterol 28mg; Calcium 175mg; Fibre 4.8g; Sodium 73mg.

AVGOLEMONO

THIS IS A GREAT FAVOURITE IN GREECE AND IS A FINE EXAMPLE OF HOW A FEW INGREDIENTS CAN MAKE A MARVELLOUS DISH IF CAREFULLY CHOSEN AND COOKED. IT IS ESSENTIAL TO USE A WELL-FLAVOURED STOCK. ADD AS LITTLE OR AS MUCH RICE AS YOU LIKE.

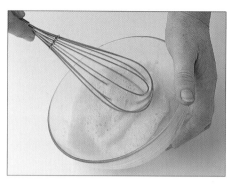

2 Whisk the egg yolks in a bowl, then add about 30ml/2 tbsp of the lemon juice, whisking constantly until the mixture is smooth and bubbly. Add a ladleful of soup and whisk again.

3 Remove the soup from the heat and slowly add the egg mixture, whisking all the time. The soup will turn a pretty lemon colour and will thicken slightly.

4 Taste and add more lemon juice if necessary. Stir in the parsley. Serve at once, without reheating, garnished with lemon slices and parsley sprigs.

SERVES 4

INGREDIENTS
  900ml/1½ pints/3¾ cups chicken
    stock, preferably home-made
  50g/2oz/generous ⅓ cup long
    grain rice
  3 egg yolks
  30–60ml/2–4 tbsp lemon juice
  30ml/2 tbsp finely chopped fresh
    parsley
  salt and freshly ground black pepper
  lemon slices and parsley sprigs,
    to garnish

1 Pour the stock into a pan, bring to simmering point, then add the drained rice. Half cover and cook for about 12 minutes until the rice is just tender. Season with salt and pepper.

COOK'S TIP
The trick here is to add the egg mixture to the soup without it curdling. Avoid whisking the mixture into boiling liquid. It is safest to remove the soup from the heat entirely and then whisk in the mixture in a slow but steady stream. Do not reheat as curdling would be almost inevitable.

Energy 96Kcal/404kJ; Protein 3.3g; Carbohydrate 10.9g, of which sugars 0.2g; Fat 4.7g, of which saturates 1.2g; Cholesterol 151mg; Calcium 39mg; Fibre 0.4g; Sodium 10mg.

PEA SOUP <u>WITH</u> PROSCIUTTO

THIS QUICK AND SIMPLE SOUP IS DELICIOUSLY CREAMY, BUT LIGHT AND REFRESHING.
USING FROZEN PEAS CUTS OUT THE LABOUR INVOLVED IN SHELLING FRESH PEAS, WITHOUT
COMPROMISING THE FLAVOUR.

SERVES 6

INGREDIENTS

25g/1oz/2 tbsp butter
1 leek, sliced
1 garlic clove, crushed
450g/1lb/4 cups frozen petits pois
  (baby peas)
1.2 litres/2 pints/5 cups
  vegetable stock
small bunch of fresh chives,
  coarsely chopped
300ml/½ pint/1¼ cups double
  (heavy) cream
90ml/6 tbsp Greek (US strained
  plain) yogurt
4 slices prosciutto, roughly chopped
salt and ground black pepper
fresh chives, to garnish

1 Melt the butter in a pan. Add the leek and garlic, cover and cook gently for 4–5 minutes, until softened.

2 Stir in the petits pois, vegetable stock and chives. Bring slowly to the boil, then simmer for 5 minutes. Set aside to cool slightly.

3 Process the soup in a food processor or blender until smooth. Pour into a bowl, stir in the cream and season to taste with salt and black pepper. Chill in the refrigerator for at least 2 hours.

4 When ready to serve, ladle the soup into bowls and add a spoonful of Greek yogurt to the centre of each bowl. Scatter the chopped prosciutto over the top of the soup and garnish with chives before serving.

COOK'S TIP
For a clever and attractive garnish, cut five lengths of chive to about 6cm/2½in long, then use another chive to tie them together. Lay a bundle of chives on top of each bowl of soup.

Energy 378Kcal/1561kJ; Protein 9.7g; Carbohydrate 10.6g, of which sugars 3.7g; Fat 33.5g, of which saturates 20g; Cholesterol 85mg; Calcium 71mg; Fibre 4.2g; Sodium 198mg.

CHILLED CUCUMBER AND PRAWN SOUP

IF YOU'VE NEVER SERVED A CHILLED SOUP BEFORE, THIS IS THE ONE TO TRY. DELICIOUS AND LIGHT, IT'S THE PERFECT WAY TO CELEBRATE SUMMER.

2 Stir in the milk, bring almost to boiling point, then lower the heat and simmer for 5 minutes. Tip the soup into a blender or food processor and purée until very smooth. Season to taste.

3 Pour the soup into a large bowl and leave to cool. When cool, stir in the prawns, chopped herbs and cream. Cover, transfer to the refrigerator and chill for at least 2 hours.

4 To serve, ladle the soup into four individual bowls, top each portion with a dollop of crème fraîche, if using, and place a prawn over the edge of each dish. Scatter over a little extra chopped dill and tuck two or three chives under the prawns on the edge of the bowls to garnish. Serve at once.

SERVES 4

INGREDIENTS
  25g/1oz/2 tbsp butter
  2 shallots, finely chopped
  2 garlic cloves, crushed
  1 cucumber, peeled, seeded
    and diced
  300ml/½ pint/1¼ cups milk
  225g/8oz cooked peeled prawns
    (shrimp)
  15ml/1 tbsp each finely chopped
    fresh mint, dill, chives and chervil
  300ml/½ pint/1¼ cups
    whipping cream
  salt and ground white pepper
For the garnish
  30ml/2 tbsp crème fraîche (optional)
  4 large, cooked prawns, peeled with
    tail intact
  fresh dill and chives

1 Melt the butter in a pan and cook the shallots and garlic over a low heat until soft but not coloured. Add the cucumber and cook gently, stirring frequently, until tender.

COOK'S TIP
If you prefer hot soup, reheat it gently until hot but not boiling. Do not boil, or the delicate flavour will be spoilt.

VARIATION
If you like, you can use other cooked shellfish in place of the peeled prawns (shrimp) – try fresh, frozen or canned crab meat or cooked, flaked salmon.

Energy 412Kcal/1704kJ; Protein 14.2g; Carbohydrate 6g, of which sugars 6g; Fat 37g, of which saturates 23g; Cholesterol 206mg; Calcium 184mg; Fibre 0.2g; Sodium 197mg.

TOMATO <u>AND</u> PEACH JUS <u>WITH</u> PRAWNS

AMERICAN-STYLE SOUPS, MADE FROM THE CLEAR JUICES EXTRACTED FROM VEGETABLES OR FRUITS AND REFERRED TO AS "WATER" SOUPS BY CHEFS, PROVIDE THE INSPIRATION FOR THIS RECIPE.

SERVES 6

INGREDIENTS

   1.5kg/3–3½lb ripe peaches
   1.2kg/2½lb beef tomatoes
   30ml/2 tbsp white wine vinegar
   1 lemon grass stalk, crushed
    and chopped
   2.5cm/1in fresh root ginger, grated
   1 bay leaf
   150ml/¼ pint/⅔ cup water
   18 tiger prawns (shrimp), shelled
    with tails on and deveined
   olive oil, for brushing
   salt and ground black pepper
   fresh coriander (cilantro) leaves and
    2 vine-ripened tomatoes, peeled,
    seeded and diced, to garnish

1 Peel the tomatoes and peaches and cut into chunks. Put into a food processor and purée them. Stir in the vinegar and seasoning.

2 Line a large bowl with muslin (cheesecloth). Pour the purée into the bowl, gather up the ends of the muslin and tie tightly. Suspend over the bowl and leave at room temperature for 3 hours or until about 1.2 litres/2 pints/ 5 cups juice have drained through.

3 Meanwhile, put the lemon grass, ginger and bay leaf into a pan with the water, and simmer for 5–6 minutes. Set aside to cool.

4 When the mixture is cool, strain into the tomato and peach juice and chill in the refrigerator for at least 4 hours.

5 Using a sharp knife, slit the prawns down their curved sides, cutting about three-quarters of the way through and keeping their tails intact. Open the prawns out flat.

6 Heat a griddle or frying pan and brush with a little oil. Sear the prawns for 1–2 minutes on each side, until tender and slightly charred. Pat dry on kitchen paper to remove any remaining oil. Cool, but do not chill.

7 When ready to serve, ladle the soup into bowls and place three prawns in each portion.

8 Add some torn coriander leaves and diced tomato to each bowl, to garnish.

Energy 188Kcal/797kJ; Protein 12.7g; Carbohydrate 25.2g, of which sugars 25.2g; Fat 4.8g, of which saturates 0.8g; Cholesterol 98mg; Calcium 71mg; Fibre 5.8g; Sodium 116mg.

SMOOTH VEGETABLE SOUPS

A bowl of smooth and creamy vegetable soup served with some

crusty bread makes an excellent light lunch at any time of year.

Choose whichever vegetables are fresh and in season — tomatoes

and herbs in the summer, pumpkins and squash for the autumn,

leeks and root vegetables during the winter months. In this

section you will find simple Chinese Egg Flower Soup and

Parsnip Soup from Ireland alongside exotic dishes such as

Spanish Sherried Onion and Almond Soup with Saffron.

CARROT AND ORANGE SOUP

*THIS TRADITIONAL BRIGHT AND SUMMERY SOUP IS ALWAYS POPULAR FOR ITS WONDERFULLY CREAMY
CONSISTENCY AND VIBRANTLY FRESH CITRUS FLAVOUR. USE A GOOD, HOME-MADE CHICKEN OR
VEGETABLE STOCK IF YOU CAN, FOR THE BEST RESULTS.*

SERVES 4

INGREDIENTS
    50g/2oz/¼ cup butter
    3 leeks, sliced
    450g/1lb carrots, sliced
    1.2 litres/2 pints/5 cups chicken or
      vegetable stock
    rind and juice of 2 oranges
    2.5ml/½ tsp freshly grated nutmeg
    150ml/¼ pint/⅔ cup Greek
      (US strained plain) yogurt
    salt and ground black pepper
    fresh sprigs of coriander (cilantro),
      to garnish

1 Melt the butter in a large pan. Add
the leeks and carrots and stir well,
coating the vegetables with the butter.
Cover and cook for about 10 minutes,
until the vegetables are beginning to
soften but not colour.

2 Pour in the stock and the orange rind
and juice. Add the nutmeg and season
to taste with salt and pepper. Bring to
the boil, lower the heat, cover and
simmer for about 40 minutes, or until
the vegetables are tender.

3 Leave to cool slightly, then purée the
soup in a food processor or blender
until smooth.

4 Return the soup to the pan and add
30ml/2 tbsp of the yogurt, then taste
the soup and adjust the seasoning, if
necessary. Reheat gently.

5 Ladle the soup into warm individual
bowls and put a swirl of yogurt in the
centre of each. Sprinkle the fresh sprigs
of coriander over each bowl to garnish,
and serve immediately.

Energy 206Kcal/856kJ; Protein 5g; Carbohydrate 15.8g, of which sugars 14.2g; Fat 14.4g, of which saturates 8.3g; Cholesterol 27mg; Calcium 111mg; Fibre 5.8g; Sodium 131mg.

PARSNIP SOUP

THIS LIGHTLY SPICED SOUP HAS BECOME VERY POPULAR IN IRELAND IN RECENT YEARS, AND MANY VARIATIONS ABOUND, INCLUDING THIS TRADITIONAL IRISH COMBINATION WHERE PARSNIP AND APPLE ARE USED IN EQUAL PROPORTIONS.

SERVES 6

INGREDIENTS

900g/2lb parsnips
50g/2oz/¼ cup butter
1 onion, chopped
2 garlic cloves, crushed
10ml/2 tsp ground cumin
5ml/1 tsp ground coriander
about 1.2 litres/2 pints/5 cups hot
 chicken stock
150ml/¼ pint/⅔ cup single
 (light) cream
salt and ground black pepper
chopped fresh chives or parsley
 and/or croûtons, to garnish

COOK'S TIP
Parsnips taste best after the first frost as the cold converts their starches into sugar, enhancing their sweetness.

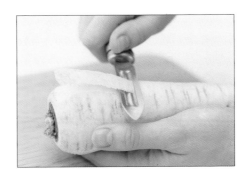

1 Peel and thinly slice the parsnips. Heat the butter in a large heavy pan and add the peeled parsnips and chopped onion with the crushed garlic. Cook until softened but not coloured, stirring occasionally. Add the ground cumin and ground coriander to the vegetable mixture and cook, stirring, for 1–2 minutes, and then gradually blend in the hot chicken stock and mix well.

2 Cover and simmer for about 20 minutes, or until the parsnip is soft. Purée the soup, adjust the texture with extra stock or water if it seems too thick, and check the seasoning. Add the cream and reheat without boiling.

3 Serve immediately, sprinkled with chopped chives or parsley and/or croûtons, to garnish.

Energy 215Kcal/899kJ; Protein 3.9g; Carbohydrate 21.3g, of which sugars 10.6g; Fat 13.3g, of which saturates 7.7g; Cholesterol 32mg; Calcium 92mg; Fibre 7.3g; Sodium 74mg.

CURRIED PARSNIP SOUP <u>WITH</u> CROÛTONS

THE MILD SWEETNESS OF PARSNIPS AND MANGO CHUTNEY IS GIVEN AN EXCITING LIFT WITH A BLEND OF SPICES IN THIS SIMPLE SOUP GARNISHED WITH NAAN CROÛTONS.

SERVES 4

INGREDIENTS
30ml/2 tbsp olive oil
1 onion, chopped
1 garlic clove, crushed
1 small green chilli, seeded and
  finely chopped
15ml/1 tbsp grated fresh
  root ginger
5 large parsnips, diced
5ml/1 tsp cumin seeds
5ml/1 tsp ground coriander
2.5ml/½ tsp ground turmeric
30ml/2 tbsp mango chutney
1.2 litres/2 pints/5 cups water
juice of 1 lime
salt and ground black pepper
60ml/4 tbsp natural (plain) yogurt
  and mango chutney, to serve
chopped fresh coriander (cilantro),
  to garnish (optional)

For the sesame naan croûtons
45ml/3 tbsp olive oil
1 large naan
15ml/1 tbsp sesame seeds

1 Heat the oil in a large pan and add the onion, garlic, chilli and ginger. Cook for 4–5 minutes, until the onion has softened. Add the parsnips and cook for 2–3 minutes. Sprinkle in the cumin seeds, coriander and turmeric and cook for 1 minute, stirring constantly.

2 Add the chutney and the water. Season well and bring to the boil. Reduce the heat and simmer for 15 minutes, until the parsnips are soft.

3 Cool the soup slightly, then process it in a food processor or blender until smooth, and return it to the saucepan. Stir in the lime juice.

4 For the naan croûtons, cut the naan into small dice. Heat the oil in a large frying pan and cook until golden all over. Remove from the heat and drain off any excess oil. Add the sesame seeds and return to the heat for 30 seconds, until the seeds are golden.

5 Ladle the soup into bowls. Add a little yogurt and top with mango chutney and naan croûtons.

Energy 189Kcal/792kJ; Protein 4g; Carbohydrate 26.6g, of which sugars 15.5g; Fat 8.2g, of which saturates 1.2g; Cholesterol 0mg; Calcium 101mg; Fibre 7.5g; Sodium 110mg.

IRISH POTATO SOUP

THIS MOST IRISH OF ALL SOUPS IS NOT ONLY EXCELLENT AS IT IS, BUT VERSATILE TOO, AS IT CAN BE USED AS A BASE FOR NUMEROUS OTHER SOUPS. USE A FLOURY POTATO, SUCH AS GOLDEN WONDER.

SERVES 6–8

INGREDIENTS
  50g/2oz/¼ cup butter
  2 large onions, peeled and
    finely chopped
  675g/1½lb potatoes, diced
  about 1.75 litres/3 pints/7½ cups
    hot chicken stock
  sea salt and ground black pepper
  a little milk, if necessary
  chopped fresh chives, to garnish

1 Melt the butter in a large heavy pan and add the onions, turning them in the butter until well coated. Cover and leave to sweat over a very low heat for about 10 mintues.

2 Add the potatoes to the pan, and mix well with the butter and onions. Season with salt and pepper, cover and cook without colouring over a gentle heat for about 10 minutes. Add the stock, bring to the boil and simmer for 25 minutes, or until the vegetables are tender.

3 Remove from the heat and allow to cool slightly. Purée the soup in batches in a blender or food processor.

4 Reheat the soup over a low heat and adjust the seasoning. If the soup seems too thick, add a little extra stock or milk to achieve the right consistency.

5 Serve the soup very hot, sprinkled with chopped chives.

COOK'S TIP
The best potatoes to use in soups are the floury ones, because they cook more quickly and disintegrate easily. Choose varieties such as Golden Wonder, Maris Piper, Estima and King Edward.

Energy 167Kcal/699kJ; Protein 2.9g; Carbohydrate 23.5g, of which sugars 5.3g; Fat 7.5g, of which saturates 4.5g; Cholesterol 18mg; Calcium 26mg; Fibre 2.1g; Sodium 201mg.

ROASTED ROOT VEGETABLE SOUP

ROASTING THE VEGETABLES GIVES THIS WINTER SOUP A WONDERFUL DEPTH OF FLAVOUR. YOU CAN USE OTHER VEGETABLES, IF YOU WISH, OR ADAPT THE QUANTITIES DEPENDING ON WHAT'S IN SEASON.

SERVES 6

INGREDIENTS

50ml/2fl oz/¼ cup olive oil
1 small butternut squash, peeled, seeded and cubed
2 carrots, cut into thick rounds
1 large parsnip, cubed
1 small swede (rutabaga), cubed
2 leeks, thickly sliced
1 onion, quartered
3 bay leaves
4 thyme sprigs, plus extra to garnish
3 rosemary sprigs
1.2 litres/2 pints/5 cups vegetable stock
salt and freshly ground black pepper
soured cream, to serve

1 Preheat the oven to 200°C/400°F/ Gas 6.

2 Pour the olive oil into a large bowl. Add the prepared vegetables and toss thoroughly with a spoon until they are all coated in the oil.

3 Spread out the vegetables in a single layer on one large or two small baking sheets. Tuck the bay leaves and the thyme and rosemary sprigs amongst the vegetables.

4 Roast the vegetables for about 50 minutes until tender, turning them occasionally to make sure they brown evenly. Remove from the oven, discard the herbs and transfer the vegetables to a large pan.

5 Pour the stock into the pan and bring to the boil. Reduce the heat, season to taste, then simmer for 10 minutes. Transfer the soup to a food processor or blender (or use a hand blender) and process for a few minutes until thick and smooth.

6 Return the soup to the pan to heat through. Season and serve with a swirl of soured cream. Garnish each serving with a sprig of thyme.

COOK'S TIP
Dried herbs can be used in place of fresh; sprinkle 2.5ml/½ tsp of each type over the vegetables in step 2 above.

Energy 65Kcal/272kJ; Protein 2.5g; Carbohydrate 11.3g, of which sugars 8.8g; Fat 1.3g, of which saturates 0.3g; Cholesterol 0mg; Calcium 93mg; Fibre 4.4g; Sodium 13mg.

LEEK, POTATO AND ROCKET SOUP

ROCKET ADDS ITS DISTINCTIVE, PEPPERY TASTE TO THIS WONDERFULLY SATISFYING SOUP.
SERVE IT HOT, GARNISHED WITH A GENEROUS SPRINKLING OF TASTY CIABATTA CROÛTONS.

SERVES 4–6

INGREDIENTS

  50g/2oz/4 tbsp butter
  1 onion, chopped
  3 leeks, chopped
  2 medium floury potatoes, diced
  900ml/1½ pints/3¾ cups light
    chicken stock or water
  2 large handfuls rocket (arugula)
  150ml/¼ pint/⅔ cup double
    (heavy) cream
  salt and ground black pepper
  garlic-flavoured ciabatta croûtons,
    to serve

1 Melt the butter in a large heavy-based pan, then add the onion, leeks and potatoes and stir until the vegetables are coated in butter. Heat the ingredients until sizzling then reduce the heat to low.

2 Cover and sweat the vegetables for 15 minutes. Pour in the stock or water and bring to the boil then reduce the heat, cover again and simmer for 20 minutes until the vegetables are tender.

3 Press the soup through a sieve (strainer) or pass through a food mill and return to the rinsed pan. (When puréeing the soup, don't use a blender or food processor, as these will give it a gluey texture.) Chop the rocket, add it to the pan and cook the soup gently, uncovered, for 5 minutes.

4 Stir in the cream, then season to taste and reheat gently. Ladle the soup into warmed soup bowls and serve with a scattering of garlic-flavoured ciabatta croûtons in each.

Energy 393Kcal/1631kJ; Protein 5.2g; Carbohydrate 23.6g, of which sugars 7.1g; Fat 31.5g, of which saturates 19.3g; Cholesterol 78mg; Calcium 87mg; Fibre 4.5g; Sodium 116mg.

CREAMY HEART OF PALM SOUP

THIS DELICATE SOUP HAS A LUXURIOUS, CREAMY, ALMOST VELVETY TEXTURE. THE SUBTLE YET DISTINCTIVE FLAVOUR OF THE PALM HEARTS IS LIKE NO OTHER, ALTHOUGH IT IS MILDLY REMINISCENT OF ARTICHOKES AND ASPARAGUS. SERVE WITH FRESH BREAD FOR A SATISFYING LUNCH.

SERVES 4

INGREDIENTS

  25g/1oz/2 tbsp butter
  10ml/2 tsp olive oil
  1 onion, finely chopped
  1 large leek, finely sliced
  15ml/1 tbsp plain (all-purpose) flour
  1 litre/1¾ pints/4 cups
    well-flavoured chicken stock
  350g/12oz potatoes, peeled
    and cubed
  2 x 400g/14oz cans hearts of palm,
    drained and sliced
  250ml/8fl oz/1 cup double
    (heavy) cream
salt and ground black pepper
cayenne pepper and chopped fresh
    chives, to garnish

1 Heat the butter and oil in a large pan over a low heat. Add the onion and leek and stir well until coated in butter. Cover and cook for 5 minutes until softened and translucent.

2 Sprinkle over the flour. Cook, stirring, for 1 minute.

3 Pour in the stock and add the potatoes. Bring to the boil, then lower the heat and simmer for 10 minutes. Stir in the hearts of palm and the cream, and simmer gently for 10 minutes.

4 Process in a blender or food processor until smooth. Return the soup to the pan and heat gently, adding a little water if necessary. The consistency should be thick but not too heavy. Season with salt and ground black pepper.

5 Ladle the soup into heated bowls and garnish each with a pinch of cayenne pepper and a scattering of fresh chives. Serve immediately.

VARIATION
For a richer, buttery flavour, add the flesh of a ripe avocado when blending.

Energy 486Kcal/2016kJ; Protein 4.9g; Carbohydrate 25.9g, of which sugars 3g; Fat 41.1g, of which saturates 24.4g; Cholesterol 99mg; Calcium 127mg; Fibre 3.7g; Sodium 97mg.

PEANUT AND POTATO SOUP

PEANUT SOUP IS A FIRM FAVOURITE THROUGHOUT CENTRAL AND SOUTH AMERICA, AND IS PARTICULARLY POPULAR IN BOLIVIA AND ECUADOR. AS IN MANY LATIN AMERICAN RECIPES, THE GROUND NUTS ARE USED AS A THICKENING AGENT, WITH UNEXPECTEDLY DELICIOUS RESULTS.

SERVES 6

INGREDIENTS
60ml/4 tbsp groundnut (peanut) oil
1 onion, finely chopped
2 garlic cloves, crushed
1 red (bell) pepper, seeded
  and chopped
250g/9oz potatoes, peeled and diced
2 fresh red chillies, seeded
  and chopped
200g/7oz canned chopped tomatoes
150g/5oz/1¼ cups unsalted peanuts
1.5 litres/2½ pints/6¼ cups beef stock
salt and ground black pepper
30ml/2 tbsp chopped fresh coriander
  (cilantro), to garnish

1 Heat the oil in a large heavy pan over a low heat. Stir in the onion and cook for 5 minutes, until beginning to soften. Add the garlic, pepper, potatoes, chillies and tomatoes. Stir well to coat the vegetables evenly in the oil, cover and cook for 5 minutes, until softened.

2 Meanwhile, toast the peanuts by gently cooking them in a large dry frying pan over a medium heat. Keep a close eye on them, moving the peanuts around the pan until they are evenly golden. Take care not to burn them.

COOK'S TIP
Replace the unsalted peanuts with peanut butter if you like. Use equal quantities of chunky and smooth peanut butter for the ideal texture.

3 Set 30ml/2 tbsp of the peanuts aside, to use as garnish. Transfer the remaining peanuts to a food processor and process until finely ground. Add the vegetables and process again until smooth.

4 Return the mixture to the pan and stir in the beef stock. Bring to the boil, then lower the heat and simmer for 10 minutes.

5 Pour the soup into heated bowls. Garnish with a generous scattering of coriander and the remaining peanuts.

Energy 260Kcal/1079kJ; Protein 8g; Carbohydrate 14.7g, of which sugars 6.2g; Fat 19.2g, of which saturates 3.6g; Cholesterol 0mg; Calcium 30mg; Fibre 3g; Sodium 20mg.

POTATO AND FENNEL SOUP WITH WARM ROSEMARY SCONES

THE SIMPLE FLAVOURS IN THIS FINE SOUP ARE ENHANCED BY THE DELICATE PERFUME OF HERB FLOWERS, AND COMPLEMENTED BY ROSEMARY-SEASONED SCONES.

SERVES 4

INGREDIENTS
75g/3oz/6 tbsp butter
2 onions, chopped
5ml/1 tsp fennel seeds, crushed
3 fennel bulbs, coarsely chopped
900g/2lb potatoes, thinly sliced
1.2 litres/2 pints/5 cups chicken
  stock
150ml/¼ pint/⅔ cup double
  (heavy) cream
salt and ground black pepper
fresh herb flowers and 15ml/
  1 tbsp chopped fresh chives,
  to garnish

For the rosemary scones (biscuits)
225g/8oz/2 cups self-raising
  (self-rising) flour
2.5ml/½ tsp salt
5ml/1 tsp baking powder
10ml/2 tsp chopped fresh
  rosemary
50g/2oz/¼ cup butter
150ml/¼ pint/⅔ cup milk
1 egg, beaten, to glaze

1 Melt the butter in a pan. Add the onions and cook gently for 10 minutes, stirring occasionally, until very soft. Add the fennel seeds and cook for 2–3 minutes. Stir in the fennel and potatoes.

2 Cover the vegetables with a sheet of wet baking parchment and put a lid on the pan. Cook gently for 10 minutes until very soft.

3 Remove the parchment. Pour in the stock, bring to the boil, cover and simmer for 35 minutes.

4 Meanwhile, make the scones. Preheat the oven to 230°C/450°F/Gas 8 and grease a baking tray. Sift the flour, salt and baking powder into a bowl. Stir in the rosemary, then rub in the butter. Add the milk and mix to form a soft dough.

5 Knead very lightly on a floured surface. Roll out to 2cm/¾in thick. Stamp out 12 rounds with a cutter.

6 Brush with the egg and bake on the prepared baking tray for 8–10 minutes, until risen and golden. Cool on a wire rack until warm.

7 Leave the soup to cool slightly, then purée it in a food processor or blender until smooth. Press through a sieve (strainer) into the rinsed pan.

8 Stir in the cream with seasoning to taste. Reheat gently but do not boil.

9 Ladle the soup into four warmed soup bowls and scatter a few herb flowers and chopped chives over each. Serve immediately with the warm rosemary scones.

Energy 797Kcal/3332kJ; Protein 12.3g; Carbohydrate 84.1g, of which sugars 8.8g; Fat 48.1g, of which saturates 29.6g; Cholesterol 120mg; Calcium 316mg; Fibre 7.6g; Sodium 703mg.

ARTICHOKE SOUP WITH ANCHOVY AND ARTICHOKE BRUSCHETTA

JERUSALEM ARTICHOKES ORIGINATE FROM NORTH AMERICA, YET LEND THEMSELVES BEAUTIFULLY TO THE METHODS AND FLAVOURS OF MEDITERRANEAN COOKING.

SERVES 6

INGREDIENTS
squeeze of lemon juice
450g/1lb Jerusalem artichokes
65g/2½oz/5 tbsp butter
175g/6oz potatoes, roughly diced
1 small onion, chopped
1 garlic clove, chopped
1 celery stick, chopped
1 small fennel bulb, halved, cored and chopped
1.2 litres/2 pints/5 cups vegetable stock
300ml/½ pint/1¼ cups double (heavy) cream
pinch of freshly grated nutmeg
salt and ground black pepper
basil leaves, to garnish

For the artichoke and anchovy bruschetta
6 thick slices French bread
1 garlic clove
50g/2oz/¼ cup unsalted butter
400g/14oz can artichoke hearts, drained and halved
45ml/3 tbsp tapenade
9 salted anchovy fillets, halved lengthways

1 Prepare a large bowl of cold water with a squeeze of lemon juice added. Peel and dice the Jerusalem artichokes, adding them to the water as soon as each one is prepared. This will prevent them from discolouring.

2 Melt the butter in a large, heavy-based saucepan. Drain the artichokes and add to the pan with the potatoes, onion, garlic, celery and fennel. Stir well and cook for 10 minutes, stirring occasionally, until beginning to soften.

3 Pour in the stock and bring to the boil, then simmer for 10–15 minutes, until all the vegetables are softened. Cool the soup slightly, then process in a food processor or blender until smooth. Press it through a sieve (strainer) into a clean pan. Add the cream and nutmeg, and season well.

4 To make the bruschetta, lightly toast the French bread slices on both sides. Rub each slice with the garlic clove and set aside. Melt the butter in a small pan. Add the artichoke hearts and cook for 3–4 minutes, turning once.

5 Spread the tapenade on the toast and arrange pieces of artichoke heart on top. Top with anchovy fillets and garnish with basil leaves.

6 Reheat the artichoke soup without allowing it to boil, then ladle it into bowls. Serve the bruschetta with the soup.

Energy 790Kcal/3303kJ; Protein 14.3g; Carbohydrate 85.6g, of which sugars 16.4g; Fat 45.8g, of which saturates 27.3g; Cholesterol 111mg; Calcium 232mg; Fibre 7.6g; Sodium 1030mg.

CREAM OF CAULIFLOWER SOUP

THIS SOUP IS LIGHT IN FLAVOUR YET SATISFYING ENOUGH FOR A LUNCHTIME SNACK.
YOU CAN TRY GREEN CAULIFLOWER FOR A COLOURFUL CHANGE.

SERVES 6

INGREDIENTS

    30ml/2 tbsp olive oil
    2 large onions, finely diced
    1 garlic clove, crushed
    3 large floury potatoes, finely diced
    3 celery sticks, finely diced
    1.75 litres/3 pints/7½ cups stock
    2 carrots, finely diced
    1 medium cauliflower, chopped
    15ml/1 tbsp chopped fresh dill
    15ml/1 tbsp lemon juice
    5ml/1 tsp mustard powder
    1.5ml/¼ tsp caraway seeds
    300ml/½ pint/1¼ cups single
     (light) cream
salt and ground black pepper
shredded spring onions (scallions)

3 Add the cauliflower, fresh dill, lemon juice, mustard powder and caraway seeds to the pan and simmer gently for 20 minutes, until the vegetables are just tender.

4 Process the soup in a blender or food processor until smooth, return to the pan and stir in the cream. Season to taste and serve garnished with shredded spring onions.

1 Heat the oil in a large pan, add the onions and garlic and fry them for a few minutes until they soften. Add the potatoes, celery and stock and simmer for 10 minutes.

2 Add the carrots and simmer for a further 10 minutes.

Energy 258Kcal/1075kJ; Protein 6.9g; Carbohydrate 26.9g, of which sugars 9.8g; Fat 14.4g, of which saturates 6.9g; Cholesterol 28mg; Calcium 95mg; Fibre 3.8g; Sodium 46mg.

CURRIED CAULIFLOWER SOUP

THIS SPICY, CREAMY SOUP IS PERFECT FOR LUNCH ON A COLD WINTER'S DAY SERVED WITH CRUSTY BREAD AND GARNISHED WITH FRESH CORIANDER.

SERVES 4

INGREDIENTS

750ml/1¼ pints/3 cups milk
1 large cauliflower
15ml/1 tbsp garam masala
salt and ground black pepper

1 Pour the milk into a large pan and place over a medium heat. Cut the cauliflower into florets and add to the milk with the garam masala and season with salt and pepper.

2 Bring the milk to the boil, then reduce the heat, partially cover the pan with a lid and simmer for about 20 minutes, or until the cauliflower is tender.

3 Let the mixture cool for a few minutes, then transfer to a food processor and process until smooth (you may have to do this in two separate batches).

4 Return the purée to the pan and heat through gently without boiling, checking and adjusting the seasoning to taste. Serve immediately.

Energy 143Kcal/601kJ; Protein 12g; Carbohydrate 13.9g, of which sugars 12.6g; Fat 4.8g, of which saturates 2.3g; Cholesterol 11mg; Calcium 271mg; Fibre 3.2g; Sodium 104mg.

SORREL, SPINACH AND DILL SOUP

THE WARM FLAVOUR OF HORSERADISH AND THE ANISEED FLAVOUR OF DILL MELD WITH SORREL AND SPINACH TO MAKE THIS UNUSUAL RUSSIAN SOUP. AN EXCELLENT SUMMER SOUP, SERVED CHILLED.

SERVES 6

INGREDIENTS
  25g/1oz/2 tbsp butter
  225g/8oz sorrel, stalks
    removed
  225g/8oz young spinach,
    stalks removed
  25g/1oz fresh horseradish,
    grated
  750ml/1¼ pints/3 cups cider
  1 pickled cucumber,
    finely chopped
  30ml/2 tbsp chopped fresh dill
  225g/8oz cooked fish, such
    as pike, perch or salmon, skinned
    and boned
  salt and ground black pepper
  sprig of dill, to garnish

1 Melt the butter in a large pan. Add the prepared sorrel and spinach leaves together with the grated fresh horseradish.

2 Cover the pan and allow to cook gently for 3–4 minutes, or until the sorrel and spinach leaves have wilted.

3 Tip into a food processor or blender and process to a fine purée (paste). Ladle into a tureen or bowl and stir in the cider, cucumber and dill.

4 Chop the fish into bitesize pieces. Add to the soup, then season well. Chill for at least 3 hours before serving, garnished with a sprig of dill.

Energy 156Kcal/653kJ; Protein 11.4g; Carbohydrate 4.8g, of which sugars 4.7g; Fat 6.6g, of which saturates 2.8g; Cholesterol 19mg; Calcium 201mg; Fibre 1.9g; Sodium 324mg.

PUMPKIN SOUP <u>WITH</u> RICE

PUMPKIN IS SO FULL OF COLOUR AND FLAVOUR THAT IT INSPIRES YOU TO BUY IT, GO HOME AND START COOKING THIS DELICIOUS WINTER SOUP.

SERVES 4

INGREDIENTS

   1.1kg/2lb 7oz pumpkin
   750ml/1¼ pints/3 cups
     chicken stock
   750ml/1¼ pints/3 cups semi-
     skimmed (low-fat) milk
   10–15ml/2–3 tsp sugar
   75g/3oz/½ cup cooked white rice
   salt and ground black pepper
   5ml/1 tsp ground cinnamon,
     to serve

1 Remove the seeds from the pumpkin, cut off the peel and chop the flesh.

2 Place in a pan and add the stock, milk, sugar and seasoning. Bring to the boil, then reduce the heat and simmer for about 20 minutes, or until the pumpkin is tender. Drain the pumpkin, reserving the liquid, and purée it in a food processor, then return it to the pan with the liquid.

3 Bring the soup back to the boil, throw in the rice and simmer for a few minutes. Check the seasoning, pour into bowls and dust with cinnamon.

Energy 202Kcal/856kJ; Protein 9.7g; Carbohydrate 33.1g, of which sugars 15.6g; Fat 4.4g, of which saturates 2.5g; Cholesterol 11mg; Calcium 315mg; Fibre 2.8g; Sodium 82mg.

ROASTED GARLIC AND BUTTERNUT SQUASH SOUP WITH TOMATO SALSA

THIS IS A WONDERFUL, RICHLY FLAVOURED DISH. A SPOONFUL OF THE HOT AND SPICY TOMATO SALSA GIVES BITE TO THE SWEET-TASTING SQUASH AND GARLIC SOUP.

SERVES 4–5

INGREDIENTS

   2 garlic bulbs, outer skin removed
   75ml/5 tbsp olive oil
   a few fresh thyme sprigs
   1 large butternut squash, halved
     and seeded
   2 onions, chopped
   5ml/1 tsp ground coriander
   1.2 litres/2 pints/5 cups vegetable
     or chicken stock
   30–45ml/2–3 tbsp chopped fresh
     oregano or marjoram
   salt and ground black pepper
For the salsa
   4 large ripe tomatoes, halved
     and seeded
   1 red (bell) pepper, halved
     and seeded
   1 large fresh red chilli, halved
     and seeded
   30–45ml/2–3 tbsp extra virgin
     olive oil
   15ml/1 tbsp balsamic vinegar
   pinch of caster (superfine) sugar

1 Preheat the oven to 220°C/425°F/ Gas 7. Place the garlic bulbs on a piece of foil and pour over half the olive oil. Add the thyme sprigs, then fold the foil around the garlic bulbs to enclose them completely. Place the foil parcel on a baking sheet with the butternut squash and brush the squash with 15ml/1 tbsp of the remaining olive oil. Add the tomatoes, red pepper and fresh chilli for the salsa.

2 Roast the vegetables for 25 minutes, then remove the tomatoes, pepper and chilli. Reduce the temperature to 190°C/375°F/Gas 5 and cook the squash and garlic for 20–25 minutes more, or until the squash is tender.

3 Heat the remaining oil in a large, heavy-based pan and cook the onions and ground coriander gently for about 10 minutes, or until softened.

4 Skin the pepper and chilli and process in a food processor or blender with the tomatoes and 30ml/2 tbsp olive oil. Stir in the vinegar and seasoning to taste, adding a pinch of caster sugar. Add the remaining oil if you think the salsa needs it.

5 Squeeze the roasted garlic out of its papery skin into the onions and scoop the squash out of its skin, adding it to the pan. Add the stock, 5ml/1 tsp salt and plenty of black pepper. Bring to the boil and simmer for 10 minutes.

6 Stir in half the oregano or marjoram and cool the soup slightly, then process it in a blender or food processor. Alternatively, press the soup through a fine sieve (strainer).

7 Reheat the soup without allowing it to boil, then taste for seasoning before ladling it into warmed bowls. Top each with a spoonful of salsa and sprinkle over the remaining chopped oregano or marjoram. Serve immediately.

Energy 303Kcal/1256kJ; Protein 4.2g; Carbohydrate 20.7g, of which sugars 16.6g; Fat 23.2g, of which saturates 3.5g; Cholesterol 0mg; Calcium 107mg; Fibre 5.7g; Sodium 15mg.

SPICY ROASTED PUMPKIN SOUP
WITH PUMPKIN CRISPS

THE PUMPKIN IS ROASTED WHOLE, THEN SPLIT OPEN AND SCOOPED OUT TO MAKE THIS DELICIOUS SOUP; TOPPED WITH CRISP STRIPS OF FRIED PUMPKIN, IT IS A REAL TREAT.

SERVES 6–8

INGREDIENTS
1.5kg/3–3½lb pumpkin
90ml/6 tbsp olive oil
2 onions, chopped
3 garlic cloves, chopped
7.5cm/3in piece fresh root
 ginger, grated
5ml/1 tsp ground coriander
2.5ml/½ tsp ground turmeric
pinch of cayenne pepper
1 litre/1¾ pints/4 cups
 vegetable stock
salt and ground black pepper
15ml/1 tbsp sesame seeds and
 fresh coriander (cilantro) leaves,
 to garnish
For the pumpkin crisps
 wedge of fresh pumpkin, seeded
 120ml/4fl oz/½ cup olive oil

1 Preheat the oven to 200°C/400°F/ Gas 6. Prick the pumpkin around the top several times with a fork. Brush the pumpkin with plenty of the oil and bake for 45 minutes or until tender. Leave until cool enough to handle.

2 Take care when cutting the pumpkin as there may still be a lot of hot steam inside. When cool enough to handle, scoop out and discard the seeds. Scoop out and chop the flesh.

3 Heat 60ml/4 tbsp of the remaining oil (you may not have to use all of it) in a large pan and add the onions, garlic and ginger, then cook gently for 4–5 minutes. Add the coriander, turmeric and cayenne, and cook for 2 minutes. Stir in the pumpkin flesh and stock. Bring to the boil, reduce the heat and simmer for 20 minutes.

COOK'S TIP
If only large pumpkins are available, cut off two or three large wedges weighing 1.5kg/3–31/2lb in total. Brush with oil and roast for 20–30 minutes until tender.

4 Cool the soup slightly, then purée it in a food processor or blender until smooth. Return the soup to the rinsed pan and season well.

5 Meanwhile, prepare the pumpkin crisps. Using a swivel-blade potato peeler, pare off long thin strips.

6 Heat the oil in a small pan and fry the strips in batches for 2–3 minutes, until crisp. Drain on kitchen paper.

7 Reheat the soup and ladle it into bowls. Top with the pumpkin crisps and garnish each portion with sesame seeds and coriander leaves.

Energy 271Kcal/1119kJ; Protein 3.1g; Carbohydrate 11.1g, of which sugars 8.2g; Fat 24.1g, of which saturates 3.6g; Cholesterol 0mg; Calcium 110mg; Fibre 3.8g; Sodium 3mg.

FRESH TOMATO SOUP

THE COMBINATION OF INTENSELY FLAVOURED SUN-RIPENED AND FRESH TOMATOES NEEDS LITTLE EMBELLISHMENT IN THIS TASTY ITALIAN SOUP. CHOOSE THE RIPEST-LOOKING TOMATOES.

SERVES 6

INGREDIENTS

   1.3–1.6kg/3–3½lb ripe tomatoes
   400ml/14fl oz/1⅔ cups chicken or
      vegetable stock
   45ml/3 tbsp sun-dried tomato
      purée (paste)
   30–45ml/2–3 tbsp balsamic vinegar
   10–15ml/2–3 tsp sugar
   a small handful of fresh basil leaves,
      plus extra to garnish
   salt and ground black pepper
   toasted cheese croûtes and crème
      fraîche, to serve

COOK'S TIP
Use a sharp knife to cut a cross in the base of each tomato before plunging it into the boiling water. The skin will then peel back easily from the crosses.

1 Plunge the tomatoes into boiling water for 30 seconds, then refresh in cold water. Peel off the skins and quarter the tomatoes. Put them in a large pan and pour over the chicken or vegetable stock. Bring just to the boil, reduce the heat, cover and simmer gently for 10 minutes until the tomatoes are pulpy.

2 Stir in the tomato purée, vinegar, sugar and basil. Season with salt and pepper, then cook gently, stirring, for 2 minutes. Process the soup in a blender or food processor, then return to a clean pan and reheat gently. Serve in bowls, topped with one or two toasted cheese croûtes and a spoonful of crème fraîche, garnished with basil leaves.

Energy 52Kcal/225kJ; Protein 1.9g; Carbohydrate 10.4g, of which sugars 10.4g; Fat 0.7g, of which saturates 0.2g; Cholesterol 0mg; Calcium 19mg; Fibre 2.4g; Sodium 38mg.

TOMATO SOUP <u>WITH</u> RED PEPPER CREAM

THIS DAZZLING SOUP CAN BE MADE AS FIERY OR AS MILD AS YOU LIKE BY INCREASING OR REDUCING THE NUMBER OF CHILLIES.

4 Transfer the pepper for the pepper cream to a bowl as soon as it is cooked. Cover with clear film (plastic wrap) and leave to cool. Peel away the skin and purée the flesh in a food processor or blender with half the crème fraîche. Pour into a bowl and stir in the remaining crème fraîche. Season and add a dash of Tabasco sauce. Chill in the refrigerator until required.

5 Process the roasted vegetables in batches, adding a ladleful of stock to each batch to make a smooth, thick purée. Depending on how juicy the tomatoes are, you may not need all the vegetable stock.

6 Press the purée through a sieve (strainer) into a pan and stir in more stock if you want to thin the soup. Heat gently and season well. Ladle the soup into bowls and spoon red pepper cream into the centre of each bowl. Pile wild rocket leaves on top to garnish.

SERVES 4

INGREDIENTS
  1.5kg/3–3½lb plum tomatoes, halved
  5 red chillies, seeded
  1 red (bell) pepper, halved
    and seeded
  2 red onions, roughly chopped
  6 garlic cloves, crushed
  30ml/2 tbsp sun-dried tomato paste
  45ml/3 tbsp olive oil
  400ml/14fl oz/1⅔ cups
    vegetable stock
  salt and ground black pepper
  wild rocket (arugula), to garnish
For the pepper cream
  1 red pepper, halved and
    seeded
  10ml/2 tsp olive oil
  120ml/4fl oz/½ cup crème fraîche
  a few drops of Tabasco sauce

1 Preheat the oven to 200°C/400°F/ Gas 6. Place the tomatoes, chillies, red pepper, onions, garlic and tomato paste in a roasting tin (pan). Toss all the vegetables, drizzle with the oil and toss again, then roast for 40 minutes, until tender and the pepper skin is slightly charred.

2 Meanwhile make the pepper cream. Lay the red pepper halves skin side up on a baking tray and brush with the olive oil.

3 Roast with the mixed vegetables for about 30–40 minutes, until blistered.

COOK'S TIP
The pepper cream may be a bit runny when first processed, but it firms up when chilled.

Energy 319Kcal/1330kJ; Protein 5.3g; Carbohydrate 23.5g, of which sugars 22g; Fat 23.4g, of which saturates 10g; Cholesterol 34mg; Calcium 67mg; Fibre 6.2g; Sodium 72mg.

TOMATO SOUP <u>WITH</u> BLACK OLIVE CIABATTA TOASTS

TOMATO SOUP IS EVERYBODY'S FAVOURITE, PARTICULARLY WHEN MADE WITH FRESH SUN-RIPENED TOMATOES. THIS DELICIOUS SOUP IS WONDERFULLY WARMING AND HAS AN EARTHY RICHNESS.

SERVES 6

INGREDIENTS

    450g/1lb very ripe fresh tomatoes
    30ml/2 tbsp olive oil
    1 onion, chopped
    1 garlic clove, crushed
    30ml/2 tbsp sherry vinegar
    30ml/2 tbsp tomato purée (paste)
    15ml/1 tbsp cornflour (cornstarch)
      or potato flour
    300ml/½ pint/1¼ cups passata
      (bottled strained tomatoes)
    1 bay leaf
    900ml/1½ pints/3¾ cups vegetable
      or chicken stock
    200ml/7fl oz/scant 1 cup crème fraîche
    salt and ground black pepper
    basil leaves, to garnish
For the black olive ciabatta toasts
    1 plain or black olive ciabatta
    1 small red (bell) pepper
    3 whole garlic cloves, skins on
    225g/8oz black olives (preferably
      a wrinkly Greek variety)
    30–45ml/2–3 tbsp salted capers or
      capers in vinegar
    12 drained canned anchovy fillets
      or 1 small can tuna in oil, drained
    about 150ml/¼ pint/⅔ cup good-
      quality olive oil
    fresh lemon juice and ground black
      pepper, to taste
    45ml/3 tbsp chopped fresh basil

1 Make the ciabatta toasts first. Preheat the oven to 200°C/400°F/Gas 6. Split the ciabatta in half and cut each half into nine fingers to give 18 in total. Arrange on a baking sheet and bake for 10–15 minutes until golden and crisp.

2 Place the whole pepper and garlic cloves under a hot grill (broiler) and cook for 15 minutes, turning, until charred all over. If you prefer, you can bake them in the oven for about 25 minutes. Once charred, put the garlic and pepper in a plastic bag, seal and leave to cool for about 10 minutes.

3 When the pepper is cool, peel off the skin (do not wash) and remove the stalk and seeds. Peel the skin off the garlic. Stone (pit) the olives. Rinse the capers under running water to remove the salt or vinegar. Place the prepared ingredients in a food processor with the anchovies or tuna and process until roughly chopped.

4 With the machine running, slowly add the olive oil until you have a fairly smooth dark paste. Alternatively, just stir in the olive oil for a chunkier result. Season to taste with lemon juice and pepper. Stir in the basil.

5 Spread the paste on the finger toasts, or, if not using immediately, transfer to a jar, cover with a layer of olive oil and keep in the refrigerator for up to three weeks.

6 For the soup, cut the tomatoes in half and remove the seeds and pulp using a lemon squeezer. Press the pulp through a sieve (strainer) and reserve the liquid.

7 Heat the oil in a pan and add the onion, garlic, sherry vinegar, tomato purée and the tomato halves. Stir, then cover the pan and cook over a low heat for 1 hour, stirring occasionally. When done, process the soup in a blender or food processor until smooth, then pass through a sieve to remove any pieces of skin. Return to the pan.

8 Mix the cornflour or potato flour with the reserved tomato pulp, then stir into the hot soup with the passata, bay leaf and stock. Simmer for 30 minutes. Stir in the crème fraîche and garnish with the basil leaves. Serve piping hot, with the ciabatta toasts.

Energy 532Kcal/2211kJ; Protein 11.9g; Carbohydrate 29.3g, of which sugars 7.6g; Fat 41.7g, of which saturates 13.2g; Cholesterol 50mg; Calcium 120mg; Fibre 3.5g; Sodium 1352mg.

BABY CHERRY TOMATO SOUP
WITH ROCKET PESTO

FOR THEIR SIZE, BABY TOMATOES ARE A POWERHOUSE OF SWEETNESS AND FLAVOUR. HERE THEY ARE COMPLEMENTED BEAUTIFULLY BY A RICH PASTE OF PEPPERY ROCKET.

SERVES 4

INGREDIENTS
   225g/8oz baby cherry
      tomatoes, halved
   225g/8oz baby plum tomatoes, halved
   225g/8oz vine-ripened
      tomatoes, halved
   2 shallots, roughly chopped
   25ml/1½ tbsp sun-dried
      tomato paste
   600ml/1 pint/2½ cups
      vegetable stock
   salt and ground black pepper
   ice cubes, to serve
For the pesto
   15g/½oz rocket (arugula) leaves
   75ml/5 tbsp olive oil
   15g/½oz/2 tbsp pine nuts
   1 garlic clove
   25g/1oz/⅓ cup freshly grated
      Parmesan cheese

1 Purée all the tomatoes and the shallots in a food processor or blender. Add the sun-dried tomato paste and process until smooth. Press the purée through a sieve (strainer) into a pan.

2 Add the vegetable stock, bring to the boil and simmer gently for 4–5 minutes. Season well with salt and black pepper. Leave to cool, then chill in the refrigerator for at least 4 hours.

3 To make the pesto, purée the rocket, oil, pine nuts and garlic using a mortar and pestle. Alternatively, use a food processor.

4 Stir the Parmesan cheese into the pesto mix, grinding it well.

5 Ladle the soup into bowls and add a few ice cubes to each. Spoon some of the rocket pesto into the centre of each portion and serve.

VARIATION
The pesto can be made with other soft-leaved herbs in place of rocket. Try fresh basil, coriander (cilantro) or mint, or use a mixture of herb leaves, if you like. Parsley and mint are a good flavour combination and make delicious pesto.

Energy 197Kcal/819kJ; Protein 4.9g; Carbohydrate 7.9g, of which sugars 7.6g; Fat 16.5g, of which saturates 3.3g; Cholesterol 6mg; Calcium 101mg; Fibre 2.4g; Sodium 105mg.

TOMATO, CIABATTA <u>AND</u> BASIL OIL SOUP

THROUGHOUT EUROPE, BREAD IS A POPULAR INGREDIENT FOR THICKENING SOUP, AND THIS RECIPE SHOWS HOW WONDERFULLY QUICK AND EASY THIS METHOD CAN BE.

SERVES 4

INGREDIENTS
  45ml/3 tbsp olive oil
  1 red onion, chopped
  6 garlic cloves, chopped
  300ml/½ pint/1¼ cups white wine
  150ml/¼ pint/⅔ cup water
  12 plum tomatoes, quartered
  2 x 400g/14oz cans plum tomatoes
  2.5ml/½ tsp sugar
  ½ ciabatta loaf
  salt and ground black pepper
  basil leaves, to garnish
For the basil oil
  115g/4oz basil leaves
  120ml/4fl oz/½ cup olive oil

1 For the basil oil, process the basil and oil in a food processor or blender to make a paste. Line a bowl with muslin (cheesecloth) and scrape the paste into it. Gather up the muslin and squeeze firmly to extract all the oil. Set aside.

2 Heat the oil in a large pan and cook the onion and garlic for 4–5 minutes until softened.

3 Add the wine, water, fresh and canned tomatoes. Bring to the boil, reduce the heat and cover the pan, then simmer for 3–4 minutes. Add the sugar and season well with salt and black pepper.

4 Break the bread into bite-sized pieces and stir into the soup.

5 Ladle the soup into bowls. Garnish with basil and drizzle the basil oil over each portion.

Energy 332Kcal/1396kJ; Protein 7.8g; Carbohydrate 35.4g, of which sugars 16.3g; Fat 13.4g, of which saturates 2g; Cholesterol 0mg; Calcium 98mg; Fibre 5g; Sodium 306mg.

ROASTED PEPPER SOUP
WITH PARMESAN TOAST

THE SECRET OF THIS SOUP IS TO SERVE IT JUST COLD, NOT OVER-CHILLED, TOPPED WITH HOT PARMESAN TOAST DRIPPING WITH CHEESE AND MELTED BUTTER.

SERVES 4

INGREDIENTS

  1 onion, quartered
  4 garlic cloves, unpeeled
  2 red (bell) peppers, seeded
    and quartered
  2 yellow (bell) peppers, seeded
    and quartered
  30–45ml/2–3 tbsp olive oil
  grated rind and juice of 1 orange
  200g/7oz can chopped tomatoes
  600ml/1 pint/2½ cups cold water
  salt and ground black pepper
  30ml/2 tbsp chopped fresh chives,
    to garnish (optional)
For the hot Parmesan toast
  1 medium baguette
  50g/2oz/¼ cup butter
  175g/6oz Parmesan cheese

1 Preheat the oven to 200°C/400°F/ Gas 6. Put the onion, garlic and peppers in a roasting tin (pan). Drizzle the oil over the vegetables and mix well, then turn the pieces of pepper skin sides up. Roast for 25–30 minutes, until slightly charred, then allow to cool slightly.

2 Squeeze the garlic flesh out of the skins into a food processor or blender. Add the roasted vegetables, orange rind and juice, tomatoes and water. Process until smooth.

COOK'S TIP
If you don't have a champignon, then use the bottom of a large ladle or the back of a wooden spoon instead.

3 Press the mixture through a sieve into a bowl using a champignon. Season well and chill for 30 minutes.

4 Make the Parmesan toasts when you are ready to serve the soup. Preheat the grill (broiler) to high. Tear the baguette in half lengthways, then tear or cut it across to give four large pieces. Spread the pieces of bread with butter.

5 Pare most of the Parmesan into thin slices or shavings using a swivel-bladed vegetable knife or a small paring knife, then finely grate the remainder.

6 Arrange the sliced Parmesan on the toasts, then dredge with the grated cheese. Transfer the cheese-topped baguette pieces to a large baking sheet or grill (broiler) rack and toast under the grill for a few minutes until the topping is well browned.

7 Ladle the chilled soup into large, shallow bowls and sprinkle with chopped fresh chives, if using, and plenty of freshly ground black pepper.

8 Serve the craggy hot Parmesan toast with the chilled soup.

Energy 124Kcal/516kJ; Protein 2.4g; Carbohydrate 15g, of which sugars 14.2g; Fat 6.4g, of which saturates 1g; Cholesterol 0mg; Calcium 23mg; Fibre 3.5g; Sodium 13mg.

SUMMER HERB SOUP <u>WITH</u> CHARGRILLED RADICCHIO

THE SWEETNESS OF SHALLOTS AND LEEKS IN THIS SOUP IS BALANCED BEAUTIFULLY BY THE SLIGHTLY ACIDIC SORREL WITH ITS HINT OF LEMON, AND A BOUQUET OF SUMMER HERBS.

SERVES 4–6

INGREDIENTS

   30ml/2 tbsp dry white wine
   2 shallots, finely chopped
   1 garlic clove, crushed
   2 leeks, sliced
   1 large potato, about 225g/8oz,
     roughly chopped
   2 courgettes (zucchini), chopped
   600ml/1 pint/2½ cups water
   115g/4oz sorrel, torn
   large handful of fresh chervil
   large handful of fresh flat leaf parsley
   large handful of fresh mint
   1 round (butterhead) lettuce,
     separated into leaves
   600ml/1 pint/2½ cups
     vegetable stock
   1 small head of radicchio
   5ml/1 tsp groundnut (peanut) oil
   salt and ground black pepper

1 Put the wine, shallots and garlic into a heavy-based pan and bring to the boil. Cook for 2–3 minutes, until softened.

2 Add the leeks, potato and courgette with enough of the water to come about halfway up the vegetables. Lay a wetted piece of greaseproof paper over the vegetables and put a lid on the pan, then cook for 10–15 minutes, until soft.

3 Remove the paper and add the fresh herbs and lettuce. Cook for 1–2 minutes, or until wilted.

4 Pour in the remaining water and the vegetable stock and simmer for 10–12 minutes. Cool the soup slightly, then process it in a food processor or blender until smooth. Return the soup to the rinsed-out pan and season well.

5 Cut the radicchio into thin wedges that hold together, then brush the cut sides with the oil. Heat a ridged griddle or frying pan until very hot and add the radicchio wedges.

6 Cook the radicchio for 1 minute on each side until slightly charred. Reheat the soup over a low heat, then ladle it into warmed shallow bowls. Serve a wedge of charred radicchio on top.

Energy 102Kcal/428kJ; Protein 5g; Carbohydrate 15.1g, of which sugars 5.7g; Fat 2.2g, of which saturates 0.4g; Cholesterol 0mg; Calcium 135mg; Fibre 4.9g; Sodium 57mg.

AUBERGINE SOUP <u>WITH</u> MOZZARELLA <u>AND</u> GREMOLATA

GREMOLATA, A CLASSIC ITALIAN MIXTURE OF GARLIC, LEMON AND PARSLEY, ADDS A FLOURISH OF FRESH FLAVOUR TO THIS RICH CREAM SOUP.

SERVES 6

INGREDIENTS
   30ml/2 tbsp olive oil
   2 shallots, chopped
   2 garlic cloves, chopped
   1kg/2¼lb aubergines (eggplant),
     trimmed and roughly chopped
   1 litre/1¾ pints/4 cups
     chicken stock
   150ml/¼ pint/⅔ cup double
     (heavy) cream
   30ml/2 tbsp chopped
     fresh parsley
   175g/6oz buffalo mozzarella,
     thinly sliced
   salt and ground black pepper

For the gremolata
   2 garlic cloves, finely chopped
   grated rind of 2 lemons
   15ml/1 tbsp chopped fresh parsley

1 Heat the oil in a large pan and add the shallots and garlic. Cook for 4–5 minutes, until soft. Add the aubergines and cook for about 25 minutes, stirring occasionally, until soft and browned.

2 Pour in the stock and cook for about 5 minutes. Leave the soup to cool slightly, then purée in a food processor or blender until smooth. Return to the rinsed pan and season. Add the cream and parsley and bring to the boil.

3 Mix the ingredients for the gremolata in a small bowl.

4 Ladle the soup into bowls and lay the mozzarella on top. Scatter with gremolata and serve.

Energy 261Kcal/1079kJ; Protein 7.5g; Carbohydrate 4.9g, of which sugars 4.3g; Fat 23.7g, of which saturates 13.1g; Cholesterol 51mg; Calcium 137mg; Fibre 3.5g; Sodium 124mg.

SIMPLE CREAM OF ONION SOUP

THIS WONDERFULLY SOOTHING SOUP HAS A DEEP, BUTTERY FLAVOUR THAT IS COMPLEMENTED BY
CRISP CROÛTONS OR CHOPPED CHIVES, SPRINKLED OVER JUST BEFORE SERVING.

SERVES 4

INGREDIENTS

115g/4oz/½ cup unsalted butter
1kg/2¼lb yellow onions, sliced
1 fresh bay leaf
105ml/7 tbsp dry white vermouth
1 litre/1¾ pints/4 cups good chicken
  or vegetable stock
150ml/¼ pint/⅔ cup double
  (heavy) cream
a little lemon juice (optional)
salt and ground black pepper
croûtons or chopped fresh chives,
  to garnish

COOK'S TIP
Adding the second batch of onions
gives texture and a buttery flavour to this
soup. Make sure they do not brown.

1 Melt 75g/3oz/6 tbsp of the butter
in a large heavy-based pan. Set about
200g/7oz of the onions aside and add
the rest to the pan with the bay leaf.
Stir to coat in the butter, then cover and
cook very gently for about 30 minutes.
The onions should be very soft and
tender, but not browned.

2 Add the vermouth, increase the heat
and boil rapidly until the liquid has
evaporated. Add the stock, 5ml/1 tsp
salt and pepper to taste. Bring to the
boil, lower the heat and simmer for
5 minutes, then remove from the heat.

3 Leave to cool, then discard the bay
leaf and process the soup in a blender
or food processor. Return the soup to
the rinsed pan.

4 Meanwhile, melt the remaining butter
in another pan and cook the remaining
onions slowly, covered, until soft but not
browned. Uncover and continue to cook
gently until golden yellow.

5 Add the cream to the soup and
reheat it gently until hot, but do not
allow it to boil. Taste and adjust the
seasoning, adding a little lemon juice if
liked. Add the buttery onions and stir
for 1–2 minutes, then ladle the soup
into bowls. Sprinkle with croûtons or
chopped chives and serve.

Energy 519Kcal/2139kJ; Protein 3.8g; Carbohydrate 21.4g, of which sugars 15.6g; Fat 44.3g, of which saturates 27.5g; Cholesterol 113mg; Calcium 88mg; Fibre 3.5g; Sodium 193mg.

SHERRIED ONION <u>AND</u> ALMOND SOUP
<u>WITH</u> SAFFRON

THE SPANISH COMBINATION OF ONIONS, SHERRY AND SAFFRON GIVES THIS PALE YELLOW SOUP
A BEGUILING FLAVOUR THAT IS PERFECT AS THE OPENING COURSE OF A SPECIAL MEAL.

2 Add the saffron strands and cook, uncovered, for 3–4 minutes, then add the ground almonds and cook, stirring constantly, for another 2–3 minutes. Pour in the stock and sherry and stir in 5ml/1 tsp salt. Season with plenty of black pepper. Bring to the boil, then lower the heat and simmer gently for about 10 minutes.

SERVES 4

INGREDIENTS
   40g/1½oz/3 tbsp butter
   2 large yellow onions, thinly sliced
   1 small garlic clove, finely chopped
   good pinch of saffron strands (about
      12 strands)
   50g/2oz blanched almonds, toasted
      and finely ground
   750ml/1¼ pints/3 cups good chicken
      or vegetable stock
   45ml/3 tbsp dry sherry
   salt and ground black pepper
   30ml/2 tbsp flaked or slivered
      almonds, toasted and chopped,
      and fresh parsley, to garnish

1 Melt the butter in a heavy-based pan over a low heat. Add the onions and garlic, stirring to coat them thoroughly in the butter, then cover the pan and cook very gently, stirring frequently, for 15–20 minutes, until the onions are a soft texture and golden yellow in colour.

VARIATION
This soup is also delicious served chilled. Use olive oil rather than butter and add a little more chicken or vegetable stock to make a slightly thinner soup, then leave to cool and chill for at least 4 hours. Just before serving, taste for seasoning. Float 1–2 ice cubes in each bowl.

3 Process the soup in a blender or food processor until smooth, then return it to the rinsed pan. Reheat slowly, stirring occasionally, but do not allow the soup to boil. Taste for seasoning, adding more salt and pepper if required.

4 Ladle the soup into heated bowls, garnish with the toasted flaked or slivered almonds and a little parsley, and serve immediately.

Energy 255Kcal/1054kJ; Protein 5.8g; Carbohydrate 11.5g, of which sugars 8.1g; Fat 19.6g, of which saturates 6.1g; Cholesterol 21mg; Calcium 82mg; Fibre 3.2g; Sodium 68mg.

POTATO AND ROASTED GARLIC BROTH

ROASTED GARLIC TAKES ON A SUBTLE, SWEET FLAVOUR IN THIS DELICIOUS VEGETARIAN SOUP. SERVE IT PIPING HOT WITH MELTED CHEDDAR OR GRUYÈRE CHEESE ON FRENCH BREAD, AS A WINTER WARMER.

SERVES 4

INGREDIENTS
    2 small or 1 large whole head of
      garlic (about 20 cloves)
    4 medium potatoes (about 500g/
      1¼lb in total), diced
    1.75 litres/3 pints/7½ cups
      good-quality hot vegetable stock
    chopped flat leaf parsley, to garnish

COOK'S TIP
Choose floury potatoes such as Maris
Piper, Estima, Cara or King Edward to
give the soup a delicious velvety texture.

VARIATION
If you are not a vegetarian, you can
use chicken or beef stock for a slightly
different flavour.

1 Preheat the oven to 190°C/375°F/
Gas 5. Place the unpeeled garlic bulbs
or bulb in a small roasting tin (pan)
and bake for 30 minutes until soft in
the centre.

2 Meanwhile, par-boil the potatoes in a
large pan of lightly salted boiling water
for 10 minutes.

3 Simmer the stock in another pan for
5 minutes. Drain the potatoes and add
them to the stock.

4 Squeeze the garlic pulp into the soup,
reserving a few whole cloves, stir and
season to taste. Simmer for 15 minutes
and serve topped with the whole garlic
cloves and parsley.

Energy 115Kcal/488kJ; Protein 4.3g; Carbohydrate 24.3g, of which sugars 2.1g; Fat 0.7g, of which saturates 0.2g; Cholesterol 0mg; Calcium 14mg; Fibre 2.3g; Sodium 219mg.

GARLIC SOUP WITH EGG AND CROÛTONS

SPANISH SOUP AND ITALIAN POLENTA MARRY WONDERFULLY WELL IN THIS RECIPE. THE DELICIOUS GARLIC SOUP ORIGINATES FROM ANDALUSIA IN SPAIN.

SERVES 4

INGREDIENTS

15ml/1 tbsp olive oil
1 garlic bulb, unpeeled and broken
  into cloves
4 slices day-old ciabatta bread,
  broken into pieces
1.2 litres/2 pints/5 cups
  chicken stock
pinch of saffron
15ml/1 tbsp white wine vinegar
4 eggs
salt and ground black pepper
chopped fresh parsley,
  to garnish
For the polenta
750ml/1¼ pints/3 cups milk
175g/6oz/1 cup quick-cook polenta
50g/2oz/¼ cup butter

1 Preheat the oven to 200°C/400°F/ Gas 6. Brush the oil over a roasting tin (pan), then add the garlic and bread, and roast for about 20 minutes, until the garlic is soft and the bread is dry. Leave until cool enough to handle.

2 Meanwhile, make the polenta. Bring the milk to the boil in a large, heavy-based pan and gradually pour in the polenta, stirring constantly. Cook for about 5 minutes, or according to the packet instructions, stirring frequently, until the polenta begins to come away from the side of the pan.

3 Spoon the polenta on to a chopping board and spread out to about 1cm/½in thick. Allow to cool and set, then cut into 1cm/½in dice.

4 Squeeze the garlic cloves from their skins into a food processor or blender. Add the dried bread and 300ml/½ pint/1¼ cups of the stock, then process until smooth. Pour into a pan. Pound the saffron in a mortar and stir in a little of the remaining stock, then add to the soup with enough of the remaining stock to thin the soup as required.

5 Melt the butter in a frying pan and cook the diced polenta over a high heat for 1–2 minutes, tossing until beginning to brown. Drain on kitchen paper.

6 Season the soup and reheat gently. Bring a large frying pan of water to the boil. Add the vinegar and reduce the heat to a simmer. Crack an egg on to a saucer. Swirl the water with a knife and drop the egg into the middle of the swirl. Repeat with the remaining eggs and poach for 2–3 minutes until set. Lift out the eggs using a draining spoon, then place one in each of four bowls.

7 Ladle the soup over the poached eggs, scatter polenta croûtons and parsley on top and serve.

Energy 415Kcal/1731kJ; Protein 13.4g; Carbohydrate 43.9g, of which sugars 0.9g; Fat 20.8g, of which saturates 8.6g; Cholesterol 217mg; Calcium 57mg; Fibre 1.9g; Sodium 247mg.

MUSHROOM SOUP

USING A MIXTURE OF MUSHROOMS GIVES THIS SOUP CHARACTER. THIS MAKES A FLAVOURSOME LIGHT MEAL SERVED WITH FRESH CRUSTY BREAD.

SERVES 4–6 AS A LIGHT MEAL
OR 6–8 AS A SOUP COURSE

INGREDIENTS
    20g/³⁄₄oz/1½ tbsp butter
    15ml/1 tbsp oil
    1 onion, roughly chopped
    4 potatoes, about 250–350g/9–12oz,
        roughly chopped
    350g/12oz mixed mushrooms, such
        as Paris Browns, field (portabello)
        and button (white), cleaned and
        roughly chopped
    1 or 2 garlic cloves, crushed
    150ml/¼ pint/²⁄₃ cup white wine or
        dry (hard) cider
    1.2 litres/2 pints/5 cups good
        chicken stock
    bunch of fresh parsley, chopped
    salt and ground black pepper
    whipped or sour cream,
        to garnish

1 Heat the butter and oil in a large pan over medium heat. Add the chopped onion, turning it in the butter until well coated. Stir in the potatoes. Cover and sweat over a low heat for 5–10 minutes until softened but not browned.

2 Add the mushrooms, garlic and white wine or cider and stock. Season, bring to the boil and cook for 15 minutes, until all the ingredients are tender.

3 Put the mixture through a mouli-legume (food mill), using the coarse blade, or liquidize (blend). Return the soup to the rinsed pan, and add three-quarters of the parsley. Bring back to the boil, season, and garnish with cream and the remaining parsley.

GARLIC SOUP

THIS INTERESTING AND SURPRISINGLY SUBTLY FLAVOURED IRISH SOUP MAKES GOOD USE OF AN ANCIENT INGREDIENT THAT IS NOT ONLY DELICIOUS BUT ALSO BELIEVED TO HAVE HEALTH-GIVING PROPERTIES. IT CERTAINLY BRINGS A GREAT SENSE OF WELL-BEING AND IS A REAL TREAT FOR GARLIC-LOVERS. SERVE IT WITH SOME CRUSTY BREAD AS A REAL WINTER WARMER .

SERVES 8

INGREDIENTS
    12 large garlic cloves, peeled
    15ml/1 tbsp olive oil
    15ml/1 tbsp melted butter
    1 small onion, finely chopped
    15g/½oz/2 tbsp plain
        (all-purpose) flour
    15ml/1 tbsp white wine vinegar
    1 litre/1¾ pints/4 cups good
        chicken stock
    2 egg yolks, lightly beaten
    bread croûtons, fried in butter,
        to serve

VARIATION
Grilled croûtes make a nice change in place of the croûtons. Toast small slices of baguette, top with grated Cheddar and grill (broil) until the cheese melts.

1 Crush the garlic. Put the oil and butter into a pan, add the garlic and onion, and cook them gently for 20 minutes, until soft but not brown.

2 Add the flour and stir to make a roux. Cook for a few minutes, then stir in the wine vinegar, stock and 1 litre/ 1¾ pints/4 cups water. Simmer for about 30 minutes.

3 When ready to serve the soup, whisk in the lightly beaten egg yolks. Put the croûtons into eight soup bowls and pour over the hot soup.

COOK'S TIP
When adding egg yolks to thicken a soup, reheat the soup gently but do not bring it back to the boil, otherwise the egg will curdle.

Top: Energy 155Kcal/648kJ; Protein 3.2g; Carbohydrate 13.6g, of which sugars 3.4g; Fat 7.6g, of which saturates 3.2g; Cholesterol 11mg; Calcium 23mg; Fibre 2.1g; Sodium 44mg.
Bottom: Energy 55Kcal/229kJ; Protein 1.6g; Carbohydrate 3.6g, of which sugars 0.6g; Fat 4g, of which saturates 1.3g; Cholesterol 53mg; Calcium 13mg; Fibre 0.4g; Sodium 11mg.

CREAM OF MUSHROOM SOUP WITH GOAT'S CHEESE CROSTINI

CLASSIC CREAM OF MUSHROOM SOUP IS STILL A FIRM FAVOURITE, ESPECIALLY WITH THE ADDITION OF LUXURIOUSLY CRISP AND GARLICKY CROÛTES.

SERVES 6

INGREDIENTS
  25g/1oz/2 tbsp butter
  1 onion, chopped
  1 garlic clove, chopped
  450g/1lb/6 cups button (white),
    chestnut or brown cap mushrooms,
    roughly chopped
  15ml/1 tbsp plain (all-purpose) flour
  45ml/3 tbsp dry sherry
  900ml/1½ pints/3¾ cups
    vegetable stock
  150ml/¼ pint/⅔ cup double
    (heavy) cream
  salt and ground black pepper
  fresh chervil sprigs, to garnish
For the crostini
  15ml/1 tbsp olive oil, plus extra
    for brushing
  1 shallot, chopped
  115g/4oz/1½ cups button (white)
    mushrooms, finely chopped
  15ml/1 tbsp chopped fresh parsley
  6 brown cap (cremini) mushrooms
  6 slices baguette
  1 small garlic clove
  115g/4oz/1 cup soft goat's cheese

1 Melt the butter in a pan and cook the onion and garlic for 5 minutes. Stir in the mushrooms, cover and cook for 10 minutes, stirring occasionally.

2 Stir in the flour and cook for 1 minute. Stir in the sherry and stock and bring to the boil, then simmer for 15 minutes. Cool slightly, then purée the soup in a food processor or blender until smooth.

3 Meanwhile, prepare the crostini. Heat the oil in a small pan. Add the shallot and button mushrooms, and cook for 8–10 minutes, until softened. Drain well and transfer to a food processor. Add the parsley and process until finely chopped.

4 Preheat the grill (broiler). Brush the brown cap mushrooms with oil and cook for 5–6 minutes.

5 Toast the slices of baguette, rub with the garlic and put a spoonful of cheese on each. Top the grilled (broiled) mushrooms with the mushroom mixture and place on the crostini.

6 Return the soup to the pan and stir in the cream. Season, then reheat gently. Ladle the soup into six bowls. Float a crostini in the centre of each and garnish with chervil.

Energy 313Kcal/1305kJ; Protein 6.2g; Carbohydrate 26.8g, of which sugars 2.5g; Fat 20g, of which saturates 11g; Cholesterol 43mg; Calcium 75mg; Fibre 2.2g; Sodium 283mg.

ASPARAGUS AND PEA SOUP WITH PARMESAN CHEESE

THIS BRIGHT AND TASTY SOUP USES EVERY INCH OF THE ASPARAGUS, INCLUDING THE WOODY ENDS, WHICH ARE USED FOR MAKING THE STOCK.

SERVES 6

INGREDIENTS

350g/12oz asparagus
2 leeks
1 bay leaf
1 carrot, roughly chopped
1 celery stick, chopped
few stalks of fresh parsley
1.75 litres/3 pints/7½ cups
   cold water
25g/1oz/2 tbsp butter
150g/5oz fresh garden peas
15ml/1 tbsp chopped fresh parsley
120ml/4fl oz/½ cup double
   (heavy) cream
grated rind of ½ lemon
salt and ground black pepper
shavings of Parmesan cheese,
   to serve

1 Cut the woody ends from the asparagus, then set the spears aside. Roughly chop the woody ends and place them in a large pan. Cut off and chop the green parts of the leeks and add to the asparagus stalks with the bay leaf, carrot, celery, parsley stalks and the cold water. Bring to the boil and simmer for 30 minutes. Strain the stock and discard the vegetables.

2 Cut the tips off the asparagus and set aside, then cut the stems into short pieces. Chop the remainder of the leeks.

3 Melt the butter in a large pan and add the leeks. Cook for 3–4 minutes until softened, then add the asparagus stems, peas and chopped parsley. Pour in 1.2 litres/2 pints/5 cups of the asparagus stock. Bring to the boil, reduce the heat and cook for 6–8 minutes, until all the vegetables are tender. Season well.

4 Cool the soup slightly, then purée it in a food processor or blender until smooth. Press the purée through a very fine sieve into the rinsed pan. Stir in the cream and lemon rind.

5 Bring a small pan of water to the boil and cook the asparagus tips for about 2–3 minutes until just tender. Drain and refresh under cold water. Reheat the soup, but do not allow it to boil.

6 Ladle the soup into six warmed bowls and garnish with the asparagus tips. Serve immediately, with shavings of Parmesan cheese and plenty of ground black pepper.

VARIATION

For a lighter soup, you could replace the cream with low-fat milk, but the finished dish will not taste as rich.

Energy 221Kcal/912kJ; Protein 8.1g; Carbohydrate 7.1g, of which sugars 4.3g; Fat 18g, of which saturates 10.8g; Cholesterol 45mg; Calcium 151mg; Fibre 3.8g; Sodium 129mg.

ITALIAN PEA AND BASIL SOUP

Energy 261Kcal/1078kJ; Protein 8.8g; Carbohydrate 22.9g, of which sugars 10.9g; Fat 15.7g, of which saturates 2.3g; Cholesterol 0mg; Calcium 73mg; Fibre 7.3g; Sodium 16mg.

*THE PUNGENT FLAVOUR OF BASIL LIFTS THIS APPETIZING ITALIAN SOUP, WHILE THE ONION AND
GARLIC GIVE DEPTH. SERVE IT WITH GOOD CRUSTY BREAD TO ENJOY IT AT ITS BEST.*

2 Add the peas and stock to the pan
and bring to the boil. Reduce the heat,
add the basil and seasoning, then
simmer for 10 minutes.

3 Spoon the soup into a food processor
or blender (you may have to do this in
batches) and process until the soup
is smooth.

4 Return the soup to the rinsed pan
and reheat gently until piping hot. Ladle
into warm bowls, sprinkle with shaved
Parmesan and garnish with basil.

VARIATION
You can also use mint or a mixture of
parsley, mint and chives in place of the
basil, if you like.

SERVES 4

INGREDIENTS
  75ml/5 tbsp olive oil
  2 large onions, chopped
  1 celery stick, chopped
  1 carrot, chopped
  1 garlic clove, finely chopped
  400g/14oz/3½ cups frozen
    petits pois (baby peas)
  900ml/1½ pints/3¾ cups
    vegetable stock
  25g/1oz/1 cup fresh basil leaves,
    roughly torn, plus extra to garnish
  salt snd ground black pepper
  shaved Parmesan cheese,
    to serve

1 Heat the oil in a large pan and add
the onions, celery, carrot and garlic.
Cover the pan and cook over a low heat
for 45 minutes, or until the vegetables
are soft, stirring occasionally to prevent
the vegetables sticking.

PEA SOUP <u>WITH</u> GARLIC

THIS DELICIOUS SOUP HAS A WONDERFULLY SWEET TASTE AND SMOOTH TEXTURE, AND IS GREAT SERVED WITH CRUSTY BREAD AND GARNISHED WITH MINT.

SERVES 4

INGREDIENTS
  25g/1oz/2 tbsp butter
  1 garlic clove, crushed
  900g/2lb/8 cups frozen peas
  1.2 litres/2 pints/5 cups
    chicken stock
  salt and ground black pepper

1 Heat the butter in a large pan and add the garlic. Fry gently for 2–3 minutes, until softened, then add the peas. Cook for 1–2 minutes more, then pour in the stock.

COOK'S TIP
If you keep a bag of frozen peas in the freezer, you can rustle up this soup at very short notice.

2 Bring the soup to the boil, then reduce the heat to a simmer. Cover and cook for 5–6 minutes, until the peas are tender. Leave to cool slightly, then transfer the mixture to a food processor and process until smooth (you may have to do this in two batches).

3 Return the soup to the pan and heat through gently. Season with salt and pepper to taste.

Energy 233Kcal/965kJ; Protein 15.6g; Carbohydrate 25.5g, of which sugars 5.2g; Fat 8.5g, of which saturates 3.9g; Cholesterol 13mg; Calcium 49mg; Fibre 10.6g; Sodium 40mg.

EGG FLOWER SOUP

THIS SIMPLE, HEALTHY SOUP IS FLAVOURED WITH FRESH ROOT GINGER AND CHINESE FIVE-SPICE POWDER. IT IS QUICK AND DELICIOUS AND CAN BE MADE AT THE LAST MINUTE.

SERVES 4

INGREDIENTS
1.2 litres/2 pints/5 cups fresh
   chicken or vegetable stock
10ml/2 tsp peeled, grated fresh
   root ginger
10ml/2 tsp light soy sauce
5ml/1 tsp sesame oil
5ml/1 tsp Chinese five-spice powder
15ml/1 tbsp cornflour (cornstarch)
2 eggs
salt and ground black pepper
1 spring onion (scallion), very finely
   sliced diagonally, and 15ml/1 tbsp
   roughly chopped coriander (cilantro)
   or flat leaf parsley, to garnish

COOK'S TIP
This soup is a good way of using up
leftover egg yolks or whites which have
been stored in the freezer.

1 Put the chicken or vegetable stock into a large pan with the ginger, soy sauce, oil and five-spice powder. Bring to the boil and allow to simmer gently for about 10 minutes.

2 Blend the cornflour in a measuring jug with 60–75ml/4–5 tbsp water and stir into the stock. Cook, stirring constantly, until slightly thickened. Season to taste with salt and pepper.

3 In a jug (pitcher), beat the eggs together with 30ml/2 tbsp cold water until the mixture becomes frothy.

4 Bring the soup back just to the boil and drizzle in the egg mixture, stirring vigorously with chopsticks. Choose a jug with a fine spout to form a very thin drizzle. Serve at once, sprinkled with the sliced spring onions and chopped coriander or parsley.

Energy 71Kcal/298kJ; Protein 3.3g; Carbohydrate 7.1g, of which sugars 0.2g; Fat 3.6g, of which saturates 0.9g; Cholesterol 95mg; Calcium 16mg; Fibre 0g; Sodium 217mg.

EGG AND CHEESE SOUP

IN THIS CLASSIC ROMAN SOUP, EGGS AND CHEESE ARE BEATEN INTO HOT SOUP, PRODUCING THE SLIGHTLY SCRAMBLED TEXTURE THAT IS CHARACTERISTIC OF THIS DISH.

SERVES 6

INGREDIENTS

3 eggs
45ml/3 tbsp fine semolina
90ml/6 tbsp freshly grated
  Parmesan cheese
pinch of nutmeg
1.5 litres/2½ pints/6¼ cups cold
  meat or chicken stock
salt and ground black pepper
12 rounds of country bread or
  ciabatta, to serve

COOK'S TIP

Once added to the hot soup, the egg will begin to cook and the soup will become less smooth. Try not to overcook the soup at this stage because it may cause the egg to curdle.

1 Beat the eggs in a bowl, then beat in the semolina and the cheese. Add the nutmeg and beat in 250ml/8fl oz/ 1 cup of the meat or chicken stock. Pour the mixture into a measuring jug (pitcher).

2 Pour the remaining stock into a large pan and bring to a gentle simmer, stirring occasionally.

3 A few minutes before you are ready to serve the soup, whisk the egg mixture into the hot stock. Raise the heat slightly, and bring it barely to the boil. Season and cook for 3–4 minutes.

4 To serve, toast the rounds of country bread or ciabatta, place two in each soup plate and ladle on the hot soup. Serve immediately.

Energy 245Kcal/1030kJ; Protein 14.1g; Carbohydrate 27.5g, of which sugars 1.3g; Fat 9.4g, of which saturates 4.1g; Cholesterol 110mg; Calcium 246mg; Fibre 1.1g; Sodium 424mg.

CHUNKY VEGETABLE SOUPS

In this section you will find a collection of traditional European soups such as French Onion Soup with Gruyère Croûtes, Irish Leek and Blue Cheese Soup and Portuguese Garlic Soup. You can also try the more exotic vegetable soups of Goa, Thailand and Bali. Ingredients such as mooli (daikon), shiitake mushrooms and Chinese leaves (Chinese cabbage) are readily available in many supermarkets these days, so be adventurous and try something new.

CORN AND POTATO CHOWDER

THIS CREAMY YET CHUNKY SOUP IS RICH WITH THE SWEET TASTE OF CORN. IT'S EXCELLENT SERVED WITH THICK CRUSTY BREAD AND TOPPED WITH SOME MELTED CHEDDAR CHEESE.

SERVES 4

INGREDIENTS

1 onion, chopped
1 garlic clove, crushed
1 medium baking potato, chopped
2 celery sticks, sliced
1 small green (bell) pepper, seeded,
  halved and sliced
30ml/2 tbsp sunflower oil
25g/1oz/2 tbsp butter
600ml/1 pint/2½ cups stock or water
300ml/½ pint/1¼ cups milk
200g/7oz can flageolet beans
300g/11oz can corn kernels
good pinch dried sage
salt and ground black pepper
Cheddar cheese, grated, to serve

1 Put the onion, garlic, potato, celery and green pepper into a large heavy-based pan with the oil and butter.

2 Heat the ingredients until sizzling then reduce the heat to low. Cover and cook gently for about 10 minutes, shaking the pan occasionally to prevent the ingredients sticking.

3 Pour in the stock or water, season with salt and pepper to taste and bring to the boil. Reduce the heat, cover again and simmer gently for about 15 minutes until the vegetables are tender.

4 Add the milk, beans and corn – including their liquids – and the sage. Simmer, uncovered, for 5 minutes. Check the seasoning and serve hot, sprinkled with grated cheese.

Energy 251Kcal/1052kJ; Protein 9.7g; Carbohydrate 25.9g, of which sugars 9.3g; Fat 12.9g, of which saturates 4.9g; Cholesterol 18mg; Calcium 128mg; Fibre 5.5g; Sodium 1154mg.

CORN AND RED CHILLI CHOWDER

CORN AND CHILLIES MAKE GOOD BEDFELLOWS, AND HERE THE COOL COMBINATION OF CREAMED CORN AND MILK IS THE PERFECT FOIL FOR THE RAGING HEAT OF THE CHILLIES.

SERVES 6

INGREDIENTS

2 tomatoes, skinned
1 onion, roughly chopped
375g/13oz can creamed
   sweetcorn (corn)
2 red (bell) peppers, halved
   and seeded
15ml/1 tbsp olive oil, plus extra
   for brushing
3 red chillies, seeded and sliced
2 garlic cloves, chopped
5ml/1 tsp ground cumin
5ml/1 tsp ground coriander
600ml/1 pint/2½ cups milk
350ml/12fl oz/1½ cups
   chicken stock
3 cobs of corn, kernels removed
450g/1lb potatoes, finely diced
60ml/4 tbsp double (heavy) cream
60ml/4 tbsp chopped fresh parsley
salt and ground black pepper

1 Process the tomatoes and onion in a food processor or blender to a smooth purée. Add the creamed sweetcorn and process again, then set aside. Preheat the grill (broiler) to high.

2 Put the peppers, skin sides up, on a grill rack and brush with oil. Grill (broil) for 8–10 minutes, until the skins blacken and blister. Transfer to a bowl and cover with clear film (plastic wrap), then leave to cool. Peel and dice the peppers, then set them aside.

3 Heat the oil in a large pan and add the chillies and garlic. Cook, stirring, for 2–3 minutes, until softened.

4 Add the ground cumin and coriander, and cook for a further 1 minute. Stir in the sweetcorn purée and cook for about 8 minutes, stirring occasionally.

5 Pour in the milk and stock, then stir in the corn kernels, potatoes, red pepper and seasoning to taste. Cook for 15–20 minutes, until the corn and potatoes are tender.

6 Pour into deep bowls and add the cream, then sprinkle over the chopped parsley and serve at once.

TORTILLA TOMATO SOUP

THERE ARE SEVERAL TORTILLA SOUPS. THIS ONE IS AN AGUADA — OR LIQUID — VERSION, AND IS INTENDED FOR SERVING AS AN APPETIZER OR LIGHT MEAL. IT IS VERY EASY AND QUICK TO PREPARE, OR MAKE IT IN ADVANCE AND FRY THE TORTILLA STRIPS AS IT REHEATS. THE CRISP TORTILLA PIECES ADD INTEREST AND GIVE THE SOUP AN UNUSUAL TEXTURE.

SERVES 4

INGREDIENTS
   4 corn tortillas
   15ml/1 tbsp vegetable oil, plus extra
     for frying
   1 small onion, chopped
   2 garlic cloves, crushed
   350g/12oz ripe plum tomatoes
   400g/14oz can plum tomatoes, drained
   1 litre/1¾ pints/4 cups chicken stock
   small bunch of fresh coriander (cilantro)
   50g/2oz/½ cup grated (shredded)
     mild Cheddar cheese
   salt and ground black pepper

1 Using a sharp knife, cut each tortilla into four or five strips, each measuring about 2cm/¾in wide. Pour vegetable oil to a depth of 2cm/¾in into a frying pan. Heat until a small piece of tortilla, added to the oil, floats on the top and bubbles at the edges.

2 Add a few tortilla strips to the hot oil and fry until crisp and golden brown.

3 Remove the tortilla chips with a slotted spoon and drain on kitchen paper. Cook the remaining tortilla strips in the same way.

4 Heat the 15ml/1 tbsp vegetable oil in a large pan. Add the onion and garlic and cook over a medium heat for 2–3 minutes, until the onion is soft and translucent. Do not let the garlic turn brown or it will give the soup a bitter taste.

5 Skin the fresh tomatoes by plunging them into boiling water for 30 seconds, refreshing them in cold water, draining them and then peeling off the skins with a sharp knife.

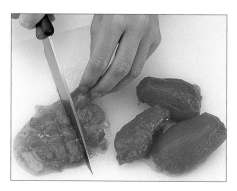

6 Chop the fresh and canned tomatoes and add them to the onion mixture. Pour in the chicken stock. Bring to the boil, then lower the heat and simmer for 10 minutes, until the liquid has reduced slightly. Stir the mixture occasionally.

7 Roughly chop or tear the coriander into pieces. Add it to the soup and season with salt and ground black pepper to taste.

8 Place a few of the crisp tortilla pieces in each of four large heated soup bowls. Ladle the soup on top. Sprinkle each portion with some of the grated mild Cheddar cheese and serve immediately.

COOK'S TIP
An easy way to chop fresh herbs is to put them in a mug and snip with a pair of scissors. Hold the scissors vertically with one hand on each handle and work the blades back and forth until the herbs are finely and evenly chopped. If you are using woody herbs, such as rosemary or thyme, remember to strip the leaves from the stalks before putting them in the mug. They are then ready to be chopped.

Energy 270Kcal/1135kJ; Protein 8.3g; Carbohydrate 36.9g, of which sugars 7.2g; Fat 10.7g, of which saturates 3.6g; Cholesterol 12mg; Calcium 164mg; Fibre 3.3g; Sodium 248mg.

IRISH LEEK AND BLUE CHEESE SOUP

THE BLUE CHEESE IS AN INTEGRAL PART OF THIS SUBSTANTIAL SOUP, WHICH MAKES FULL USE OF INGREDIENTS THAT HAVE ALWAYS BEEN IMPORTANT IN IRISH COOKING. IT CAN BE A GOOD WAY TO USE UP CHEESES LEFT OVER FROM THE CHEESEBOARD. SERVE WITH FRESHLY BAKED BROWN BREAD.

SERVES 6

INGREDIENTS

3 large leeks
50g/2oz/¼ cup butter
30ml/2 tbsp oil
115g/4oz Irish blue cheese,
  such as Cashel Blue
15g/½oz/2 tbsp plain
  (all-purpose) flour
15ml/1 tbsp wholegrain Irish
  mustard, or to taste
1.5 litres/2½ pints/6¼ cups
  chicken stock
ground black pepper
50g/2oz/½ cup grated cheese and
  chopped chives or spring onion
  (scallion) greens, to garnish

VARIATION
Any melting blue-veined cheese can be used in this recipe, such as Cabrales, Gorgonzola or Picon.

1 Slice the leeks thinly. Heat the butter and oil together in a large heavy pan and gently cook the leeks in it, covered, for 10–15 minutes, or until just softened but not brown.

2 Grate the cheese coarsely and add it to the pan, stirring over a low heat until it is melted. Add the flour and cook for 2 minutes, stirring constantly with a wooden spoon, then add ground black pepper and mustard to taste.

3 Gradually add the stock, stirring constantly and blending it in well; bring the soup to the boil.

4 Reduce the heat, cover and simmer very gently for about 15 minutes. Check the seasoning.

5 Serve the soup garnished with the extra grated cheese and the chopped chives or spring onion greens, and hand fresh bread around separately.

Energy 205Kcal/852kJ; Protein 8.2g; Carbohydrate 7.9g, of which sugars 2.2g; Fat 15.7g, of which saturates 9.9g; Cholesterol 40mg; Calcium 188mg; Fibre 2.2g; Sodium 347mg.

LEEK AND OATMEAL SOUP

THIS TRADITIONAL IRISH SOUP IS KNOWN AS BROTCHÁN FOLTCHEP OR BROTCHÁN ROY, AND COMBINES LEEKS, OATMEAL AND MILK — THREE INGREDIENTS THAT HAVE BEEN STAPLE FOODS IN IRELAND FOR CENTURIES. SERVE WITH FRESHLY BAKED BREAD AND BUTTER.

SERVES 4–6

INGREDIENTS

about 1.2 litres/2 pints/5 cups
    chicken stock and milk, mixed
30ml/2 tbsp medium pinhead
    oatmeal
25g/1oz/2 tbsp butter
6 large leeks, sliced into 2cm/¾in
    pieces and washed
sea salt and ground black pepper
pinch of ground mace
30ml/2 tbsp chopped fresh parsley
single (light) cream and chopped
    fresh parsley leaves or chives,
    to garnish

1 Bring the stock and milk mixture to the boil over medium heat and sprinkle in the oatmeal. Stir well to prevent lumps forming, and then simmer gently.

2 Melt the butter in a separate pan and cook the leeks over a gentle heat until softened slightly, then add them to the stock. Simmer for 15–20 minutes, until the oatmeal is cooked.

VARIATION

Make nettle soup in the spring, when the nettle tops are young and tender. Strip about 10oz/275g nettle tops from the stems, chop them and add to the leeks.

3 Season with salt, pepper and mace, stir in the parsley and serve in warmed bowls. Decorate with a swirl of cream and some chopped fresh parsley or chives, if you like.

Energy 121Kcal/505kJ; Protein 4.2g; Carbohydrate 11.3g, of which sugars 4.5g; Fat 6.8g, of which saturates 3.5g; Cholesterol 13mg; Calcium 53mg; Fibre 4.9g; Sodium 44mg.

FRENCH ONION SOUP
WITH GRUYÈRE CROÛTES

THIS IS PERHAPS THE MOST FAMOUS OF ALL ONION SOUPS. TRADITIONALLY, IT WAS SERVED AS A SUSTAINING EARLY MORNING MEAL TO THE PORTERS AND WORKERS OF LES HALLES MARKET IN PARIS.

SERVES 6

INGREDIENTS

50g/2oz/¼ cup butter
15ml/1 tbsp olive oil
2kg/4½lb yellow onions, peeled
   and sliced
5ml/1 tsp chopped fresh thyme
5ml/1 tsp caster (superfine) sugar
15ml/1 tbsp sherry vinegar
1.5 litres/2½ pints/6¼ cups good
   beef, chicken or duck stock
25ml/1½ tbsp plain (all-purpose) flour
150ml/¼ pint/⅔ cup dry white wine
45ml/3 tbsp brandy
salt and ground black pepper
For the croûtes
6–12 thick slices day-old French
   stick or baguette, about 2.5cm/
   1in thick
1 garlic clove, halved
15ml/1 tbsp French mustard
115g/4oz/1 cup coarsely grated
   Gruyère cheese

1 Melt the butter with the oil in a large pan. Add the onions and stir to coat them in the fat. Cook over a medium heat for 5–8 minutes, stirring once or twice, until the onions begin to soften. Stir in the thyme.

2 Reduce the heat to very low, cover the pan and cook the onions for 20–30 minutes, stirring frequently, until they are very soft and golden yellow.

3 Uncover the pan and increase the heat slightly. Stir in the sugar and cook for 5–10 minutes, until the onions start to brown. Add the sherry vinegar and increase the heat again, then continue cooking, stirring frequently, until the onions turn a deep, golden brown – this could take up to 20 minutes.

COOK'S TIP
The long slow cooking of the onions is the key to success with this soup. If the onions brown too quickly the soup will be bitter.

4 Meanwhile, bring the stock to the boil in another pan. Stir the flour into the onions and cook for about 2 minutes, then gradually pour in the hot stock. Add the wine and brandy and season the soup to taste with salt and pepper. Simmer for 10–15 minutes.

5 For the croûtes, preheat the oven to 150°C/300°F/Gas 2. Place the slices of bread on a greased baking tray and bake for 15–20 minutes, until dry and lightly browned. Rub the bread with the cut surface of the garlic and spread with the mustard, then sprinkle the grated Gruyère cheese over the slices.

6 Preheat the grill (broiler) on the hottest setting. Ladle the soup into a large flameproof pan or six flameproof bowls. Float the croûtes on the soup, then grill until the cheese melts, bubbles and browns. Serve immediately.

Energy 484Kcal/2030kJ; Protein 15.3g; Carbohydrate 67.2g, of which sugars 21.5g; Fat 15.1g, of which saturates 8.7g; Cholesterol 36mg; Calcium 314mg; Fibre 6.4g; Sodium 611mg.

PORTUGUESE GARLIC SOUP

THIS RECIPE IS BASED ON THE WONDERFUL BREAD SOUPS OR AÇORDAS OF PORTUGAL. BEING A SIMPLE SOUP IT SHOULD BE MADE WITH THE BEST INGREDIENTS — PLUMP GARLIC, FRESH CORIANDER, HIGH-QUALITY CRUSTY COUNTRY BREAD AND EXTRA VIRGIN OLIVE OIL.

SERVES 6

INGREDIENTS

25g/1oz fresh coriander (cilantro),
  leaves and stalks chopped separately
1.5 litres/2½ pints/6¼ cups vegetable
  or chicken stock, or water
5–6 plump garlic cloves, peeled
6 eggs
275g/10oz day-old bread, most
  of the crust removed, torn into
  bite-size pieces
salt and ground black pepper
90ml/6 tbsp extra virgin olive oil,
  plus extra to serve

1 Place the coriander stalks in a pan. Add the stock or water and bring to the boil. Lower the heat and simmer for 10 minutes, then process in a blender or food processor and sieve (strain) back into the pan.

2 Crush the garlic with 5ml/1 tsp salt, then stir in 120ml/4fl oz/½ cup hot soup. Return the mixture to the pan.

3 Meanwhile, poach the eggs in a frying pan of simmering water for about 3–4 minutes, until just set. Use a slotted spoon to remove them from the pan and transfer to a warmed plate. Trim off any untidy bits of white.

4 Bring the soup back to the boil and add seasoning. Stir in the chopped coriander leaves and remove from the heat.

5 Place the bread in six soup plates or bowls and drizzle the oil over it. Ladle in the soup and stir. Add a poached egg to each bowl and serve immediately, offering olive oil at the table so that it can be drizzled over the soup to taste.

Energy 299Kcal/1249kJ; Protein 11.6g; Carbohydrate 24.6g, of which sugars 2.8g; Fat 18g, of which saturates 3.1g; Cholesterol 190mg; Calcium 170mg; Fibre 3g; Sodium 323mg.

CASTILIAN GARLIC SOUP

THIS RICH, DARK GARLIC SOUP COMES FROM LA MANCHA IN CENTRAL SPAIN, AND IS SIMILAR TO PORTUGUESE GARLIC SOUP. THE REGION IS FAMOUS FOR ITS SUMMER SUNSHINE, AND THE LOCAL SOUP HAS A HARSH, STRONG TASTE TO MATCH THE CLIMATE.

SERVES 4

INGREDIENTS
    30ml/2 tbsp olive oil
    4 large garlic cloves, peeled
    4 slices stale country bread
    20ml/4 tbsp paprika
    1 litre/1¾ pints/4 cups
      beef stock
    1.5ml/¼ tsp ground cumin
    4 free-range (farm-fresh) eggs
    salt and ground black pepper
    chopped fresh parsley, to garnish

VARIATION
If you prefer, you can simply whisk the eggs into the hot soup.

1 Preheat the oven to 230°C/450°F/ Gas 8. Heat the olive oil in a large pan. Add the whole peeled garlic cloves and cook until they are golden, then remove and set aside. Fry the slices of bread in the oil until golden, then set these aside.

2 Add 15ml/1 tbsp of the paprika to the pan, and fry for a few seconds. Stir in the beef stock, cumin and remaining paprika, then add the reserved garlic, crushing the cloves with the back of a wooden spoon. Season to taste, then cook for about 5 minutes.

3 Break up the slices of fried bread into bitesize pieces and stir them into the soup. Ladle the soup into four ovenproof bowls. Carefully break an egg into each bowl of soup and place in the oven for about 3 minutes, until the eggs are set. Sprinkle the soup with chopped fresh parsley and serve immediately.

Energy 202Kcal/843kJ; Protein 9.3g; Carbohydrate 15.3g, of which sugars 1.5g; Fat 12.2g, of which saturates 2.4g; Cholesterol 190mg; Calcium 69mg; Fibre 0.6g; Sodium 202mg.

SUMMER VEGETABLE SOUP

THIS BRIGHTLY COLOURED, FRESH-TASTING TOMATO SOUP MAKES THE MOST OF SUMMER VEGETABLES IN SEASON. ADD LOTS OF RED AND YELLOW PEPPERS TO MAKE A SWEETER VERSION.

SERVES 4

INGREDIENTS

450g/1lb ripe plum tomatoes
225g/8oz ripe yellow tomatoes
45ml/3 tbsp olive oil
1 large onion, finely chopped
15ml/1 tbsp sun-dried tomato
  purée (paste)
225g/8oz courgettes (zucchini),
  trimmed and chopped
225g/8oz yellow courgettes,
  trimmed and chopped
3 waxy new potatoes, diced
2 garlic cloves, crushed
about 1.2 litres/2 pints/5 cups
  chicken stock or water
60ml/4 tbsp shredded fresh basil
50g/2oz/⅔ cup freshly grated
  (shredded) Parmesan cheese
sea salt and freshly ground
  black pepper

1 Plunge all the tomatoes in boiling water for 30 seconds, refresh in cold water, then peel and chop finely. Heat the oil in a large pan, add the onion and cook gently for about 5 minutes, stirring constantly, until softened. Stir in the sun-dried tomato purée, chopped tomatoes, courgettes, diced potatoes and garlic. Mix well and cook gently for 10 minutes, shaking the pan often.

2 Pour in the stock or water. Bring to the boil, lower the heat, half cover the pan and simmer gently for 15 minutes or until the vegetables are just tender. Add more stock or water if necessary.

3 Remove the pan from the heat and stir in the basil and half the cheese. Taste for seasoning. Serve hot, sprinkled with the remaining cheese.

GREEK AUBERGINE AND COURGETTE SOUP

A FUSION OF FLAVOURS FROM THE SUNNY GREEK ISLANDS CREATES THIS FABULOUS SOUP, WHICH IS SERVED WITH TZATZIKI, THE POPULAR COMBINATION OF CUCUMBER AND CREAMY YOGURT.

SERVES 4

INGREDIENTS
   2 large aubergines (eggplant),
     roughly diced
   4 large courgettes (zucchini),
     roughly diced
   1 onion, roughly chopped
   4 garlic cloves, roughly chopped
   45ml/3 tbsp olive oil
   1.2 litres/2 pints/5 cups
     vegetable stock
   15ml/1 tbsp chopped fresh oregano
   salt and ground black pepper
   mint sprigs, to garnish
For the tzatziki
   1 cucumber
   10ml/2 tsp salt
   2 garlic cloves, crushed
   5ml/1 tsp white wine vinegar
   225g/8oz/1 cup Greek (US strained
     plain) yogurt
   small bunch of fresh mint leaves,
     chopped

1 Preheat the oven to 200°C/400°F/Gas 6. Place the aubergines and courgettes in a roasting tin (pan). Add the onion and garlic, and drizzle over the olive oil. Roast for 35 minutes, turning once, until tender and slightly charred.

2 Place half the roasted vegetables in a food processor or blender. Add the stock and process until almost smooth. Pour into a large pan and add the remaining vegetables. Bring to the boil, season and stir in the chopped oregano.

3 For the tzatziki, peel, seed and dice the cucumber. Place the flesh in a colander and sprinkle with salt. Leave for 30 minutes. Mix the garlic with the vinegar and stir into the yogurt. Pat the cucumber dry on kitchen paper and fold it into the yogurt. Season to taste and stir in the mint. Chill until required.

4 Ladle the soup into bowls and garnish with mint sprigs. Hand round the bowl of tzatziki so that your guests can add a dollop or two to their soup.

Energy 188Kcal/778kJ; Protein 6.9g; Carbohydrate 8.5g, of which sugars 7.3g; Fat 14.9g, of which saturates 4.3g; Cholesterol 0mg; Calcium 134mg; Fibre 3.6g; Sodium 1027mg.

ROAST VEGETABLE MEDLEY WITH SUN-DRIED TOMATO BREAD

WINTER MEETS SUMMER IN THIS SOUP RECIPE FOR CHUNKY ROASTED ROOTS. SERVE IT WITH BREAD BAKED WITH A HINT OF ADDED SUMMER FLAVOUR IN THE FORM OF SUN-DRIED TOMATOES.

SERVES 4

INGREDIENTS
  4 parsnips, quartered lengthways
  2 red onions, cut into thin wedges
  4 carrots, thickly sliced
  2 leeks, thickly sliced
  1 small swede (rutabaga), cut into
    bite-size pieces
  4 potatoes, cut into chunks
  60ml/4 tbsp olive oil
  few sprigs of fresh thyme
  1 garlic bulb, broken into
    cloves, unpeeled
  1 litre/1¾ pints/4 cups
    vegetable stock
  salt and ground black pepper
  fresh thyme sprigs, to garnish
For the sun-dried tomato bread
  1 ciabatta loaf (about 275g/10oz)
  75g/3oz/6 tbsp butter, softened
  1 garlic clove, crushed
  4 sun-dried tomatoes, finely chopped
  30ml/2 tbsp chopped fresh parsley

1 Preheat the oven to 200°C/400°F/ Gas 6. Cut the thick ends of the parsnip quarters into four, then place them in a large roasting tin (pan). Add the onions, carrots, leeks, swede and potatoes, and spread them in an even layer.

2 Drizzle the olive oil over the vegetables. Add the thyme sprigs and the unpeeled garlic cloves. Toss well to coat with oil and roast for about 45 minutes, until all the vegetables are tender and slightly charred.

3 Meanwhile, to make the sun-dried tomato bread, cut diagonal slits along the loaf, taking care not to cut right through it. Mix the butter with the garlic, sun-dried tomatoes and parsley. Spread the mixture into each slit, then press the bread back together. Wrap the loaf in foil and bake for 15 minutes, opening the foil for the last 5 minutes.

4 Discard the thyme from the roasted vegetables. Squeeze the garlic cloves from their skins over the vegetables.

5 Process about half the vegetables with the stock in a food processor or blender until almost smooth. Pour into a pan and add the remaining vegetables. Bring to the boil and season well with salt and black pepper.

6 Ladle the soup into bowls and garnish with fresh thyme leaves. Serve the hot bread with the soup.

Energy 511Kcal/2146kJ; Protein 13.9g; Carbohydrate 72.6g, of which sugars 18.9g; Fat 20.4g, of which saturates 10.6g; Cholesterol 40mg; Calcium 218mg; Fibre 12.1g; Sodium 521mg.

BUTTERNUT SQUASH AND BLUE CHEESE RISOTTO SOUP

THIS IS, IN FACT, A VERY WET RISOTTO, BUT IT BEARS MORE THAN A PASSING RESEMBLANCE TO SOUP AND MAKES A VERY SMART FIRST COURSE FOR A DINNER PARTY.

SERVES 4

INGREDIENTS
25g/1oz/2 tbsp butter
30ml/2 tbsp olive oil
2 onions, finely chopped
½ celery stick, finely sliced
1 small butternut squash, peeled,
 seeded and cut into small cubes
15ml/1 tbsp chopped sage
300g/11oz/1½ cups risotto rice
1.2 litres/2 pints/5 cups hot
 chicken stock
30ml/2 tbsp double (heavy) cream
115g/4oz blue cheese, finely diced
30ml/2 tbsp olive oil
4 large sage leaves
salt and ground black pepper

1 Place the butter in a large pan with the oil and heat gently. Add the onions and celery, and cook for 4–5 minutes, until softened.

2 Stir in the butternut squash and cook for 3–4 minutes, then add the sage.

3 Add the rice and cook for 1–2 minutes, stirring, until the grains are slightly translucent. Add the chicken stock a ladleful at a time.

4 Cook until each ladleful of stock has been absorbed before adding the next. Continue adding the stock in this way until you have a very wet rice mixture. Season and stir in the cream.

5 Meanwhile, heat the oil in a frying pan and fry the sage leaves for a few seconds until crisp. Drain.

6 Stir the blue cheese into the risotto soup and ladle it into bowls. Garnish with a fried sage leaf.

Energy 505Kcal/2100kJ; Protein 9.2g; Carbohydrate 63.7g, of which sugars 5.7g; Fat 23g, of which saturates 8.3g; Cholesterol 26mg; Calcium 110mg; Fibre 2.7g; Sodium 91mg.

RUSSIAN BORSCHT WITH *KVAS* AND SOURED CREAM

BEETROOT IS THE MAIN INGREDIENT OF BORSCHT, AND ITS FLAVOUR AND COLOUR DOMINATE THIS WELL-KNOWN SOUP. IT IS A CLASSIC OF BOTH RUSSIA AND POLAND.

SERVES 4–6

INGREDIENTS

900g/2lb uncooked beetroot, peeled
2 carrots, peeled
2 celery sticks
40g/1½oz/3 tbsp butter
2 onions, sliced
2 garlic cloves, crushed
4 tomatoes, peeled, seeded
  and chopped
1 bay leaf
1 large parsley sprig
2 cloves
4 whole peppercorns
1.2 litres/2 pints/5 cups beef or
  chicken stock
150ml/¼ pint/⅔ cup beetroot *kvas*
  (see Cook's Tip) or the liquid from
  pickled beetroot
salt and freshly ground black pepper
soured cream, garnished with chopped
  fresh chives or sprigs of dill, to serve

1 Cut the beetroot, carrots and celery into thick strips. Melt the butter in a pan and cook the onions over a low heat for 5 minutes, stirring occasionally.

2 Add the beetroot, carrots and celery and cook for a further 5 minutes.

COOK'S TIP

Beetroot *kvas* adds an intense colour and a slight tartness. If unavailable, peel and grate 1 beetroot, add 150ml/¼ pint/⅔ cup stock and 10ml/2 tsp lemon juice. Bring to the boil, cover and leave for 30 minutes. Strain before using.

3 Add the crushed garlic and chopped tomatoes to the pan and cook, stirring, for 2 more minutes.

4 Place the bay leaf, parsley, cloves and peppercorns in a piece of muslin (cheesecloth) and tie with string.

5 Add the muslin bag to the pan with the stock. Bring to the boil, reduce the heat, cover and simmer for 1¼ hours, until the vegetables are tender. Discard the bag. Stir in the beetroot *kvas* and season. Ladle into bowls and serve with soured cream. Garnish with chives or dill.

Energy 125Kcal/532kJ; Protein 5.3g; Carbohydrate 26.2g, of which sugars 23.5g; Fat 0.7g, of which saturates 0.1g; Cholesterol 0mg; Calcium 71mg; Fibre 6.6g; Sodium 166mg.

SWEET AND SOUR CABBAGE, BEETROOT AND TOMATO BORSCHT

THERE ARE MANY VARIATIONS OF THIS CLASSIC JEWISH SOUP, WHICH MAY BE SERVED HOT OR COLD. THIS VERSION INCLUDES PLENTIFUL AMOUNTS OF CABBAGE, TOMATOES AND POTATOES.

SERVES 6

INGREDIENTS

1 onion, chopped
1 carrot, chopped
4–6 raw or vacuum-packed (cooked, not pickled) beetroot (beets), 3–4 diced and 1–2 coarsely grated
400g/14oz can tomatoes
4–6 new potatoes, cut into bitesize pieces
1 small white cabbage, thinly sliced
1 litre/1¾ pints/4 cups vegetable stock
45ml/3 tbsp sugar
30–45ml/2–3 tbsp white wine, cider vinegar or sour salt (citric acid)
45ml/3 tbsp chopped fresh dill, plus extra to garnish
salt and ground black pepper
sour cream, to garnish
buttered rye bread, to serve

1 Put the onion, carrot, diced beetroot, tomatoes, potatoes, cabbage and stock in a large pan. Bring to the boil, reduce the heat and simmer for 30 minutes, or until the potatoes are tender.

VARIATION

To make meat borscht, place 1kg/2¼lb chopped beef in a large pan. Pour over water to cover and crumble in 1 beef stock (bouillon) cube. Bring to the boil, then reduce the heat and simmer until tender. Skim any fat from the surface, then add the vegetables and proceed as above. For Kashrut, omit the sour cream and serve with unbuttered rye bread.

2 Add the grated beetroot, sugar and wine, vinegar or sour salt to the soup and cook for 10 minutes. Taste for a good sweet-sour balance and add more sugar and/or vinegar if necessary. Season.

3 Stir the chopped dill into the soup and ladle into warmed bowls immediately. Garnish each bowl with a generous spoonful of sour cream and more dill and serve with buttered rye bread.

Energy 111Kcal/470kJ; Protein 3.2g; Carbohydrate 24.6g, of which sugars 17.8g; Fat 0.6g, of which saturates 0.1g; Cholesterol 0mg; Calcium 65mg; Fibre 3.8g; Sodium 52mg.

HUNGARIAN CHERRY SOUP

SOUPS MADE FROM SEASONAL FRUITS ARE A FAVOURITE CENTRAL EUROPEAN TREAT, AND CHERRY SOUP IS ONE OF THE GLORIES OF THE HUNGARIAN TABLE. IT IS OFTEN SERVED AT THE START OF A DAIRY MEAL, SUCH AS AT THE FESTIVAL OF SHAVUOT WHEN DAIRY FOODS ARE TRADITIONALLY FEASTED UPON, AND IS DELICIOUS SERVED WITH AN EXTRA SPOONFUL OR TWO OF SOUR CREAM.

SERVES 6

INGREDIENTS

1kg/2¼lb fresh, frozen or canned
  sour cherries, such as Morello or
  Montmorency, pitted
250ml/8fl oz/1 cup water
175–250g/6–9oz/about 1 cup sugar,
  to taste
1–2 cinnamon sticks, each about
  5cm/2in long
750ml/1¼ pints/3 cups dry red wine
5ml/1 tsp almond essence (extract),
  or to taste
250ml/8fl oz/1 cup single
  (light) cream
250ml/8fl oz/1 cup sour cream or
  crème fraîche

1 Put the pitted cherries, water, sugar, cinnamon and wine in a large pan. Bring to the boil, reduce the heat and simmer for 20–30 minutes, until the cherries are tender. Remove from the heat and add the almond essence.

2 In a bowl, stir a few tablespoons of single cream into the sour cream or crème fraîche to thin it down, then stir in the rest until the mixture is smooth. Stir the mixture into the cherry soup, then chill until ready to serve.

Energy 518Kcal/2163kJ; Protein 4.1g; Carbohydrate 51.8g, of which sugars 51.7g; Fat 24.8g, of which saturates 16.4g; Cholesterol 70mg; Calcium 107mg; Fibre 1.5g; Sodium 34mg.

GRANDFATHER'S SOUP

THIS TRADITIONAL EASTERN EUROPEAN SOUP DERIVES ITS NAME FROM THE FACT THAT IT IS EASILY DIGESTED AND THEREFORE THOUGHT TO BE SUITABLE FOR THE ELDERLY. TO GET THE CORRECT TEXTURE FOR THE DISH, USE OLD POTATOES OF A FLOURY TEXTURE, SUCH AS KING EDWARD, MARIS PIPER OR ESTIMA.

SERVES 4

INGREDIENTS
   1 large onion, finely sliced
   25g/1oz/2 tbsp butter
   350g/12oz potatoes, peeled
      and diced
   900ml/1½ pints/3¾ cups
      beef stock
   1 bay leaf
   salt and freshly ground
      black pepper
For the drop noodles
   75g/3oz/⅔ cup self-raising
      (self-rising) flour
   pinch of salt
   15g/½oz/1 tbsp butter
   15ml/1 tbsp chopped fresh parsley,
      plus a little extra to garnish
   1 egg, beaten
   chunks of bread, to serve

1 In a wide heavy-based pan, cook the onion gently in the butter for 10 minutes, or until it begins to soften and go golden brown.

2 Add the diced potatoes and cook for 2–3 minutes, then pour in the stock. Add the bay leaf, salt and pepper. Bring to the boil, then reduce the heat, cover and simmer for about 10 minutes.

3 To make the noodles, sift the flour and salt into a bowl and rub in the butter. Stir in the parsley, then add the egg and mix to a soft dough.

4 Drop half-teaspoonfuls of the dough into the simmering soup. Cover and simmer gently for a further 10 minutes. Ladle into warmed soup bowls, sprinkle over a little parsley, and serve.

Energy 239Kcal/1001kJ; Protein 5.5g; Carbohydrate 33.3g, of which sugars 5g; Fat 10.2g, of which saturates 5.7g; Cholesterol 69mg; Calcium 96mg; Fibre 2.3g; Sodium 157mg.

MIXED MUSHROOM SOLYANKA
WITH PICKLED CUCUMBER

THE TART FLAVOURS OF PICKLED CUCUMBER, CAPERS AND LEMON ADD EXTRA BITE TO THIS TRADITIONAL RUSSIAN SOUP. THIS IS THE PERFECT DISH TO SERVE WHEN YOU WANT TO OFFER SOMETHING A LITTLE DIFFERENT.

2 Add the remaining vegetable stock with the sliced mushrooms, bring to the boil, cover and simmer gently for about 30 minutes.

3 In a small bowl, blend the tomato purée with 30ml/2 tbsp of stock.

4 Add the tomato purée to the pan with the pickled cucumber, bay leaf, capers, salt and peppercorns. Cook gently for a further 10 minutes.

5 Ladle the soup into warmed bowls and sprinkle lemon rind curls, a few olives and a sprig of flat leaf parsley over each bowl before serving.

SERVES 4

INGREDIENTS
  2 onions, chopped
  1.2 litres/2 pints/5 cups
    vegetable stock
  450g/1lb/6 cups mushrooms, sliced
  20ml/4 tsp tomato purée (paste)
  1 pickled cucumber, chopped
  1 bay leaf
  15ml/1 tbsp capers in brine, drained
  pinch of salt
  6 peppercorns, crushed
  lemon rind curls, green olives and
    sprigs of flat leaf parsley, to garnish

1 Put the onions in a large pan with 50ml/2fl oz/¼ cup of the stock. Cook, stirring occasionally, until all the liquid has evaporated.

COOK'S TIP
Using a mixture of mushrooms gives this soup its character. Try using varieties such as Paris Browns, field (portabello) and button (white) mushrooms.

Energy 35Kcal/147kJ; Protein 3g; Carbohydrate 4.6g, of which sugars 3.6g; Fat 0.7g, of which saturates 0.1g; Cholesterol 0mg; Calcium 20mg; Fibre 2g; Sodium 34mg.

RUSSIAN SPINACH AND ROOT VEGETABLE SOUP WITH DILL

THIS IS A TYPICAL RUSSIAN SOUP, TRADITIONALLY PREPARED WHEN THE FIRST VEGETABLES OF SPRINGTIME APPEAR. EARTHY ROOT VEGETABLES, COOKED WITH FRESH SPINACH LEAVES, ARE ENLIVENED WITH A TART, FRESH TOPPING OF DILL, LEMON AND SOUR CREAM.

SERVES 4–6

INGREDIENTS

  1 small turnip, cut into chunks
  2 carrots, sliced or diced
  1 small parsnip, cut into large dice
  1 potato, peeled and diced
  1 onion, chopped or cut into chunks
  1 garlic clove, finely chopped
  ¼ celeriac bulb, diced
  1 litre/1¾ pints/4 cups vegetable
    or chicken stock
  200g/7oz spinach, washed and
    roughly chopped
  1 small bunch fresh dill, chopped
  salt and ground black pepper
For the garnish
  2 hard-boiled eggs, sliced
  1 lemon, cut into slices
  250ml/8fl oz/1 cup sour cream
  30ml/2 tbsp fresh parsley and dill

1 Put the turnip, carrots, parsnip, potato, onion, garlic, celeriac and stock into a large pan. Bring to the boil, then simmer for 25–30 minutes, or until the vegetables are very tender.

COOK'S TIP
For the best results, use a really good-quality vegetable stock.

2 Add the spinach to the pan and cook for a further 5 minutes, or until the spinach is tender but still green and leafy. Season with salt and pepper.

3 Stir the dill into the soup, then ladle into bowls and serve garnished with egg, lemon, sour cream and a sprinkling of parsley and dill.

Energy 229Kcal/952kJ; Protein 7.8g; Carbohydrate 14.3g, of which sugars 9.2g; Fat 16.2g, of which saturates 8.7g; Cholesterol 133mg; Calcium 197mg; Fibre 4.1g; Sodium 148mg.

THAI OMELETTE SOUP

THIS IS A SURPRISINGLY SATISFYING SOUP FROM THAILAND THAT IS VERY QUICK AND EASY TO PREPARE. IT IS A VERSATILE RECIPE, TOO, IN THAT YOU CAN VARY THE VEGETABLES YOU USE ACCORDING TO WHAT IS SEASONALLY AVAILABLE.

SERVES 4

INGREDIENTS

1 egg
15ml/1 tbsp groundnut (peanut) oil
900ml/1½ pints/3¾ cups
  vegetable stock
2 large carrots, finely diced
4 outer leaves Savoy
  cabbage, shredded
30ml/2 tbsp soy sauce
2.5ml/½ tsp granulated sugar
2.5ml/½ tsp ground black pepper
fresh coriander (cilantro) leaves,
  to garnish

VARIATION

Use pak choi (bok choy) instead of Savoy cabbage. In Thailand there are about forty different types of pak choi, including miniature versions.

1 Put the egg in a bowl and beat lightly with a fork. Heat the oil in a small frying pan until it is hot, but not smoking. Pour in the egg and swirl the pan so that it coats the base evenly. Cook over a medium heat until the omelette has set and the underside is golden. Slide it out of the pan and roll it up like a pancake. Slice into 5mm/¼in rounds and set aside for the garnish.

2 Put the stock into a large pan. Add the carrots and cabbage and bring to the boil. Reduce the heat and simmer for 5 minutes, then add the soy sauce, granulated sugar and pepper.

3 Stir well, then pour into warmed bowls. Lay a few omelette rounds on the surface of each portion and complete the garnish with the coriander leaves.

Energy 64Kcal/264kJ; Protein 2.3g; Carbohydrate 4.3g, of which sugars 4.1g; Fat 4.3g, of which saturates 0.7g; Cholesterol 48mg; Calcium 27mg; Fibre 1.1g; Sodium 560mg.

THAI MIXED VEGETABLE SOUP

IN THAILAND, THIS TYPE OF SOUP IS USUALLY MADE IN LARGE QUANTITIES AND THEN REHEATED FOR CONSUMPTION OVER SEVERAL DAYS. IF YOU WOULD LIKE TO DO THE SAME, DOUBLE OR TREBLE THE QUANTITIES. CHILL LEFTOVER SOUP RAPIDLY AND REHEAT THOROUGHLY BEFORE SERVING.

SERVES 4

INGREDIENTS
  30ml/2 tbsp groundnut (peanut) oil
  15ml/1 tbsp magic paste (see
    Cook's Tip)
  90g/3½oz Savoy cabbage or
    Chinese leaves (Chinese cabbage),
    finely shredded
  90g/3½oz mooli (daikon),
    finely diced
  1 medium cauliflower,
    coarsely chopped
  4 celery sticks, coarsely chopped
  1.2 litres/2 pints/5 cups
    vegetable stock
  130g/4½oz fried tofu, cut into
    2.5cm/1in cubes
  5ml/1 tsp palm sugar or light
    muscovado (brown) sugar
  45ml/3 tbsp light soy sauce

1 Heat the groundnut oil in a large, heavy pan or wok. Add the magic paste and cook over a low heat, stirring frequently, until it gives off its aroma. Add the shredded Savoy cabbage or Chinese leaves, mooli, cauliflower and celery. Pour in the vegetable stock, increase the heat to medium and bring to the boil, stirring occasionally. Gently stir in the tofu cubes.

2 Add the sugar and soy sauce. Reduce the heat and simmer for 15 minutes, until the vegetables are cooked and tender. Taste and add a little more soy sauce if needed. Serve hot.

COOK'S TIP
Magic paste is a mixture of crushed garlic, white pepper and coriander (cilantro). Look for it at Thai markets.

Energy 167Kcal/693kJ; Protein 10.4g; Carbohydrate 4.9g, of which sugars 4.2g; Fat 11.9g, of which saturates 0.8g; Cholesterol 0mg; Calcium 521mg; Fibre 1.9g; Sodium 832mg.

BALINESE VEGETABLE SOUP

THE BALINESE BASE THIS POPULAR SOUP ON BEANS, BUT ANY SEASONAL VEGETABLES CAN BE ADDED OR SUBSTITUTED. THE RECIPE ALSO INCLUDES SHRIMP PASTE, WHICH IS KNOWN LOCALLY AS TERASI.

2 Finely grind the chopped garlic, macadamia nuts or almonds, shrimp paste (blachan) and the coriander seeds to a paste using a pestle and mortar or in a food processor.

3 Heat the oil in a wok, and fry the onion until transparent. Remove with a slotted spoon. Add the nut paste to the wok and fry it for 2 minutes without allowing it to brown.

4 Pour in the reserved vegetable water. Spoon off 45–60ml/3–4 tbsp of the cream from the top of the coconut milk and set it aside. Add the remaining coconut milk to the wok, bring to the boil and add the bay leaves. Cook, uncovered, for 15–20 minutes.

SERVES 8

INGREDIENTS
225g/8oz green beans
1.2 litres/2 pints/5 cups lightly
  salted water
1 garlic clove, roughly
  chopped
2 macadamia nuts or 4 almonds,
  finely chopped
1cm/¹/₂in cube shrimp paste
  (blachan)
10–15ml/2–3 tsp coriander seeds,
  dry fried
30ml/2 tbsp vegetable oil
1 onion, finely sliced
400ml/14fl oz can coconut milk
2 bay leaves
225g/8oz/4 cups beansprouts
8 thin lemon wedges
30ml/2 tbsp lemon juice
salt and ground black pepper

1 Top and tail the beans, then cut them into small pieces. Bring the lightly salted water to the boil, add the beans to the pan and cook for 3–4 minutes. Drain, reserving the cooking water. Set the beans aside.

COOK'S TIP
Dry fry the coriander seeds for about 2 minutes until the aroma is released.

5 Just before serving, reserve a few beans, fried onions and beansprouts to garnish and stir the rest into the soup. Add the lemon wedges, reserved coconut cream, lemon juice and seasoning; stir well. Pour into individual soup bowls and serve, garnished with the reserved beans, onion and beansprouts.

Energy 54Kcal/224kJ; Protein 2.1g; Carbohydrate 5.2g, of which sugars 4.2g; Fat 2.8g, of which saturates 0.4g; Cholesterol 0mg; Calcium 38mg; Fibre 1.3g; Sodium 57mg.

SHIITAKE MUSHROOM LAKSA

"NOODLES" OF FINELY SLICED RED ONIONS ENHANCE THE TRADITIONAL FLOUR NOODLES IN THIS SOUP, WHICH IS BASED ON THE CLASSIC MALAYSIAN SOUP KNOWN AS PENANG LAKSA.

SERVES 6

INGREDIENTS

150g/5oz/2½ cups dried shiitake
   mushrooms
1.2 litres/2 pints/5 cups boiling
   vegetable stock
30ml/2 tbsp tamarind paste
250ml/8fl oz/1 cup hot water
6 large dried red chillies, stems
   removed and seeded
2 lemon grass stalks, finely sliced
5ml/1 tsp ground turmeric
15ml/1 tbsp grated fresh galangal
1 onion, chopped
5ml/1 tsp dried shrimp paste
30ml/2 tbsp oil
10ml/2 tsp palm sugar
175g/6oz rice vermicelli
1 red onion, peeled and very
   finely sliced
1 small cucumber, seeded and
   cut into strips
handful of fresh mint leaves,
   to garnish

1 Place the mushrooms in a bowl and pour in enough boiling stock to cover them. Set aside and leave to soak for 30 minutes.

2 Put the tamarind paste into a small bowl and pour in the hot water. Mash the paste against the side of the bowl with a fork to extract as much flavour as possible, then strain and reserve the liquid, discarding the pulp.

3 Soak the chillies in enough hot water to cover for 5 minutes, then drain, reserving the liquid.

4 Process the lemon grass, turmeric, galangal, onion, soaked chillies and shrimp paste in a food processor or blender, adding a little soaking water from the chillies to form a paste.

5 Heat the oil in a large, heavy-based pan and cook the paste over a low heat for 4–5 minutes until fragrant. Add the tamarind liquid and bring to the boil, then simmer for 5 minutes. Remove from the heat.

6 Drain the mushrooms and reserve the stock. Discard the stems, then halve or quarter the mushrooms, if large. Add the mushrooms to the pan with their soaking liquid, the remaining stock and the palm sugar. Simmer for 25–30 minutes or until tender.

7 Put the rice vermicelli into a large bowl and cover with boiling water, then leave to soak for 4 minutes or according to the packet instructions. Drain well, then divide among six bowls. Top with onion and cucumber, then ladle in the boiling shiitake soup. Add a small bunch of mint leaves to each bowl and serve immediately.

Energy 152Kcal/635kJ; Protein 3.2g; Carbohydrate 25.9g, of which sugars 2.6g; Fat 4g, of which saturates 0.5g; Cholesterol 0mg; Calcium 14mg; Fibre 0.6g; Sodium 4mg.

WILD MUSHROOM SOUP
WITH SOFT POLENTA

THIS RICH SOUP, SERVED WITH SOFT PARMESAN-ENRICHED POLENTA, PROVIDES PLENTY OF SCOPE FOR INDIVIDUAL VARIATIONS, DEPENDING ON YOUR CHOICE OF WILD MUSHROOMS.

SERVES 6

INGREDIENTS
  20g/¾oz/scant ½ cup dried
    porcini mushrooms
  175ml/6fl oz/¾ cup hot water
  50g/2oz/¼ cup butter
  1 large red onion, chopped
  3 garlic cloves, chopped
  115g/4oz/1¾ cups mixed wild
    mushrooms, trimmed
  120ml/4fl oz/½ cup light red wine
  1.2 litres/2 pints/5 cups
    vegetable stock
  2.5ml/½ tsp wholegrain mustard
  salt and ground black pepper
  chopped fresh parsley, to garnish
For the polenta
  750ml/1¼ pints/3 cups milk
  175g/6oz/1 cup quick-cook polenta
  50g/2oz/¼ cup butter
  50g/2oz/⅔ cup freshly grated
    Parmesan cheese, plus extra to serve

1 Put the dried porcini in a bowl and pour over the hot water. Leave them to soak for about 30 minutes. Drain, then strain the liquid through a fine sieve (strainer); reserve both the liquid and the mushrooms.

2 Melt the butter in a large pan. Add the onion and garlic and cook for 4–5 minutes, until softened. Add the mixed wild mushrooms and cook for a further 3–4 minutes.

3 Add the dried mushrooms and strain in the soaking liquid through a sieve (strainer) lined with muslin (cheesecloth) or a coffee filter. Pour in the wine and stock, and cook for 15 minutes or until the liquid has reduced by half. Remove from the heat and cool slightly.

4 Ladle half the soup into a food processor or blender and process until almost smooth. Pour the processed soup back into the soup remaining in the pan and set aside.

5 To make the polenta, bring the milk to the boil and pour in the polenta in a steady stream, stirring continuously. Cook for about 5 minutes, or until the polenta begins to come away from the side of the pan. Beat in the butter, then stir in the Parmesan.

6 Return the soup to the heat and bring just to the boil. Stir in the wholegrain mustard and season well.

7 Divide the polenta among six bowls and ladle the soup around it. Sprinkle over the grated Parmesan and the chopped parsley. Serve immediately.

COOK'S TIP
Many large supermarkets now sell a range of wild and cultivated mushrooms, both fresh and dried. If you can't find any, then substitute a mixture of well-flavoured cultivated varieties such as shiitake and chestnut.

GOAN POTATO SOUP WITH SPICED PEA SAMOSAS

IN GOA THIS SOUP WOULD BE SERVED AS A COMPLETE MEAL. BOTH SOUP AND SAMOSAS ARE SIMPLE TO PREPARE, AND MAKE A SUBSTANTIAL VEGETARIAN LUNCH.

SERVES 4

INGREDIENTS
  60ml/4 tbsp sunflower oil
  10ml/2 tsp black mustard seeds
  1 large onion, chopped
  1 red chilli, seeded and chopped
  2.5ml/½ tsp ground turmeric
  1.5ml/¼ tsp cayenne pepper
  900g/2lb potatoes, cut into cubes
  4 fresh curry leaves
  750ml/1¼ pint/3 cups water
  225g/8oz spinach leaves, torn if large
  400ml/14fl oz/1⅔ cups coconut milk
  handful of fresh coriander
    (cilantro) leaves
  salt and ground black pepper
For the samosa dough
  275g/10oz/2½ cups plain
    (all-purpose) flour
  1.5ml/¼ tsp salt
  30ml/2 tbsp sunflower oil
  150ml/¼ pint/⅔ cup warm water
For the samosa filling
  60ml/4 tbsp sunflower oil
  1 small onion, finely chopped
  175g/6oz/1½ cups frozen peas,
    thawed
  15ml/1 tbsp grated fresh root ginger
  1 green chilli, seeded and
    finely chopped
  45ml/3 tbsp water
  350g/12oz cooked potatoes,
    finely diced
  7.5ml/1½ tsp ground coriander
  5ml/1 tsp garam masala
  7.5ml/1½ tsp ground cumin
  1.5ml/¼ tsp cayenne pepper
  10ml/2 tsp lemon juice
  30ml/2 tbsp chopped fresh
    coriander
  vegetable oil, for deep frying

1 Make the samosa dough. Mix the flour and salt in a bowl and make a well in the middle. Add the oil and water and mix in the flour to make a soft dough. Knead briefly on a lightly floured surface. Wrap in clear film (plastic wrap) and chill for 30 minutes.

2 To make the filling, heat the oil in a frying pan and add the onion. Cook for 6–7 minutes until golden. Add the peas, ginger, chilli and water. Cover and simmer for 5–6 minutes, until the peas are cooked. Add the potatoes, spices and lemon juice. Cook over a low heat for 2–3 minutes. Stir in the coriander and season well. Leave to cool.

3 Divide the dough into eight. On a floured surface, roll out one piece into an 18cm/7in round. Keep the remaining dough covered. Cut the round in half and place 30ml/2 tbsp of the filling on each half towards one corner.

4 Dampen the edges and fold the dough over the filling. Pinch the edges together to form triangles. Repeat with the remaining dough and filling.

5 Heat the oil for deep frying to 190°C/375°F, or until a cube of bread rises and sizzles in 30 seconds. Fry the samosas for 4–5 minutes, turning once. Drain on kitchen paper.

6 To make the soup, heat the oil in a large pan. Add the mustard seeds, cover and cook until they begin to pop. Add the onion and chilli and cook for 5–6 minutes, until softened. Stir in the turmeric, cayenne, potatoes, curry leaves and water. Cover and cook over a low heat for 15 minutes, stirring occasionally, until the potatoes are soft.

7 Add the spinach and cook for 5 minutes. Stir in the coconut milk and cook for a further 5 minutes. Season and add the coriander leaves before ladling the soup into bowls. Serve with the vegetable samosas.

Energy 836Kcal/3503kJ; Protein 16.7g; Carbohydrate 112g, of which sugars 8.6g; Fat 38.7g, of which saturates 4.9g; Cholesterol 0mg; Calcium 227mg; Fibre 8.9g; Sodium 117mg.

LEGUME SOUPS

Soups made with legumes — peas, beans and lentils — are very nutritious as they contain protein, fibre, minerals and B vitamins, and are low in fat. The recipes in this section are particularly suitable for vegetarians, if made with vegetable stock. For a quick and easy lunch, try a simple Potage of Lentils or Catalan Potato Broad Bean Soup. On special occasions, impress your guests with cinnamon-scented Chickpea and Lentil Soup with Honey Buns.

BROAD BEAN MINESTRONE

THE CLASSIC, WINTRY MINESTRONE SOUP TAKES ON A SUMMER-FRESH IMAGE IN THIS LIGHT RECIPE. ANY SMALL PASTA SHAPES CAN BE USED INSTEAD OF THE SPAGHETTINI IF YOU PREFER.

SERVES 6

INGREDIENTS
  30ml/2 tbsp olive oil
  2 onions, peeled and finely chopped
  2 garlic cloves, peeled and
    finely chopped
  2 carrots, very finely chopped
  1 celery stick, very finely chopped
  1.27 litres/2¼ pints/5⅔ cups
    boiling water
  450g/1lb shelled fresh broad
    (fava) beans
  225g/8oz mangetouts (snow peas),
    cut into fine strips
  3 tomatoes, peeled and chopped
  5ml/1 tsp tomato purée (paste)
  50g/2oz spaghettini, broken into
    4cm/1½in lengths
  225g/8oz baby spinach
  30ml/2 tbsp chopped fresh parsley
  handful of fresh basil leaves
  salt and ground black pepper
  basil sprigs, to garnish
  freshly grated Parmesan cheese,
    to serve

4 Bring the pan of water back to the boil, add the mangetouts and cook for 1 minute until just tender. Drain, then refresh under cold water and set aside.

5 Add the tomatoes and the tomato purée to the soup. Cook for 1 minute. Purée two or three large ladlefuls of the soup and a quarter of the broad beans in a food processor or blender until smooth. Set aside.

6 Add the spaghettini to the remaining soup and cook for 6–8 minutes, until tender. Stir in the purée and spinach and cook for 2–3 minutes. Add the rest of the broad beans, the mangetouts and parsley, and season well.

7 When you are ready to serve the soup, stir in the basil leaves, ladle the soup into deep cups or bowls and garnish with sprigs of basil. Serve a little grated Parmesan with the soup.

1 Heat the oil in a pan and add the chopped onions and garlic. Cook over a low heat for 4–5 minutes, until softened but not browned.

2 Add the carrots and celery, and cook for 2–3 minutes. Add the boiling water and simmer for 15 minutes, until the vegetables are tender.

3 Cook the broad beans in boiling salted water for 4–5 minutes. Remove with a slotted spoon, refresh under cold water and set aside.

CATALAN POTATO AND BROAD BEAN SOUP

BROAD BEANS ARE ALSO KNOWN AS FAVA BEANS. WHILE THEY ARE IN SEASON, FRESH BEANS ARE IDEAL, BUT TINNED OR FROZEN WILL MAKE A PERFECTLY GOOD SUBSTITUTE.

SERVES 6

INGREDIENTS
    30ml/2 tbsp olive oil
    2 onions, chopped
    3 large floury potatoes, diced
    450g/1lb fresh broad (fava) beans
    1.75 litres/3 pints/7½ cups
      vegetable stock
    1 bunch coriander (cilantro),
      finely chopped
    150ml/¼ pint/⅔ cup single
      (light) cream
    salt and ground black pepper
    fresh coriander, to garnish

COOK'S TIP
Broad (fava) beans sometimes have a tough outer skin, particularly if they are large. To remove this, first cook the beans briefly, peel off the skin, and add the tender centre part to the soup.

1 Heat the oil in a large pan and fry the onions, stirring occasionally, for about 5 minutes until softened but not brown.

2 Add the potatoes, beans (reserving a few for garnishing) and stock to the mixture in the pan and bring to the boil, then simmer for 5 minutes.

3 Stir in the coriander and simmer for a further 10 minutes.

4 Process the mixture in a blender or food processor (you may have to do this in batches) then return the soup to the pan.

5 Stir in the cream (reserving a little for garnishing). Season to taste with salt and pepper, and bring to a simmer.

6 Serve garnished with more coriander leaves, beans and cream.

Energy 187Kcal/784kJ; Protein 8.1g; Carbohydrate 19.2g, of which sugars 3.5g; Fat 9.2g, of which saturates 3.7g; Cholesterol 14mg; Calcium 89mg; Fibre 6.1g; Sodium 22mg.

AMERICAN RED BEAN SOUP
WITH GUACAMOLE SALSA

THIS SOUP IS IN TEX-MEX STYLE, AND IT IS SERVED WITH A COOLING AVOCADO AND LIME SALSA. IF YOU RELISH CHILLIES, ADD A LITTLE MORE CAYENNE FOR A TRULY FIERY EXPERIENCE.

SERVES 6

INGREDIENTS
    30ml/2 tbsp olive oil
    2 onions, chopped
    2 garlic cloves, chopped
    10ml/2 tsp ground cumin
    1.5ml/¼ tsp cayenne pepper
    15ml/1 tbsp paprika
    15ml/1 tbsp tomato purée (paste)
    2.5ml/½ tsp dried oregano
    400g/14oz can chopped tomatoes
    2 x 400g/14oz cans red kidney
      beans, drained and rinsed
    900ml/1½ pints/3¾ cups water
    salt and ground black pepper
    Tabasco sauce, to serve
For the guacamole salsa
    2 avocados
    1 small red onion, finely chopped
    1 green chilli, seeded and chopped
    15ml/1 tbsp chopped fresh
      coriander (cilantro)
    juice of 1 lime

1 Heat the oil in a pan and add the onions and garlic. Cook for 4–5 minutes, until softened. Add the cumin, cayenne and paprika, and cook for 1 minute.

2 Stir in the tomato purée and cook for a few seconds, then stir in the oregano. Add the chopped tomatoes, kidney beans and water. Bring to the boil and simmer for 15–20 minutes.

3 Cool the soup slightly, then purée it in a food processor or blender until smooth. Return to the pan and season.

4 To make the guacamole salsa, halve, stone (pit) and peel the avocados, then dice them finely. Place in a small bowl and gently, but thoroughly, mix with the finely chopped red onion and chilli, and the coriander and lime juice.

5 Reheat the soup and ladle into bowls. Spoon a little guacamole salsa into the middle of each and serve, offering Tabasco sauce separately.

Energy 244Kcal/1023kJ; Protein 10.5g; Carbohydrate 27.5g, of which sugars 7.4g; Fat 11g, of which saturates 2g; Cholesterol 0mg; Calcium 108mg; Fibre 10g; Sodium 535mg.

BUTTER BEAN, SUN-DRIED TOMATO AND PESTO SOUP

THIS SOUP IS SO QUICK AND EASY TO MAKE, AND USING PLENTY OF PESTO AND SUN-DRIED TOMATO PASTE GIVES IT A RICH, MINESTRONE-LIKE FLAVOUR.

SERVES 4

INGREDIENTS

900ml/1½ pints/3¾ cups chicken
  or vegetable stock
2 x 400g/14oz cans butter
  (lima) beans
60ml/4 tbsp sun-dried tomato
  purée (paste)
75ml/5 tbsp pesto

COOK'S TIP
Use a good-quality home-made or
bought fresh stock for the best results.
Vegetarians should use vegetable stock.

VARIATION
As an alternative to butter beans, use
haricot (navy) or cannellini beans.

1 Drain and rinse the butter beans. Put the drained beans in a large pan with the stock and bring just to the boil.

2 Reduce the heat and stir in the tomato purée and pesto. Cover, bring back to simmering point and cook gently for 5 minutes.

3 Transfer six ladlefuls of the soup to a blender or food processor, scooping up plenty of the beans. Process until smooth, then return to the pan.

4 Heat gently, stirring frequently, for 5 minutes, then season if necessary. Ladle into four warmed soup bowls.

Energy 264Kcal/1109kJ; Protein 14.8g; Carbohydrate 27.4g, of which sugars 3.6g; Fat 11.3g, of which saturates 2.7g; Cholesterol 6mg; Calcium 109mg; Fibre 9.5g; Sodium 932mg.

OLD COUNTRY MUSHROOM, BEAN AND BARLEY SOUP

THIS HEARTY JEWISH SOUP IS PERFECT ON A FREEZING COLD DAY. SERVE IN WARMED BOWLS, WITH PLENTY OF RYE OR PUMPERNICKEL BREAD.

SERVES 6–8

INGREDIENTS

30–45ml/2–3 tbsp small haricot
   (navy) beans, soaked overnight
45–60ml/3–4 tbsp green split peas
45–60ml/3–4 tbsp yellow split peas
90–105ml/6–7 tbsp pearl barley
1 onion, chopped
2 carrots, sliced
3 celery sticks, diced or sliced
½ baking potato, peeled and cut
   into chunks
10g/¼oz or 45ml/3 tbsp mixed
   flavourful dried mushrooms
5 garlic cloves, sliced
2 litres/3½ pints/8 cups water
2 vegetable stock (bouillon) cubes
salt and ground black pepper
30–45ml/2–3 tbsp chopped fresh
   parsley, to garnish

1 In a large pan, put the beans, green and yellow split peas, pearl barley, onion, carrots, celery, potato, mushrooms, garlic and water.

2 Bring the mixture to the boil, then reduce the heat, cover and simmer gently for about 1½ hours, or until the beans are tender.

3 Crumble the stock cubes into the soup and taste for seasoning. Ladle into warmed bowls, garnish with parsley and serve with rye or pumpernickel bread.

COOK'S TIP
Do not add the stock (bouillon) cubes until the end of cooking as the salt will stop the beans from becoming tender.

Energy 171Kcal/726kJ; Protein 7.7g; Carbohydrate 35.4g, of which sugars 3.7g; Fat 0.8g, of which saturates 0.1g; Cholesterol 0mg; Calcium 37mg; Fibre 3.3g; Sodium 27mg.

TUSCAN CANNELLINI BEAN SOUP
WITH CAVOLO NERO

CAVOLO NERO IS A VERY DARK GREEN CABBAGE WITH A NUTTY FLAVOUR FROM TUSCANY AND SOUTHERN ITALY. IT IS IDEAL FOR THIS TRADITIONAL RECIPE.

SERVES 4

INGREDIENTS

2 x 400g/14oz cans chopped
  tomatoes with herbs
250g/9oz cavolo nero leaves, or
  Savoy cabbage
400g/14oz can cannellini beans,
  drained and rinsed
60ml/4 tbsp extra virgin olive oil
salt and ground black pepper

1 Pour the tomatoes into a large pan
and add a can of cold water. Season
with salt and pepper and bring to the
boil, then reduce the heat to a simmer.

2 Roughly shred the cabbage leaves
and add them to the pan. Partially
cover the pan and simmer gently for
about 15 minutes, or until the cabbage
is tender.

3 Add the cannellini beans to the pan
and warm through for a few minutes.
Check and adjust the seasoning, then
ladle the soup into bowls, drizzle each
one with a little olive oil and serve.

Energy 227Kcal/950kJ; Protein 8.2g; Carbohydrate 22.3g, of which sugars 10.4g; Fat 12.2g, of which saturates 1.9g; Cholesterol 0mg; Calcium 60mg; Fibre 7.9g; Sodium 443mg.

TUSCAN BEAN SOUP

THIS ITALIAN SOUP IS KNOWN AS RIBOLLITA. IT IS RATHER LIKE MINESTRONE, BUT MADE WITH BEANS INSTEAD OF PASTA, AND IS TRADITIONALLY LADLED OVER A RICH GREEN VEGETABLE, SUCH AS SPINACH.

SERVES 6

INGREDIENTS
    45ml/3 tbsp olive oil
    2 onions, chopped
    2 carrots, sliced
    4 garlic cloves, crushed
    2 celery sticks, thinly sliced
    1 fennel bulb, trimmed and chopped
    2 large courgettes (zucchini),
        thinly sliced
    400g/14oz can chopped tomatoes
    30ml/2 tbsp home-made or
        bought pesto
    900ml/1½ pints/3¾ cups
        vegetable stock
    400g/14oz can haricot (navy) or
        borlotti beans, drained
    salt and ground black pepper
For the base
    15ml/1 tbsp extra virgin olive oil,
        plus extra for drizzling
    450g/1lb fresh young spinach
    ground black pepper

1 Heat the oil in a large pan. Add the chopped onions, carrots, crushed garlic, celery and fennel and fry gently for about 10 minutes. Add the courgettes and fry for a further 2 minutes.

2 Stir in the chopped tomatoes, pesto, stock and beans and bring to the boil. Lower the heat, cover and simmer gently for 25–30 minutes, until the vegetables are completely tender. Season with salt and black pepper to taste.

3 Heat the oil in a frying pan and fry the spinach for 2 minutes, or until wilted. Spoon the spinach into heated soup bowls, then ladle the soup over the spinach. Just before serving, drizzle with olive oil and sprinkle with ground black pepper.

VARIATION
Use other dark greens, such as chard or cabbage, instead of the spinach; simply shred and cook until tender, then ladle the soup over the top.

Energy 197Kcal/822kJ; Protein 6.8g; Carbohydrate 20.8g, of which sugars 10.3g; Fat 10.2g, of which saturates 1.5g; Cholesterol 0mg; Calcium 93mg; Fibre 7.7g; Sodium 287mg.

BEAN AND PISTOU SOUP

*THIS HEARTY VEGETARIAN SOUP IS A TYPICAL PROVENÇAL-STYLE SOUP, RICHLY FLAVOURED WITH
A HOME-MADE GARLIC AND FRESH BASIL PISTOU SAUCE.*

SERVES 4–6

INGREDIENTS

150g/5oz/scant 1 cup dried haricot
   (navy) beans, soaked overnight
150g/5oz/scant 1 cup dried flageolet
   or cannellini beans, soaked overnight
1 onion, chopped
1.2 litres/2 pints/5 cups hot
   vegetable stock
2 carrots, roughly chopped
225g/8oz Savoy cabbage, shredded
1 large potato, about 225g/8oz,
   roughly chopped
225g/8oz French (green) beans,
   chopped
salt and ground black pepper
basil leaves, to garnish

For the pistou
4 garlic cloves
8 large sprigs basil leaves
90ml/6 tbsp olive oil
60ml/4 tbsp freshly grated
   Parmesan cheese

3 Add the chopped carrots, shredded
cabbage, chopped potato and French
beans to the bean pot. Season with salt
and pepper, cover and return the pot to
the oven. Reduce the oven temperature
to 180°C/350°F/Gas 4 and cook for
1 hour, or until all the vegetables are
cooked right through.

4 Meanwhile place the garlic and basil
in a mortar and pound with a pestle,
then gradually beat in the oil. Stir in the
grated Parmesan. Stir half the pistou
into the soup and then ladle into
warmed soup bowls. Top each bowl of
soup with a spoonful of the remaining
pistou and serve garnished with basil.

1 Soak a bean pot in cold water for 20
minutes, then drain. Drain the soaked
haricot and flageolet or cannellini beans
and place in the bean pot. Add the
chopped onion and pour over sufficient
cold water to come 5cm/2in above the
beans. Cover and place the pot in an
unheated oven. Set the oven to 200°C/
400°F/Gas 6 and cook for about 1½
hours, or until the beans are tender.

2 Drain the beans and onions. Place
half the beans and onions in a food
processor or blender and process to a
paste. Return the beans and paste to
the bean pot. Add the vegetable stock.

Energy 286Kcal/1214kJ; Protein 19.8g; Carbohydrate 50.9g, of which sugars 11.1g; Fat 1.8g, of which saturates 0.3g; Cholesterol 0mg; Calcium 142mg; Fibre 16.1g; Sodium 36mg.

BLACK-EYED BEAN
AND TOMATO BROTH

THIS DELICIOUS BLACK-EYED BEAN SOUP — KNOWN AS LUBIYA IN ISRAEL — IS FLAVOURED WITH TANGY LEMON AND SPECKLED WITH CHOPPED FRESH CORIANDER. IT IS IDEAL FOR SERVING AT PARTIES; SIMPLY MULTIPLY THE QUANTITIES AS REQUIRED.

SERVES 4

INGREDIENTS

175g/6oz/1 cup black-eyed
  beans (peas)
15ml/1 tbsp olive oil
2 onions, chopped
4 garlic cloves, chopped
1 medium-hot or 2–3 mild fresh
  chillies, chopped
5ml/1 tsp ground cumin
5ml/1 tsp ground turmeric
250g/9oz fresh or canned
  tomatoes, diced
600ml/1 pint/2½ cups chicken,
  beef or vegetable stock
25g/1oz fresh coriander (cilantro)
  leaves, roughly chopped
juice of ½ lemon
pitta bread, to serve

1 Put the beans in a pan, cover with cold water, bring to the boil and cook for 5 minutes. Remove from the heat, cover and leave to stand for 2 hours. Drain the beans, return to the pan, cover with fresh cold water, then simmer for 35–40 minutes, or until the beans are tender. Drain and set aside.

2 Heat the oil in a pan, add the onions, garlic and chilli and cook for 5 minutes, or until the onion is soft. Stir in the cumin, turmeric, tomatoes, stock, half the coriander and the beans and simmer for 20–30 minutes. Stir in the lemon juice and remaining coriander and serve at once with pitta bread.

Energy 168Kcal/712kJ; Protein 10.7g; Carbohydrate 25g, of which sugars 2.3g; Fat 3.6g, of which saturates 0.6g; Cholesterol 0mg; Calcium 52mg; Fibre 4.1g; Sodium 10mg.

MOROCCAN CHICKPEA AND LENTIL SOUP WITH HONEY BUNS

THIS THICK PULSE AND VEGETABLE SOUP IS SAID TO ORIGINATE FROM A SEMOLINA GRUEL THAT THE BERBERS ATE DURING THE COLD WINTERS IN THE ATLAS MOUNTAINS. TODAY, IT IS SERVED IN RESTAURANTS AND CAFÉS AS A HEARTY SNACK WITH HONEY-SWEETENED SPICED BREAD OR BUNS.

SERVES 8

INGREDIENTS

30–45ml/2–3 tbsp olive oil
2 onions, halved and sliced
2.5ml/½ tsp ground ginger
2.5ml/½ tsp ground turmeric
5ml/1 tsp ground cinnamon
pinch of saffron threads
2 x 400g/14oz cans chopped
  tomatoes
5–10ml/1–2 tsp caster
  (superfine) sugar
175g/6oz/¾ cup brown or green
  lentils, picked over and rinsed
about 1.75 litres/3 pints/7½ cups
  meat or vegetable stock, or water
200g/7oz/1 generous cup dried
  chickpeas, soaked overnight,
  drained and boiled until tender
200g/7oz/1 generous cup dried broad
  (fava) beans, soaked overnight,
  drained and boiled until tender
small bunch of fresh coriander
  (cilantro), chopped
small bunch of flat leaf
  parsley, chopped
salt and ground black pepper
for the buns
2.5ml/½ tsp dried yeast
300g/11oz/1¼ cups unbleached
  strong white bread flour
15–30ml/1–2 tbsp clear honey
5ml/1 tsp fennel seeds
250ml/8fl oz/1 cup milk
1 egg yolk, stirred with a little milk
salt

1 Make the buns. Dissolve the yeast in about 15ml/1 tbsp lukewarm water. Sift the flour and a pinch of salt into a bowl. Make a well in the centre and add the dissolved yeast, honey and fennel seeds. Gradually pour in the milk, using your hands to work it into the flour along with the honey and yeast, until the mixture forms a dough – if the dough becomes too sticky to handle, add more flour.

2 Turn the dough out on to a floured surface and knead well for about 10 minutes, until it is smooth and elastic. Flour the surface under the dough and cover it with a damp cloth, then leave the dough to rise until it has doubled in size.

3 Preheat the oven to 230ºC/450ºF/ Gas 8. Grease two baking sheets. Divide the dough into 12 balls. On a floured surface, flatten the balls of dough with the palm of your hand, then place them on a baking sheet. Brush the tops of the buns with egg yolk and bake for about 15 minutes until they are risen slightly and sound hollow when tapped underneath. Transfer to a wire rack to cool.

4 To make the soup, heat the olive oil in a stockpot or large pan. Add the onions and stir for about 15 minutes, or until they are soft.

5 Add the ginger, turmeric, cinnamon, saffron, tomatoes and sugar. Stir in the lentils and pour in the stock or water. Bring to the boil, then reduce the heat, cover and simmer for about 25 minutes, or until the lentils are tender.

6 Stir in the cooked chickpeas and beans, bring back to the boil, then cover and simmer for a further 10–15 minutes. Stir in the fresh herbs and season the soup to taste. Serve piping hot, with the honey buns.

Energy 368Kcal/1558kJ; Protein 18.3g; Carbohydrate 64.9g, of which sugars 9.7g; Fat 5.7g, of which saturates 1g; Cholesterol 2mg; Calcium 172mg; Fibre 7.5g; Sodium 74mg.

NORTH AFRICAN SPICED SOUP

CLASSICALLY KNOWN AS HARIRA, THIS SOUP IS OFTEN SERVED IN THE EVENING DURING RAMADAN, THE MUSLIM RELIGIOUS FESTIVAL WHEN FOLLOWERS FAST DURING THE DAYTIME FOR A MONTH.

SERVES 6

INGREDIENTS

    1 large onion, chopped
    1.2 litres/2 pints/5 cups stock
    5ml/1 tsp ground cinnamon
    5ml/1 tsp turmeric
    15ml/1 tbsp grated ginger
    pinch of cayenne pepper
    2 carrots, diced
    2 celery sticks, diced
    400g/14oz can chopped tomatoes
    450g/1lb floury potatoes, diced
    5 strands saffron
    400g/14oz can chickpeas, drained
    30ml/2 tbsp chopped fresh
      coriander (cilantro)
    15ml/1 tbsp lemon juice
    salt and ground black pepper
    fried wedges of lemon, to serve

1 Place the chopped onion in a large pot with 300ml/½ pint/1¼ cups of the vegetable stock. Bring the mixture to the boil and simmer gently for about 10 minutes.

2 Meanwhile, mix together the cinnamon, turmeric, ginger, cayenne pepper and 30ml/2 tbsp of stock to form a paste. Stir into the onion mixture with the carrots, celery and remaining stock.

3 Bring the mixture to a boil, reduce the heat, then cover and gently simmer for 5 minutes.

4 Add the tomatoes and potatoes and simmer gently, covered, for 20 minutes. Add the saffron, chickpeas, coriander and lemon juice. Season to taste and when piping hot serve with fried wedges of lemon.

Energy 158Kcal/668kJ; Protein 7.2g; Carbohydrate 28.4g, of which sugars 7g; Fat 2.5g, of which saturates 0.4g; Cholesterol 0mg; Calcium 64mg; Fibre 5.4g; Sodium 173mg.

POTAGE OF LENTILS

This traditional Jewish soup is sometimes known as Esau's soup. Red lentils and vegetables are cooked and puréed, then sharpened with lots of lemon juice.

SERVES 4

INGREDIENTS
45ml/3 tbsp olive oil
1 onion, chopped
2 celery sticks, chopped
1–2 carrots, sliced
8 garlic cloves, chopped
1 potato, peeled and diced
250g/9oz/generous 1 cup red lentils,
  picked over and rinsed
1 litre/1¾ pints/4 cups
  vegetable stock
2 bay leaves
1–2 lemons, halved
2.5ml/½ tsp ground cumin, or
  to taste
cayenne pepper or Tabasco sauce,
  to taste
salt and ground black pepper
lemon slices and chopped
  fresh flat leaf parsley, to serve

1 Heat the oil in a large pan. Add the onion and cook for about 5 minutes, or until softened. Stir in the celery, carrots, half the garlic and all the potato. Cook for a few minutes until beginning to soften.

2 Add the lentils and stock to the pan and bring to the boil. Reduce the heat, cover and simmer for about 30 minutes, until the potato and lentils are tender.

3 Add the bay leaves, remaining garlic and half the lemons to the pan and cook the soup for a further 10 minutes. Remove the bay leaves. Squeeze the juice from the remaining lemons, then stir into the soup, to taste.

4 Pour the soup into a food processor or blender and process until smooth. (You may need to do this in batches.) Tip the soup back into the pan, stir in the cumin, cayenne pepper or Tabasco sauce, and season with salt and pepper.

5 Ladle the soup into bowls and top each portion with lemon slices and a sprinkling of chopped fresh flat leaf parsley.

VARIATION
On a hot day, serve this soup cold, with even more lemon juice.

Energy 330Kcal/1391kJ; Protein 16.3g; Carbohydrate 48.1g, of which sugars 4.7g; Fat 9.4g, of which saturates 1.4g; Cholesterol 0mg; Calcium 50mg; Fibre 4.5g; Sodium 44mg.

THAI-STYLE LENTIL AND COCONUT SOUP

HOT, SPICY AND RICHLY FLAVOURED, THIS SUBSTANTIAL SOUP IS ALMOST A MEAL IN ITSELF. IF YOU ARE REALLY HUNGRY, SERVE WITH CHUNKS OF WARMED NAAN BREAD OR THICK SLICES OF TOAST.

SERVES 4

INGREDIENTS
  30ml/2 tbsp sunflower oil
  2 red onions, finely chopped
  1 bird's eye chilli, seeded and
    finely sliced
  2 garlic cloves, chopped
  2.5cm/1in piece fresh lemon grass,
    outer layers removed and inside
    finely sliced
  200g/7oz/scant 1 cup red
    lentils, rinsed
  5ml/1 tsp ground coriander
  5ml/1 tsp paprika
  400ml/14fl oz/1⅔ cups coconut milk
  juice of 1 lime
  3 spring onions (scallions), chopped
  20g/¾oz/scant 1 cup fresh coriander
    (cilantro), finely chopped
  salt and freshly ground black pepper

1 Heat the oil in a large pan and add the onions, chilli, garlic and lemon grass. Cook for 5 minutes or until the onions have softened but not browned, stirring occasionally.

COOK'S TIP
When using canned coconut milk, shake it before opening. This ensures that the layers of milk are well combined.

2 Add the lentils and spices. Pour in the coconut milk and 900ml/1½ pints/3¾ cups water, and stir. Bring to the boil, reduce the heat and simmer for 40–45 minutes, until the lentils are soft.

3 Pour in the lime juice and add the spring onions and coriander, reserving a little of each for the garnish. Season, ladle into bowls and garnish.

Energy 245Kcal/1034kJ; Protein 12.9g; Carbohydrate 35.8g, of which sugars 8.1g; Fat 6.6g, of which saturates 1g; Cholesterol 0mg; Calcium 75mg; Fibre 3.2g; Sodium 131mg.

SPICED LENTIL SOUP WITH PARSLEY CREAM

CRISPY SHALLOTS AND A PARSLEY CREAM TOP THIS RICH SOUP, WHICH IS INSPIRED BY THE DHALS OF INDIAN COOKING. CHUNKS OF SMOKED BACON ADD TEXTURE.

SERVES 6

INGREDIENTS

    5ml/1 tsp cumin seeds
    2.5ml/½ tsp coriander seeds
    5ml/1 tsp ground turmeric
    30ml/2 tbsp olive oil
    1 onion, chopped
    2 garlic cloves, chopped
    1 smoked bacon hock
    1.2 litres/2 pints/5 cups
      vegetable stock
    275g/10oz/1¼ cups red lentils
    400g/14oz can chopped tomatoes
    15ml/1 tbsp vegetable oil
    3 shallots, thinly sliced
For the parsley cream
    45ml/3 tbsp chopped
      fresh parsley
    150ml/¼ pint/⅔ cup Greek
      (US strained plain) yogurt
    salt and ground black pepper

1 Heat a frying pan and add the cumin and coriander seeds. Roast them over a high heat for a few seconds, shaking the pan until they smell aromatic. Transfer to a mortar and crush using a pestle. Mix in the turmeric. Set aside.

2 Heat the oil in a large pan. Add the onion and garlic and cook for 4–5 minutes, until softened.

3 Add the spice mixture and cook for 2 minutes, stirring continuously.

COOK'S TIP
Tip lentils into a sieve (strainer) or colander and pick them over to remove any pieces of grit before rinsing.

4 Place the bacon in the pan and pour in the stock. Bring to the boil, cover and simmer gently for 30 minutes.

5 Add the red lentils and cook for 20 minutes or until the lentils and bacon hock are tender. Stir in the tomatoes and cook for a further 5 minutes.

6 Remove the bacon from the pan and set it aside until cool enough to handle. Leave the soup to cool slightly, then process in a food processor or blender until almost smooth. Return the soup to the rinsed-out pan. Cut the meat from the hock, discarding skin and fat, then stir it into the soup and reheat.

7 Heat the oil in a frying pan and fry the shallots for 10 minutes until crisp and golden. Remove using a slotted spoon and drain on kitchen paper.

8 To make the parsley cream, stir the chopped parsley into the yogurt and season well. Ladle the soup into bowls and add a dollop of the parsley cream to each. Pile some crisp shallots on to each portion and serve at once.

Energy 235Kcal/991kJ; Protein 13g; Carbohydrate 28.4g, of which sugars 3.7g; Fat 8.8g, of which saturates 2.2g; Cholesterol 0mg; Calcium 66mg; Fibre 2.9g; Sodium 40mg.

PASTA AND NOODLE SOUPS

In Italy hearty pasta soups are often served with bread for a light supper. There are hundreds of little pasta shapes, called pastina, to choose from — which means an endless variety of dishes is possible. In this section you will find Pasta, Bean and Vegetable Soup, Meatballs in Pasta Soup with Basil and Avgolemono with Pasta. Noodles are a key ingredient in many Asian soups. Why not try Tokyo-style Ramen Noodles in Soup, or Thai Cellophane Noodle Soup.

BORLOTTI BEAN AND PASTA SOUP

A COMPLETE MEAL IN A BOWL, THIS IS A VERSION OF A CLASSIC ITALIAN SOUP. TRADITIONALLY, THE PERSON WHO FINDS THE BAY LEAF IS HONOURED WITH A KISS FROM THE COOK.

SERVES 4

INGREDIENTS

   1 onion, chopped
   1 celery stick, chopped
   2 carrots, chopped
   75ml/5 tbsp olive oil
   1 bay leaf
   1 glass white wine (optional)
   1 litre/1¾ pints/4 cups
     vegetable stock
   400g/14oz can chopped tomatoes
   300ml/½ pint/1¼ cups passata
     (bottled strained tomatoes)
   175g/6oz/1½ cups dried pasta shapes,
     such as farfalle or conchiglie
   400g/14oz can borlotti
     beans, drained
   salt and ground black pepper
   250g/9oz spinach, washed
     and drained
   50g/2oz/⅔ cup freshly grated
     (shredded) Parmesan cheese, to serve

VARIATION
Other pulses, such as cannellini beans, haricot (navy) beans or chickpeas, are equally good in this soup.

1 Place the chopped onion, celery and carrots in a large pan with the olive oil. Cook over a medium heat for 5 minutes or until the vegetables soften, stirring occasionally.

2 Add the bay leaf, wine, vegetable stock, tomatoes and passata, and bring to the boil. Lower the heat and simmer for 10 minutes until the vegetables are just tender.

3 Add the pasta and beans, and bring the soup back to the boil, then simmer for 8 minutes until the pasta is *al dente*. Stir frequently to prevent the pasta from sticking.

4 Season to taste with salt and pepper. Remove any thick stalks from the spinach and add it to the mixture. Cook for a further 2 minutes. Serve in heated soup bowls sprinkled with the freshly grated Parmesan.

VARIATIONS
• This soup is also delicious with chunks of cooked spicy sausage or pieces of crispy cooked pancetta or bacon – simply add to the soup at the end of Step 3 and stir in, ensuring that the meat is piping hot before serving.
• For vegetarians, you could use fried chunks of smoked or marinated tofu as an alternative to meat.

Energy 488Kcal/2049kJ; Protein 20.5g; Carbohydrate 59.8g, of which sugars 14.1g; Fat 20.1g, of which saturates 4.9g; Cholesterol 13mg; Calcium 366mg; Fibre 11.1g; Sodium 808mg.

PASTA, BEAN AND VEGETABLE SOUP

This is a Calabrian speciality known as Millecosedde. The name comes from the Italian word millecose, meaning "a thousand things". Literally anything edible can go in this soup.

SERVES 4-6

INGREDIENTS

75g/3oz/scant ½ cup brown lentils
15g/½oz dried mushrooms
60ml/4 tbsp olive oil
1 carrot, diced
1 celery stick, diced
1 onion, finely chopped
1 garlic clove, finely chopped
a little chopped fresh flat leaf parsley
a good pinch of crushed red chillies (optional)
1.5 litres/2½ pints/6¼ cups vegetable stock
150g/5oz/scant 1 cup each canned red kidney beans, cannellini beans and chickpeas, rinsed and drained
115g/4oz/1 cup dried small pasta shapes, such as rigatoni, penne or penne rigate
salt and ground black pepper
freshly grated Pecorino cheese, to serve
chopped flat leaf parsley, to garnish

3 Heat the oil in a large pan and add the carrot, celery, onion, garlic, parsley and chillies, if using. Cook over a low heat, stirring constantly, for 5–7 minutes, until the vegetables are soft.

4 Add the stock, then the mushrooms and their soaking liquid. Bring to the boil, then add the beans, chickpeas and lentils. Season to taste. Cover, and simmer gently for 20 minutes.

5 Add the pasta and bring back to the boil, stirring. Simmer for 7–8 minutes, until the pasta is *al dente*. Season, then serve hot in soup bowls, with grated Pecorino and chopped parsley.

COOK'S TIP
You can freeze the soup at the end of Step 4. Thaw and bring to the boil, add the pasta and simmer until tender.

1 Put the lentils in a medium pan, add 475ml/16fl oz/2 cups water and bring to the boil over a high heat. Lower the heat to a gentle simmer and cook, stirring occasionally, for 15–20 minutes or until the lentils are just tender. Meanwhile, soak the dried mushrooms in 175ml/6fl oz/¾ cup warm water for 15–20 minutes.

2 Put the lentils in a sieve (strainer) to drain, then rinse under the cold tap. Drain the soaked mushrooms and reserve the soaking liquid. Finely chop the mushrooms and set aside.

Energy 668Kcal/2831kJ; Protein 41.4g; Carbohydrate 100.8g, of which sugars 7.5g; Fat 14g, of which saturates 2g; Cholesterol 0mg; Calcium 178mg; Fibre 26.1g; Sodium 44mg.

TOMATO SOUP <u>WITH</u> ISRAELI COUSCOUS

NEWLY POPULAR ISRAELI COUSCOUS IS A TOASTED, ROUND PASTA WHICH IS MUCH LARGER THAN REGULAR COUSCOUS. IT MAKES A WONDERFUL ADDITION TO THIS WARM AND COMFORTING SOUP. IF YOU LIKE YOUR SOUP REALLY GARLICKY, ADD AN EXTRA CLOVE OF CHOPPED GARLIC BEFORE SERVING.

SERVES 4–6

INGREDIENTS
    30ml/2 tbsp olive oil
    1 onion, chopped
    1–2 carrots, diced
    400g/14oz can chopped tomatoes
    6 garlic cloves, roughly chopped
    1.5 litres/2½ pints/6¼ cups
        vegetable or chicken stock
    200–250g/7–9oz/1–1½ cups
        Israeli couscous
    2–3 mint sprigs, chopped, or several
        pinches of dried mint
    1.5ml/¼ tsp ground cumin
    ¼ bunch fresh coriander (cilantro),
        or about 5 sprigs, chopped
    cayenne pepper, to taste
    salt and ground black pepper

1 Heat the oil in a large pan, add the onion and carrots and cook gently for about 10 minutes until softened. Add the tomatoes, half the garlic, stock, couscous, mint, ground cumin, coriander, and cayenne pepper, salt and pepper to taste.

2 Bring the soup to the boil, add the remaining chopped garlic, then reduce the heat slightly and simmer gently for 7–10 minutes, stirring occasionally, or until the couscous is just tender. Serve piping hot, ladled into individual serving bowls.

Energy 191Kcal/797kJ; Protein 4.2g; Carbohydrate 31.3g, of which sugars 5g; Fat 6.2g, of which saturates 0.8g; Cholesterol 0mg; Calcium 30mg; Fibre 1.4g; Sodium 44mg.

MEATBALLS IN PASTA SOUP WITH BASIL

THESE HOME-MADE MEATBALLS ARE DELICIOUS — SCENTED WITH ORANGE AND GARLIC, THEY ARE SERVED IN A RUSTIC PASTA SOUP, WHICH IS THICKENED WITH PURÉED CANNELLINI BEANS. THE DISH IS A FILLING AND SATISFYING ITALIAN CLASSIC.

SERVES 4

INGREDIENTS
    400g/14oz can cannellini beans,
      drained and rinsed
    1 litre/1¾ pints/4 cups
      vegetable stock
    45ml/3 tbsp olive oil
    1 onion, finely chopped
    2 garlic cloves, chopped
    1 small red chilli, seeded and chopped
    2 celery sticks, finely chopped
    1 carrot, finely chopped
    15ml/1 tbsp tomato purée (paste)
    300g/11oz small pasta shapes
    large handful of fresh basil, torn
    salt and ground black pepper
    basil leaves, to garnish
    freshly grated Parmesan cheese,
      to serve
For the meatballs
    1 thick slice white bread,
      crusts removed
    60ml/4 tbsp milk
    350g/12oz lean minced (ground)
      beef or veal
    30ml/2 tbsp chopped fresh parsley
    grated rind of 1 orange
    2 garlic cloves, crushed
    1 egg, beaten
    30ml/2 tbsp olive oil

1 First prepare the meatballs. Break the bread into small pieces and place them in a bowl. Add the milk and leave to soak for about 10 minutes. Add the minced beef or veal, parsley, orange rind and garlic, and season well. Mix well with your hands.

2 When the bread is thoroughly incorporated with the meat, add enough beaten egg to bind the mixture. Shape small spoonfuls of the mixture into balls about the size of a large olive.

COOK'S TIP
Choose hollow pasta shapes for this soup, which will scoop up the soup as you eat. Look for small and medium-size shapes that are made especially for soup.

3 Heat the oil in a frying pan and fry the meatballs in batches for 6–8 minutes until browned all over. Use tongs or a draining spoon to remove them from the pan, and set them aside.

4 Purée the cannellini beans with a little of the stock in a food processor or blender until smooth. Set aside.

5 Heat the olive oil in a large pan. Add the chopped onion and garlic, chilli, celery and carrot, and cook for 4–5 minutes. Cover and cook gently for a further 5 minutes.

6 Stir in the tomato purée, the bean purée and the remaining vegetable stock. Bring the soup to the boil and cook for about 10 minutes.

7 Stir in the pasta shapes and simmer for 8–10 minutes, until the pasta is tender, but not soft. Add the meatballs and basil and cook for a further 5 minutes. Season the soup well before ladling it into warmed bowls. Garnish each bowl of soup with a basil leaf, and serve freshly grated Parmesan cheese with the soup.

Energy 718Kcal/3014kJ; Protein 35g; Carbohydrate 80.9g, of which sugars 10g; Fat 30.5g, of which saturates 8.5g; Cholesterol 53mg; Calcium 152mg; Fibre 9.7g; Sodium 529mg.

AVGOLEMONO WITH PASTA

THIS IS THE MOST POPULAR OF GREEK SOUPS. THE NAME MEANS EGG AND LEMON, THE TWO MOST IMPORTANT INGREDIENTS, WHICH PRODUCE A LIGHT, NOURISHING SOUP. ORZO IS A GREEK RICE-SHAPED PASTA, BUT YOU CAN USE ANY SMALL SOUP PASTA.

SERVES 4–6

INGREDIENTS
    1.75 litres/3 pints/7½ cups
      chicken stock
    115g/4oz/½ cup orzo pasta
    3 eggs
    juice of 1 large lemon
    salt and ground black pepper
    lemon slices, to garnish

COOK'S TIP
This egg and lemon combination is also widely used in Greece as a sauce for pasta or with meatballs.

1 Pour the stock into a large pan, and bring it to a rolling boil. Add the pasta and cook for 5 minutes.

2 Beat the eggs until frothy, then add the lemon juice and 15ml/ 1 tbsp of cold water. Slowly stir in a ladleful of the hot chicken stock, then add one or two more.

3 Return this mixture to the pan, remove from the heat and stir well. (Do not let the soup boil once the eggs have been added or it will curdle.)

4 Season the soup to taste with salt and freshly ground black pepper and serve immediately, garnished with a few lemon slices.

OLD-FASHIONED CHICKEN NOODLE SOUP

THIS IS A REALLY TRADITIONAL CHICKEN NOODLE SOUP — CLEAR, GOLDEN AND WARMING, AND FILLED WITH LIGHTLY COOKED PASTA. IT IS GUARANTEED TO MAKE YOU FEEL BETTER WHENEVER YOU HAVE A COLD. THE SECRET LIES IN BEGINNING WITH A GOOD-QUALITY STOCK.

SERVES 4–6

INGREDIENTS

2kg/4½lb boiling fowl (stewing chicken) with the giblets (except the liver)
1 large onion, peeled and halved
2 large carrots, halved lengthways
6 celery sticks, roughly chopped
1 bay leaf
175g/6oz vermicelli pasta
45ml/3 tbsp chopped fresh parsley or whole parsley leaves
salt and ground black pepper

1 Put the chicken into a large pan with all the vegetables and the bay leaf. Cover with 2.4 litres/4 pints/10 cups cold water. Bring slowly to the boil, carefully skimming off any scum that rises to the top. Add 5ml/1 tsp salt and some ground black pepper.

2 Turn down the heat and simmer the soup slowly for at least 2 hours, or until the fowl is tender. When simmering, the surface of the liquid should just tremble. If it is allowed to boil, the soup will become cloudy.

3 When tender, remove the bird from the broth and strip the flesh off the carcass. (Use the meat in sandwiches or a risotto.) Return the bones to the soup and simmer for another hour.

VARIATION
For a change you can use the same weight of guinea fowl and chicken wings and thighs, mixed.

4 Strain the soup into a bowl, cool, then chill overnight. The next day the soup should have set to a solid jelly and will be covered with a thin layer of solidified chicken fat. Carefully remove the fat.

5 To serve the soup, reheat in a large pan. Add the vermicelli and chopped parsley, and simmer for 6–8 minutes until the pasta is cooked. Taste and season well. Serve piping hot.

Energy 176Kcal/748kJ; Protein 6.3g; Carbohydrate 37.5g, of which sugars 5.7g; Fat 1.2g, of which saturates 0.1g; Cholesterol 0mg; Calcium 66mg; Fibre 3.4g; Sodium 39mg.

THAI CHICKEN NOODLE SOUP
WITH LITTLE CRAB CAKES

THIS SOUP IS A MEAL IN ITSELF. LOOK FOR STORES THAT SELL BUNCHES OF CORIANDER WITH THE ROOTS STILL ATTACHED, AS THEY ADD EXCELLENT FLAVOUR TO THE STOCK.

SERVES 6

INGREDIENTS
    8 garlic cloves
    small bunch of coriander (cilantro),
      with roots on
    1.2–1.4kg/2½–3lb chicken
    2 star anise
    2 carrots, chopped
    2 celery sticks, chopped
    1 onion, chopped
    30ml/2 tbsp soy sauce
    150g/5oz egg noodles
    30ml/2 tbsp vegetable oil
    60ml/4 tbsp Thai fish sauce (nam pla)
    1.5ml/¼ tsp chilli powder
    150g/5oz/1½ cups beansprouts
    2 spring onions (scallions), sliced
    herb sprigs, to garnish
    salt and ground black pepper
For the crab cakes
    5ml/1 tsp Thai red curry paste
    5ml/1 tsp cornflour (cornstarch)
    5ml/1 tsp Thai fish sauce (nam pla)
    1 small egg yolk
    15ml/1 tbsp chopped fresh
      coriander
    175g/6oz white crab meat
    50g/2oz/1 cup fresh white
      breadcrumbs
    30ml/2 tbsp vegetable oil

1 Chop four of the garlic cloves, thinly slice the remainder and set aside. Cut the roots off the coriander stems and place in a large pan with the garlic. Pick the coriander leaves off their stems and set aside; discard the stems. Place the chicken in the pan and add the star anise, carrots, celery and onion and soy sauce. Pour in enough water to cover the chicken. Bring to the boil, reduce the heat, cover and simmer for 1 hour.

2 For the crab cakes, mix the curry paste, cornflour, fish sauce and egg yolk in a bowl. Add the coriander, crab meat, breadcrumbs and seasoning, then mix well. Divide the mixture into 12 portions and form each into a small cake.

3 Cook the egg noodles according to the packet instructions. Drain and set aside. Heat the oil in a small pan and fry the sliced garlic until golden brown. Drain and set aside.

4 Remove the chicken from its stock and leave until cool enough to handle. (Reserve the stock.) Discard the chicken skin, take the meat off the bones and tear it into large strips. Set aside. Strain the stock and pour 1.2 litres/2 pints/5 cups into a pan. Stir in the fish sauce, chilli powder and seasoning, then bring to the boil. Reduce the heat and keep hot.

5 To cook the crab cakes, heat the vegetable oil in a large frying pan and fry the crab cakes for 2–3 minutes on each side until golden.

6 Divide the cooked noodles, fried garlic slices, beansprouts, sliced spring onions and chicken strips among six shallow soup bowls.

7 Arrange two of the crab cakes on top of the noodles, then ladle the hot chicken broth into the bowls. Scatter a few fresh coriander leaves over the soups, then garnish with the herb sprigs and serve immediately.

Energy 250Kcal/1049kJ; Protein 10.9g; Carbohydrate 28.8g, of which sugars 3.5g; Fat 10.9g, of which saturates 1.8g; Cholesterol 62mg; Calcium 74mg; Fibre 1.9g; Sodium 638mg.

CHICKEN AND CRAB NOODLE SOUP WITH CORIANDER OMELETTE

THE CHICKEN MAKES A DELICIOUS STOCK FOR THIS LIGHT NOODLE SOUP WITH ITS ELUSIVE HINT OF ENTICING AROMATIC CHINESE FLAVOURS.

SERVES 6

INGREDIENTS
    2 chicken legs, skinned
    1.75 litres/3 pints/7½ cups water
    bunch of spring onions (scallions)
    2.5cm/1in piece fresh root
      ginger, sliced
    5ml/1 tsp black peppercorns
    2 garlic cloves, halved
    75g/3oz rice noodles
    115g/4oz fresh white crab meat
    30ml/2 tbsp light soy sauce
    salt and ground black pepper
    coriander (cilantro) leaves, to garnish
For the omelettes
    4 eggs
    30ml/2 tbsp chopped fresh
      coriander leaves
    15ml/1 tbsp extra virgin olive oil

1 Put the chicken and water in a pan. Bring to the boil, reduce the heat and cook gently for 20 minutes; skim the surface occasionally.

2 Slice half the spring onions and add to the pan with the ginger, peppercorns, garlic and salt to taste. Cover and simmer for 1½ hours.

3 Meanwhile, soak the noodles in boiling water for 4 minutes, or according to the packet instructions. Drain and refresh under cold water. Shred the remaining spring onions and set aside.

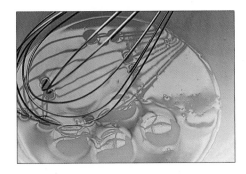

4 To make the omelettes, beat the eggs with the coriander and seasoning.

5 Heat a little of the olive oil in a small frying pan. Add a third of the egg and swirl the pan to coat the base evenly. Cook for 1 minute. Flip over and cook for 30 seconds. Turn the omelette out on to a plate and leave to cool. Repeat twice more to make three omelettes.

6 Roll up the omelettes tightly one at a time and slice thinly.

7 Remove the chicken from the stock and leave to cool. Strain the stock through a sieve (strainer) lined with muslin (cheesecloth) into a clean pan. When the chicken is cool enough to handle, remove and finely shred the meat, discarding the bones.

8 Bring the stock to the boil. Add the noodles, chicken, spring onions and crab meat, then simmer for 1–2 minutes. Stir in the soy sauce and season. Ladle the soup into bowls and top each with sliced omelette and coriander leaves.

Energy 159Kcal/664kJ; Protein 13.5g; Carbohydrate 10.6g, of which sugars 0.4g; Fat 6.9g, of which saturates 1.7g; Cholesterol 157mg; Calcium 46mg; Fibre 0g; Sodium 526mg.

CRAB SOUP WITH CORIANDER RELISH

*PREPARED FRESH CRAB IS READILY AVAILABLE, HIGH QUALITY AND CONVENIENT — PERFECT FOR
CREATING AN EXOTIC SEAFOOD AND NOODLE SOUP IN MINUTES. HERE IT IS ACCOMPANIED BY
A HOT CORIANDER AND CHILLI RELISH THAT GIVES IT A SPICY TANG.*

SERVES 4

INGREDIENTS

  45ml/3 tbsp olive oil
  1 red onion, finely chopped
  2 red chillies, seeded and
    finely chopped
  1 garlic clove, finely chopped
  450g/1lb fresh white crab meat
  30ml/2 tbsp chopped fresh parsley
  30ml/2 tbsp chopped fresh
    coriander (cilantro)
  juice of 2 lemons
  1 lemon grass stalk
  1 litre/1¾ pints/4 cups good fish
    or chicken stock
  15ml/1 tbsp Thai fish sauce
    (nam pla)
  150g/5oz vermicelli or angel hair
    pasta, broken into 5–7.5cm/
    2–3in lengths
  salt and ground black pepper
For the relish
  50g/2oz/1 cup fresh coriander
    leaves
  1 green chilli, seeded and chopped
  15ml/1 tbsp sunflower oil
  25ml/1½ tbsp lemon juice
  2.5ml/½ tsp ground roasted
    cumin seeds

1 Heat the oil in a pan and add the onion, chillies and garlic. Cook over a gentle heat for 10 minutes until the onion is very soft.

3 Lay the lemon grass on a chopping board and bruise it with a rolling pin or pestle. Pour the stock and fish sauce into a pan. Add the lemon grass and bring to the boil, then add the pasta. Simmer, uncovered, for 3–4 minutes or until the pasta is just tender.

5 Remove and discard the lemon grass from the soup. Stir the chilli and crab mixture into the soup and season it well. Bring to the boil, then reduce the heat and simmer for 2 minutes.

6 Ladle the soup into four deep, warmed bowls and put a spoonful of the coriander relish in the centre of each. Serve at once.

2 Transfer the cooked onion and chillies to a bowl and stir in the crab meat, parsley, coriander and lemon juice, then set aside.

4 Meanwhile, make the relish. Using a mortar and pestle, make a coarse paste with the fresh coriander, chilli, oil, lemon juice and cumin.

Energy 425Kcal/1773kJ; Protein 26.7g; Carbohydrate 50.7g, of which sugars 1.4g; Fat 12.6g, of which saturates 1.6g; Cholesterol 81mg; Calcium 198mg; Fibre 1.3g; Sodium 632mg.

MALAYSIAN PRAWN LAKSA

THIS SPICY PRAWN AND NOODLE SOUP TASTES JUST AS GOOD WHEN MADE WITH FRESH CRAB MEAT OR ANY FLAKED COOKED FISH INSTEAD OF THE PRAWNS. IF YOU ARE SHORT OF TIME, BUY READY-MADE LAKSA PASTE, WHICH YOU WILL FIND IN ORIENTAL STORES.

SERVES 2–3

INGREDIENTS

 115g/4oz rice vermicelli or stir-fry
  rice noodles
 15ml/1 tbsp vegetable or groundnut
  (peanut) oil
 600ml/1 pint/2½ cups fish stock
 400ml/14fl oz/1⅔ cups thin
  coconut milk
 30ml/2 tbsp Thai fish sauce
  (nam pla)
 ½ lime
 16–24 cooked peeled prawns
  (shrimp)
 salt
 cayenne pepper
 60ml/4 tbsp fresh coriander (cilantro)
  sprigs and leaves, chopped,
  to garnish
For the spicy paste
 2 lemon grass stalks,
  finely chopped
 2 fresh red chillies, seeded
  and chopped
 2.5cm/1in piece fresh root ginger,
  peeled and sliced
 2.5ml/½ tsp shrimp paste
 2 garlic cloves, chopped
 2.5ml/½ tsp ground turmeric
 30ml/2 tbsp tamarind paste

1 Cook the rice vermicelli or noodles in a large pan of boiling salted water for 3–4 minutes, or according to the instructions on the packet.

2 Tip the noodles into a large sieve (strainer) or colander, then rinse under cold water and drain. Set aside.

3 To make the spicy paste, place all the prepared ingredients in a mortar and pound with a pestle. Alternatively, put the ingredients in a food processor until a smooth paste is formed.

4 Heat the vegetable or groundnut oil in a large saucepan, add the spicy paste and fry, stirring constantly, for a few moments to release all the flavours. Be careful not to let it burn.

5 Add the fish stock and coconut milk and bring to the boil. Stir in the fish sauce, then simmer for 5 minutes. Season with salt and cayenne to taste, adding a squeeze of lime. Add the prawns and heat through for a few seconds.

6 Divide the noodles among two or three soup plates. Pour over the soup. Garnish with fresh coriander and serve piping hot.

Energy 436Kcal/1830kJ; Protein 36.9g; Carbohydrate 55.3g, of which sugars 10.2g; Fat 7.6g, of which saturates 1.2g; Cholesterol 341mg; Calcium 239mg; Fibre 0.8g; Sodium 562mg.

CHIANG MAI NOODLE SOUP

NOWADAYS A SIGNATURE DISH OF THE CITY OF CHIANG MAI, THIS DELICIOUS NOODLE SOUP ORIGINATED IN BURMA, NOW CALLED MYANMAR, WHICH LIES ONLY A LITTLE TO THE NORTH OF THE CITY. IT IS ALSO THE THAI EQUIVALENT OF THE FAMOUS MALAYSIAN "LAKSA".

SERVES 4–6

INGREDIENTS
    600ml/1 pint/2½ cups coconut milk
    30ml/2 tbsp Thai red curry paste
    5ml/1 tsp ground turmeric
    450g/1lb chicken thighs, boned and
      cut into bitesize chunks
    600ml/1 pint/2½ cups
      chicken stock
    60ml/4 tbsp Thai fish sauce (nam pla)
    15ml/1 tbsp dark soy sauce
    juice of ½–1 lime
    450g/1lb fresh egg noodles, blanched
      briefly in boiling water
    salt and ground black pepper
To garnish
    3 spring onions (scallions), chopped
    4 fresh red chillies, chopped
    4 shallots, chopped
    60ml/4 tbsp sliced pickled mustard
      leaves, rinsed
    30ml/2 tbsp fried sliced garlic
    coriander (cilantro) leaves
    4–6 fried noodle nests (optional)

1 Pour about one-third of the coconut milk into a large, heavy pan or wok. Bring to the boil over a medium heat, stirring frequently with a wooden spoon until the milk separates.

2 Add the curry paste and ground turmeric, stir to mix completely and cook until the mixture is fragrant.

3 Add the chunks of chicken and toss over the heat for about 2 minutes, making sure that all the chunks are thoroughly coated with the paste.

4 Add the remaining coconut milk, the chicken stock, fish sauce and soy sauce. Season with salt and pepper to taste. Bring to simmering point, stirring frequently, then lower the heat and cook gently for 7–10 minutes. Remove from the heat and stir in lime juice to taste.

5 Reheat the fresh egg noodles in boiling water, drain and divide among four to six warmed bowls. Divide the chunks of chicken among the bowls and ladle in the hot soup. Top each serving with spring onions, chillies, shallots, pickled mustard leaves, fried garlic, coriander leaves and a fried noodle nest, if using. Serve immediately.

Energy 679Kcal/2873kJ; Protein 43.2g; Carbohydrate 88.7g, of which sugars 10.1g; Fat 19.4g, of which saturates 5.6g; Cholesterol 180mg; Calcium 95mg; Fibre 3.4g; Sodium 769mg.

THAI CELLOPHANE NOODLE SOUP

THE THAI NOODLES USED IN THIS SOUP GO BY VARIOUS NAMES: GLASS NOODLES, CELLOPHANE NOODLES, BEAN THREAD OR TRANSPARENT NOODLES. THEY ARE MADE FROM MUNG BEAN FLOUR, AND ARE ESPECIALLY VALUED FOR THEIR BRITTLE TEXTURE.

SERVES 4

INGREDIENTS

   4 large dried shiitake mushrooms
   15g/½oz dried lily buds
   ½ cucumber, coarsely chopped
   2 garlic cloves, halved
   90g/3½oz white cabbage, chopped
   1.2 litres/2 pints/5 cups boiling water
   115g/4oz cellophane noodles
   30ml/2 tbsp soy sauce
   15ml/1 tbsp palm sugar or light
     muscovado (brown) sugar
   90g/3½oz block silken tofu, diced
   fresh coriander (cilantro), to garnish

1 Soak the shiitake mushrooms and dried lily buds in two separate bowls of warm water for 30 minutes.

COOK'S TIP
Dried lily buds are the unopened flowers of day lilies. They must always be soaked in warm water before use.

2 Meanwhile, put the chopped cucumber, garlic and cabbage in a food processor or blender and process to a smooth paste. Scrape the mixture into a large pan and add the measured boiling water.

3 Bring to the boil, then reduce the heat and cook for 2 minutes, stirring the mixture occasionally. Strain this warm stock into another pan, return to a low heat and gently bring to simmering point.

4 Drain the soaked lily buds, rinse under cold running water, then drain again. Cut off any hard ends. Add the lily buds to the stock with the noodles, soy sauce and sugar and cook for 5 minutes more.

5 Strain the liquid from the soaked mushrooms into the soup. Discard the mushroom stems, then slice the caps. Divide them and the tofu among four bowls. Pour the soup over, garnish with fresh coriander leaves and serve.

Energy 143Kcal/598kJ; Protein 4.9g; Carbohydrate 28.3g, of which sugars 5.6g; Fat 1.1g, of which saturates 0.1g; Cholesterol 0mg; Calcium 137mg; Fibre 0.6g; Sodium 362mg.

TOKYO-STYLE RAMEN NOODLES IN SOUP

RAMEN IS A HYBRID CHINESE NOODLE DISH PRESENTED IN A JAPANESE WAY, AND THERE ARE MANY REGIONAL VARIATIONS FEATURING LOCAL SPECIALITIES. THIS IS A LEGENDARY TOKYO VERSION.

SERVES 4

INGREDIENTS
250g/9oz dried ramen noodles
For the soup stock
   4 spring onions (scallions)
   7.5cm/3in fresh root ginger, quartered
   raw bones from 2 chickens, washed
   1 large onion, quartered
   4 garlic cloves, peeled
   1 large carrot, roughly chopped
   1 egg shell
   120ml/4fl oz/½ cup sake
   about 60ml/4 tbsp Japanese soy
     sauce (shoyu)
   2.5ml/½ tsp salt
For the *cha-shu* (pot-roast pork)
   500g/1¼lb pork shoulder, boned
   30ml/2 tbsp vegetable oil
   2 spring onions, chopped
   2.5cm/1in fresh root ginger, peeled
     and sliced
   15ml/1 tbsp sake
   45ml/3 tbsp Japanese soy sauce
   15ml/1 tbsp caster (superfine) sugar
For the toppings
   2 hard-boiled (hard-cooked) eggs
   150g/5oz menma, soaked for
     30 minutes and drained
   ½ nori sheet, broken into pieces
   2 spring onions, chopped
   ground white pepper
   sesame oil or chilli oil

1 To make the soup stock, bruise the spring onions and ginger by hitting with the side of a large knife. Pour 1.5 litres/ 2½ pints/6¼ cups water into a wok and bring to the boil. Add the chicken bones and boil until meat changes colour. Discard the water and wash the bones.

2 Wash the wok, bring 2 litres/ 3½ pints/ 9 cups water to the boil and add the bones and other stock ingredients, except the soy sauce and salt. Reduce the heat to low, and simmer until the water has reduced by half, skimming off any scum. Strain into a bowl through a sieve (strainer) lined with muslin (cheesecloth). This will take 1–2 hours.

3 Make the *cha-shu*. Roll the meat up tightly, 8cm/3½in in diameter, and tie it with kitchen string.

4 Wash the wok and dry over a high heat. Heat the oil to smoking point in the wok and add the chopped spring onions and ginger. Cook briefly, then add the meat. Turn often to brown the outside evenly.

5 Sprinkle with sake and add 400ml/ 14fl oz/1⅔ cups water, the soy sauce and sugar. Boil, then reduce the heat to low and cover. Cook for 25–30 minutes, turning every 5 minutes. Remove from the heat.

6 Slice the pork into 12 fine slices. Use any leftover pork for another recipe.

7 Shell and halve the boiled eggs, and sprinkle some salt on to the yolks.

8 Pour 1 litre/1¾ pints/4 cups soup stock from the bowl into a large pan. Boil and add the soy sauce and salt. Check the seasoning; add more sauce if required.

9 Wash the wok again and bring 2 litres/ 3½ pints/9 cups water to the boil. Cook the ramen noodles according to the packet instructions until just soft. Stir constantly to prevent sticking. If the water bubbles up, pour in 50ml/2fl oz/ ¼ cup cold water. Drain well and divide among four bowls.

10 Pour the soup over the noodles to cover. Arrange half a boiled egg, pork slices, menma and nori on top, and sprinkle with spring onions. Serve with pepper and sesame or chilli oil. Season to taste with a little salt, if you like.

COOK'S TIPS
• Sake, made from fermented rice, can be stored in the refrigerator for at least 3 weeks in a sealed container.
• Menma are pickled bamboo shoots, and need soaking before use.

Energy 466Kcal/1947kJ; Protein 35.1g; Carbohydrate 49.9g, of which sugars 0.9g; Fat 13.9g, of which saturates 3.2g; Cholesterol 175mg; Calcium 43mg; Fibre 0.3g; Sodium 489mg.

SOBA NOODLES IN HOT SOUP WITH TEMPURA

WHEN YOU COOK JAPANESE NOODLE DISHES, EVERYONE SHOULD BE READY AT THE DINNER TABLE,
BECAUSE COOKED NOODLES START TO SOFTEN AND LOSE THEIR TASTE AND TEXTURE QUITE QUICKLY.

SERVES 4

INGREDIENTS
400g/14oz dried soba noodles
1 spring onion (scallion), sliced
shichimi togarashi (optional)
For the tempura
16 medium raw tiger or king prawns
    (jumbo shrimp), heads and shell
    removed, tails intact
400ml/14fl oz/1⅔ cups ice-cold water
1 large (US extra large) egg, beaten
200g/7oz/scant 2 cups plain
    (all-purpose) flour
vegetable oil, for deep-frying
For the soup
150ml/¼ pint/⅔ cup mirin
150ml/¼ pint/⅔ cup shoyu
900ml/1½ pints/3¾ cups water
25g/1oz kezuri-bushi or 2 × 15g/
    ½oz packets
15ml/1 tbsp caster (superfine) sugar
5ml/1 tsp salt
900ml/1½ pints/3¾ cups first dashi
    stock or the same amount of water
    and 12.5ml/2½ tsp dashi-no-moto

1 To make the soup, put the mirin in a large pan. Bring to the boil, then add the rest of the soup ingredients apart from the dashi stock. Bring back to the boil, then reduce the heat to low. Skim off the scum and cook for 2 minutes. Strain the soup and put back into a clean pan with the dashi stock.

2 Remove the vein from the prawns, then make five shallow cuts into each prawn's belly. Clip the tip of the tail with scissors and squeeze out any moisture from the tail.

3 To make the batter, pour the ice-cold water into a bowl and mix in the beaten egg. Sift in the flour and stir briefly; it should remain fairly lumpy.

4 Heat the oil in a wok or deep-fryer to 180°C/350°F. Hold the tail of a prawn, dunk it in the batter, then plunge it into the hot oil. Deep-fry two prawns at a time until crisp and golden. Drain on kitchen paper and keep warm.

5 Put the noodles in a large pan with at least 2 litres/3½ pints/9 cups rapidly boiling water, and stir frequently to stop them sticking.

6 When the water foams, pour in about 50ml/2fl oz/¼ cup cold water to lower the temperature. Repeat when the water foams once again. The noodles should be slightly softer than *al dente* pasta.

7 Tip the noodles into a sieve (strainer) and wash under cold water with your hands to rinse off any oil.

8 Heat the soup. Warm the noodles with hot water, and divide among individual serving bowls. Place the prawns attractively on the noodles and add the soup. Sprinkle with sliced spring onion and some shichimi togarashi, if you like. Serve immediately.

COOK'S TIPS
• Shichimi togarashi is a peppery condiment made of seven seasonings.
• Kezuri-bushi is ready-shaved dried fish, one of the main ingredients used in dashi stock.
• Dashi is a fish stock that is frequently used in Japanese cooking. Freeze-dried granules are called dashi-no-moto, and these can be used to make a quick dashi.

Energy 728Kcal/3053kJ; Protein 30.7g; Carbohydrate 121.8g, of which sugars 5.3g; Fat 14g, of which saturates 1.9g; Cholesterol 218mg; Calcium 173mg; Fibre 1.6g; Sodium 728mg.

SAPPORO-STYLE RAMEN NOODLES IN SOUP

THIS IS A RICH AND TANGY SOUP FROM SAPPORO, THE CAPITAL OF HOKKAIDO, WHICH IS JAPAN'S MOST NORTHERLY ISLAND. RAW GRATED GARLIC AND CHILLI OIL ARE ADDED TO WARM THE BODY.

SERVES 4

INGREDIENTS
250g/9oz dried ramen noodles
For the soup stock
   4 spring onions (scallions)
   6cm/2½in fresh root ginger, quartered
   raw bones from 2 chickens, washed
   1 large onion, quartered
   4 garlic cloves
   1 large carrot, roughly chopped
   1 egg shell
   120ml/4fl oz/½ cup sake
   90ml/6 tbsp miso (any colour)
   30ml/2 tbsp Japanese soy sauce
   (shoyu)
For the toppings
   115g/4oz pork belly
   5cm/2in carrot
   12 mangetouts (snow peas)
   8 baby corn
   15ml/1 tbsp sesame oil
   1 dried red chilli, seeded and crushed
   225g/8oz/1 cup beansprouts
   2 spring onions, chopped
   2 garlic cloves, finely grated
   chilli oil
   salt

1 To make the soup stock, bruise the spring onions and ginger by hitting with a rolling pin. Boil 1.5 litres/2½ pints/6¼ cups water in a heavy pan, add the bones, and cook until the meat changes colour. Discard the water and wash the bones under running water.

2 Wash the pan and boil 2 litres/3½ pints/9 cups water, then add the bones and other stock ingredients except for the miso and soy sauce. Reduce the heat to low, and simmer for 2 hours, skimming any scum off. Strain into a bowl through a sieve (strainer) lined with muslin (cheesecloth); this will take about 1–2 hours. Do not squeeze the muslin.

3 Cut the pork into 5mm/¼in slices. Peel and halve the carrot lengthways then cut into 3mm/⅛in thick, 5cm/2in long slices. Boil the carrot, mangetouts and corn for 3 minutes in water. Drain.

4 Heat the sesame oil in a wok and fry the pork slices and chilli. When the colour of the meat has changed, add the beansprouts. Reduce the heat to medium and add 1 litre/1¾ pints/4 cups soup stock. Cook for 5 minutes.

5 Scoop 60ml/4 tbsp soup stock from the wok and mix well with the miso and soy sauce in a bowl. Stir back into the soup. Reduce the heat to low.

6 Bring 2 litres/3½ pints/9 cups water to the boil. Cook the noodles until just soft, following the instructions on the packet. Stir constantly. If the water bubbles up, pour in 50ml/2fl oz/¼ cup cold water. Drain well and divide among four bowls.

7 Pour the hot soup on to the noodles and heap the beansprouts and pork on top. Add the carrot, mangetouts and corn. Sprinkle with the spring onions and serve with garlic and chilli oil.

Energy 365Kcal/1522kJ; Protein 12.5g; Carbohydrate 54.1g, of which sugars 3.9g; Fat 10.9g, of which saturates 3.9g; Cholesterol 21mg; Calcium 43mg; Fibre 1.7g; Sodium 569mg.

UDON NOODLES WITH EGG BROTH AND GINGER

IN THIS DISH, CALLED ANKAKE UDON, THE SOUP FOR THE UDON IS THICKENED WITH CORNFLOUR AND RETAINS ITS HEAT FOR A LONG TIME. A PERFECT LUNCH FOR A FREEZING COLD DAY.

2 Heat at least 2 litres/3½ pints/9 cups water in a large pan, and cook the udon for 8 minutes or according to the packet instructions. Drain under cold running water and wash off the starch with your hands. Leave in the sieve (strainer).

3 Pour the soup into a large pan and bring to the boil. Blend the cornflour with 60ml/4 tbsp water. Reduce the heat to medium and gradually add the cornflour mixture to the hot soup. Stir constantly. The soup will thicken after a few minutes. Reduce the heat to low.

4 Mix the egg, mustard and cress, and spring onions in a small bowl. Stir the soup once again to create a whirlpool. Pour the eggs slowly into the soup pan.

5 Reheat the udon with hot water from a kettle. Divide among four bowls and pour the soup over the top. Garnish with the ginger and serve hot.

SERVES 4

INGREDIENTS
- 400g/14oz dried udon noodles
- 30ml/2 tbsp cornflour (cornstarch)
- 4 eggs, beaten
- 50g/2oz mustard and cress
- 2 spring onions (scallions), finely chopped
- 2.5cm/1in fresh root ginger, peeled and finely grated, to garnish

For the soup
- 1 litre/1¾ pints/4 cups water
- 40g/1½oz kezuri-bushi
- 25ml/1½ tbsp mirin
- 25ml/1½ tbsp Japanese soy sauce (shoyu)
- 7.5ml/1½ tsp salt

1 To make the soup, place the water and the soup ingredients in a pan and bring to the boil on a medium heat. Remove from the heat when it starts boiling. Stand for 1 minute, then strain through muslin (cheesecloth). Check the taste and add more salt if required.

COOK'S TIPS
- You can use ready-made noodle soup, available from Japanese food stores.
- Kezuri-bushi, or shaved, dried fish, is available in various graded packets.

Energy 487Kcal/2038kJ; Protein 15.5g; Carbohydrate 92.8g, of which sugars 0.6g; Fat 6.1g, of which saturates 1.6g; Cholesterol 190mg; Calcium 61mg; Fibre 0.2g; Sodium 1359mg.

POT-COOKED UDON IN MISO SOUP

UDON IS A WHITE WHEAT NOODLE EATEN WITH VARIOUS HOT AND COLD SOUPS. IN THIS DISH, KNOWN AS MISO NIKOMI UDON, THE NOODLES ARE COOKED IN A CLAY POT WITH A RICH MISO SOUP.

SERVES 4

INGREDIENTS
200g/7oz chicken breast portion, boned and skinned
10ml/2 tsp sake
2 abura-age
900ml/1½ pints/3¾ cups second dashi stock, or the same amount of water and 7.5ml/1½ tsp dashi-no-moto
6 large fresh shiitake mushrooms, stalks removed, quartered
4 spring onions (scallions), trimmed and chopped into 3mm/⅛in lengths
30ml/2 tbsp mirin
about 90g/3½oz aka miso or hatcho miso
300g/11oz dried udon noodles
4 eggs
shichimi togarashi (optional)

1 Cut the chicken into bitesize pieces. Sprinkle with sake and leave to marinate for 15 minutes.

2 Put the abura-age in a sieve (strainer) and thoroughly rinse with hot water from the kettle to wash off the oil. Drain on kitchen paper and cut each abura-age into 4 squares.

3 To make the soup, heat the second dashi stock in a large pan. When it has come to the boil, add the chicken pieces, shiitake mushrooms and abura-age and cook for 5 minutes. Remove the pan from the heat and add the spring onions.

COOK'S TIPS
Look for the traditional ingredients in Japanese food stores:
• Abura-age is a thin deep-fried tofu, used in traditional Japanese soups.
• Dashi-no-moto are freeze-dried granules of dashi fish stock.
• Hatcho miso is a paste made from soybeans using traditional methods.
• Shichimi togarashi is a peppery condiment made of seven seasonings.

4 Put the mirin and miso paste into a small bowl. Scoop 30ml/2 tbsp soup from the pan and mix this in well.

5 To cook the udon, boil at least 2 litres/3½ pints/9 cups water in a large pan. The water should not come higher than two-thirds the depth of the pan. Cook the udon for 6 minutes and drain.

6 Put the udon in one large flameproof clay pot or casserole (or divide among four small pots). Mix the miso paste into the soup and check the taste. Add more miso if required. Ladle in enough soup to cover the udon, and arrange the soup ingredients on top of the udon.

7 Put the soup on a medium heat and break an egg on top. When the soup bubbles, wait for 1 minute, then cover and remove from the heat. Leave to stand for 2 minutes. Serve with shichimi togarashi, if you like.

Energy 431Kcal/1819kJ; Protein 28.6g; Carbohydrate 54.7g, of which sugars 2.2g; Fat 12.6g, of which saturates 3.5g; Cholesterol 248mg; Calcium 60mg; Fibre 2.9g; Sodium 594mg.

NOODLE, PAK CHOI AND SALMON RAMEN

THIS LIGHTLY SPICED JAPANESE NOODLE SOUP IS ENHANCED BY SLICES OF SEARED FRESH SALMON AND CRISP VEGETABLES. THE CONTRASTS IN TEXTURE ARE AS APPEALING AS THE DELICIOUS TASTE.

SERVES 4

INGREDIENTS

   1.5 litres/2½ pints/6 cups good
      vegetable stock
   2.5cm/1in piece fresh root ginger,
      finely sliced
   2 garlic cloves, crushed
   6 spring onions (scallions), sliced
   45ml/3 tbsp soy sauce
   45ml/3 tbsp sake
   450g/1lb salmon fillet, skinned
   5ml/1 tsp groundnut (peanut) oil
   350g/12oz ramen or udon noodles
   4 small heads pak choi (bok choy),
      broken into leaves
   1 fresh red chilli, seeded and sliced
   50g/2oz/1 cup beansprouts
   salt and ground black pepper

1 Pour the stock into a large pan and add the ginger, garlic, and a third of the spring onions.

2 Add the soy sauce and sake. Bring to the boil, then reduce the heat and simmer for 30 minutes.

3 Meanwhile, remove any pin bones from the salmon using tweezers, then cut the salmon on the slant into 12 slices, using a very sharp knife.

4 Brush a ridged griddle or frying pan with the oil and heat until very hot. Sear the salmon slices for 1–2 minutes on each side until tender and marked by the ridges of the pan. Set aside.

COOK'S TIP

To obtain the distinctive stripes on the slices of salmon, it is important that the ridged pan or griddle is very hot before they are added. Avoid moving the slices, or the stripes will become blurred.

5 Cook the ramen or udon noodles in a large pan of boiling water for 4–5 minutes or according to the instructions on the packet. Tip into a colander, drain well and refresh under cold running water. Drain again and set aside.

6 Strain the broth into a clean pan and season, then bring to the boil. Add the pak choi. Using a fork, twist the noodles into four nests and put these into deep bowls. Divide the salmon slices, spring onions, chilli and beansprouts among the bowls. Ladle in the broth.

Energy 569Kcal/2394kJ; Protein 34.6g; Carbohydrate 65.6g, of which sugars 4.1g; Fat 20.5g, of which saturates 4.3g; Cholesterol 83mg; Calcium 70mg; Fibre 3.5g; Sodium 746mg.

JAPANESE-STYLE NOODLE SOUP

THIS DELICATE, FRAGRANT SOUP IS FLAVOURED WITH JUST A SUBTLE HINT OF CHILLI. IT IS BEST SERVED AS A LIGHT LUNCH OR FIRST COURSE.

SERVES 4

INGREDIENTS

    45ml/3 tbsp mugi miso
    200g/7oz/scant 2 cups udon noodles,
      soba noodles or Chinese noodles
    30ml/2 tbsp sake or dry sherry
    15ml/1 tbsp rice or wine vinegar
    45ml/3 tbsp Japanese soy sauce
    115g/4oz asparagus tips or
      mangetouts (snow peas), thinly
      sliced diagonally
    50g/2oz/scant 1 cup shiitake
      mushrooms, stalks removed and
      thinly sliced
    1 carrot, sliced into julienne strips
    3 spring onions (scallions), thinly
      sliced diagonally
    salt and freshly ground black pepper
    5ml/1 tsp dried chilli flakes, to serve

1 Bring 1 litre/1¾ pints/4 cups water to the boil in a pan. Pour 150ml/¼ pint/⅔ cup boiling water over the miso and stir until dissolved, then set aside.

2 Meanwhile, bring another large pan of lightly salted water to the boil, add the noodles and cook until just tender.

3 Drain the noodles in a colander. Rinse under cold running water, then drain again. Set aside.

COOK'S TIPS
• Mugi miso is the fermented paste of soybeans and barley.
• If fresh shiitake mushrooms are not available, use dried ones instead. Put them in a bowl, pour over boiling water and leave to stand for 30 minutes.

4 Add the sake or sherry, rice or wine vinegar and soy sauce to the pan of boiling water. Boil gently for 3 minutes or until the alcohol has evaporated, then reduce the heat and stir in the miso mixture.

5 Add the asparagus or mangetouts, mushrooms, carrot and spring onions, and simmer for 2 minutes until the vegetables are tender. Season to taste.

6 Divide the noodles among four warm bowls and pour the soup over the top. Sprinkle with the chilli flakes to serve.

Energy 220Kcal/929kJ; Protein 7.9g; Carbohydrate 39.7g, of which sugars 4.4g; Fat 4.3g, of which saturates 1.2g; Cholesterol 15mg; Calcium 37mg; Fibre 2.8g; Sodium 898mg.

CHICKEN AND DUCK SOUPS

A substantial chicken soup such as Chicken, Leek and Celery
Soup, Chicken Soup with Knaidlach, or Pumpkin, Rice and
Chicken Soup can be a meal in itself, served with crusty bread
and some fresh fruit to follow. Chicken soups from Asia are
usually lighter and refreshing, often served as an appetizer or
as part of the meal. Duck makes a rich soup, and there are two
exotic recipes to try – Cream of Duck Soup with Blueberry
Relish and Duck Broth with Orange Spiced Dumplings.

PUMPKIN, RICE AND CHICKEN SOUP

THIS IS A WARM, COMFORTING SOUP WHICH, DESPITE THE SPICE AND BASMATI RICE, IS QUINTESSENTIALLY ENGLISH. FOR AN EVEN MORE SUBSTANTIAL MEAL, ADD A LITTLE MORE RICE AND MAKE SURE YOU USE ALL THE CHICKEN FROM THE STOCK.

SERVES 4

INGREDIENTS

1 wedge of pumpkin, about 450g/1lb
15ml/1 tbsp sunflower oil
25g/1oz/2 tbsp butter
6 green cardamom pods
2 leeks, chopped
115g/4oz/generous ½ cup basmati
   rice, soaked
350ml/12fl oz/1½ cups milk
salt and freshly ground black pepper
generous strips of pared orange rind,
   to garnish

For the chicken stock
2 chicken quarters
1 onion, quartered
2 carrots, chopped
1 celery stalk, chopped
6–8 peppercorns
900ml/1½ pints/3¾ cups water

1 First make the chicken stock. Place the chicken quarters, onion, carrots, celery stalk and peppercorns in a large pan. Pour in the water and slowly bring to the boil. Skim the surface of the stock if necessary, then lower the heat, cover and simmer gently for 1 hour.

2 Strain the chicken stock into a clean, large bowl, discarding the vegetables. Skin and bone one or both chicken pieces and cut the flesh into strips. (If not using both chicken pieces for the soup, reserve the other piece for another recipe.)

3 Skin the pumpkin and remove all the seeds and pith, so that you have about 350g/12oz flesh. Cut the flesh into 2.5cm/1in cubes.

4 Heat the oil and butter in a pan and fry the cardamom pods for 2–3 minutes until slightly swollen. Add the leeks and pumpkin. Cook, stirring, for 3–4 minutes over a medium heat, then lower the heat, cover and sweat for 5 minutes more or until the pumpkin is quite soft, stirring once or twice.

5 Measure out 600ml/1 pint/2½ cups of the stock and add to the pumpkin mixture. Bring to the boil, then lower the heat, cover and simmer gently for 10–15 minutes, until the pumpkin is soft.

6 Pour the remaining stock into a measuring jug and make up with water to 300ml/½ pint/1¼ cups. Drain the rice and put it into a pan. Pour in the stock, bring to the boil, then simmer for about 10 minutes until the rice is tender. Add seasoning to taste.

7 Remove the cardamom pods, then process the soup in a blender or food processor until smooth. Pour back into a clean pan and stir in the milk, chicken and rice (with any stock that has not been absorbed). Heat until simmering. Garnish with the strips of pared orange rind and freshly ground black pepper, and serve with granary or wholemeal bread.

COOK'S TIP
Once made, chicken stock will keep in an airtight container in the refrigerator for 3–4 days.

Energy 315Kcal/1320kJ; Protein 24.6g; Carbohydrate 29.9g, of which sugars 6.3g; Fat 10.8g, of which saturates 4.9g; Cholesterol 71mg; Calcium 140mg; Fibre 2.1g; Sodium 122mg.

CHICKEN AND LEEK SOUP
WITH PRUNES AND BARLEY

THIS RECIPE IS BASED ON THE TRADITIONAL SCOTTISH SOUP, COCK-A-LEEKIE. THE UNUSUAL COMBINATION OF LEEKS AND PRUNES IS SURPRISINGLY DELICIOUS.

SERVES 6

INGREDIENTS
1 chicken, weighing about 2kg/4¼lb
900g/2lb leeks
1 fresh bay leaf
a few each fresh parsley stalks and
  thyme sprigs
1 large carrot, thickly sliced
2.4 litres/4 pints/10 cups chicken
  or beef stock
115g/4oz/generous ½ cup
  pearl barley
400g/14oz ready-to-eat prunes
salt and ground black pepper
chopped fresh parsley, to garnish

1 Cut the breasts off the chicken and set aside. Place the remaining chicken carcass in a large pan. Cut half the leeks into 5cm/2in lengths and add them to the pan. Tie the bay leaf, parsley and thyme into a bouquet garni and add to the pan with the carrot and the stock. Bring to the boil, then reduce the heat and cover. Simmer gently for 1 hour. Skim off any scum when the water first boils and occasionally during simmering.

2 Add the chicken breasts and cook for another 30 minutes, until they are just cooked. Leave until cool enough to handle, then strain the stock. Reserve the chicken breasts and meat from the chicken carcass. Discard all the skin, bones, cooked vegetables and herbs. Skim as much fat as you can from the stock, then return it to the pan.

3 Meanwhile, rinse the pearl barley thoroughly in a sieve (strainer) under cold running water, then cook it in a large pan of boiling water for about 10 minutes. Drain, rinse well again and drain thoroughly.

4 Add the pearl barley to the stock. Bring to the boil over a medium heat, then lower the heat and cook very gently for 15–20 minutes, until the barley is just cooked and tender. Season the soup with 5ml/1 tsp salt and black pepper.

5 Add the prunes. Slice the remaining leeks and add them to the pan. Bring to the boil, then simmer for 10 minutes or until the leeks are just cooked.

6 Slice the chicken breasts and add them to the soup with the remaining chicken meat, sliced or cut into neat pieces. Reheat if necessary, then ladle the soup into deep plates and sprinkle with chopped parsley.

Energy 359Kcal/1526kJ; Protein 41.7g; Carbohydrate 44g, of which sugars 26.9g; Fat 3g, of which saturates 0.6g; Cholesterol 105mg; Calcium 73mg; Fibre 7.4g; Sodium 104mg.

CHICKEN, LEEK AND CELERY SOUP

THIS MAKES A SUBSTANTIAL MAIN COURSE SOUP WITH FRESH CRUSTY BREAD. YOU WILL NEED NOTHING MORE THAN A SALAD AND CHEESE, OR JUST FRESH FRUIT TO FOLLOW THIS DISH.

SERVES 4–6

INGREDIENTS

1.4kg/3lb free-range chicken
1 small head of celery, trimmed
1 onion, coarsely chopped
1 fresh bay leaf
a few fresh parsley stalks
a few fresh tarragon sprigs
2.4 litres/4 pints/10 cups cold water
3 large leeks
65g/2½oz/5 tbsp butter
2 potatoes, cut into chunks
150ml/¼ pint/⅔ cup dry white wine
30–45ml/2–3 tbsp single (light)
  cream (optional)
salt and ground black pepper
90g/3½oz pancetta, grilled until
  crisp, to garnish

1 Cut the breasts off the chicken and set aside. Chop the rest of the chicken carcass into 8–10 pieces and place in a large pan.

2 Chop 4–5 of the outer sticks of the celery and add them to the pan with the onion. Tie the bay leaf, parsley and tarragon together and add to the pan. Pour in the cold water to cover the ingredients and bring to the boil. Reduce the heat and cover the pan, then simmer for 1½ hours.

3 Remove the chicken and cut off and reserve the meat. Strain the stock, then return it to the pan and boil rapidly until it has reduced to about 1.5 litres/ 2½ pints/6¼ cups.

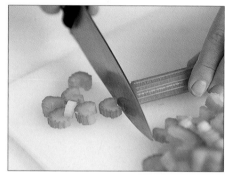

4 Meanwhile, set about 150g/5oz of the leeks aside. Slice the remaining leeks and the remaining celery, reserving any celery leaves. Chop the celery leaves and set aside to garnish the soup.

5 Melt half the butter in a large, heavy-based pan. Add the sliced leeks and celery, cover and cook over a low heat for about 10 minutes, or until softened but not browned. Add the potatoes, wine and 1.2 litres/2 pints/ 5 cups of the stock.

6 Season well with salt and pepper, bring to the boil and reduce the heat. Part-cover the pan and simmer the soup for 15–20 minutes, or until the potatoes are cooked.

7 Meanwhile, skin the reserved chicken breasts and cut the flesh into small pieces. Melt the remaining butter in a frying pan, add the chicken and fry for 5–7 minutes, until cooked.

8 Thickly slice the remaining leeks, add to the pan and cook, stirring occasionally, for a further 3–4 minutes, until just cooked.

9 Process the soup with the cooked chicken from the stock in a blender or food processor. Taste and adjust the seasoning, and add more stock if the soup is very thick.

10 Stir in the cream, if using, and the chicken and leek mixture. Reheat gently and serve in warmed bowls. Crumble the pancetta over the soup and sprinkle with the chopped celery leaves.

Energy 294Kcal/1246kJ; Protein 40.5g; Carbohydrate 22.1g, of which sugars 5.9g; Fat 2.8g, of which saturates 0.7g; Cholesterol 105mg; Calcium 69mg; Fibre 4.9g; Sodium 124mg.

MOROCCAN CHICKEN SOUP
WITH CHARMOULA BUTTER

THIS TASTY SOUP, INSPIRED BY THE INGREDIENTS OF NORTH AFRICA, IS SPICED WITH CHILLI AND SERVED WITH A RICH AND PUNGENT LEMON BUTTER CREAMED WITH CRISP BREADCRUMBS.

SERVES 6

INGREDIENTS
  50g/2oz/¼ cup butter
  450g/1lb chicken breasts, cut
    into strips
  1 onion, chopped
  2 garlic cloves, crushed
  7.5ml/1½ tsp plain (all-purpose) flour
  15ml/1 tbsp harissa
  1 litre/1¾ pints/4 cups chicken stock
  400g/14oz can chopped tomatoes
  400g/14oz can chickpeas, drained
    and rinsed
  salt and ground black pepper
  lemon wedges, to serve
For the charmoula
  50g/2oz/¼ cup slightly salted butter,
    at room temperature
  30ml/2 tbsp chopped fresh
    coriander (cilantro)
  2 garlic cloves, crushed
  5ml/1 tsp ground cumin
  1 red chilli, seeded and chopped
  pinch of saffron strands
  finely grated rind of ½ lemon
  5ml/1 tsp paprika
  25g/1oz/1 cup dried breadcrumbs

1 Melt the butter in a large, heavy-based pan. Add the chicken strips and cook for 5–6 minutes, turning with a wooden spatula, until beginning to brown. Use a slotted spoon to remove the chicken from the pan and set aside.

2 Add the onion and garlic to the pan and cook over a gentle heat for 4–5 minutes, until softened but not brown.

3 Stir in the flour and cook for 3–4 minutes, stirring continuously, until beginning to brown.

4 Stir in the harissa and cook for a further 1 minute. Gradually pour in the stock and cook for 2–3 minutes, until slightly thickened. Stir in the tomatoes.

5 Return the chicken to the soup and add the chickpeas. Cover and cook over a low heat for 20 minutes. Season well with salt and black pepper.

6 Meanwhile, to make the charmoula, put the butter into a bowl and beat in the coriander, garlic, cumin, chilli, saffron strands, lemon rind and paprika. When the mixture is well combined, stir in the coarse breadcrumbs.

7 Ladle the soup into six warmed bowls. Spoon a little of the charmoula into the centre of each and leave for a few seconds to allow the butter to melt into the soup before serving with lemon wedges.

Energy 313Kcal/1312kJ; Protein 25g; Carbohydrate 18.3g, of which sugars 3.3g; Fat 16.1g, of which saturates 9g; Cholesterol 88mg; Calcium 53mg; Fibre 3.6g; Sodium 207mg.

SOUTHERN AMERICAN SUCCOTASH SOUP
WITH CHICKEN

BASED ON A VEGETABLE DISH FROM THE SOUTHERN STATES OF AMERICA, THIS SOUP INCLUDES SUCCULENT FRESH CORN KERNELS, WHICH GIVE IT A RICHNESS THAT COMPLEMENTS THE CHICKEN.

SERVES 4

INGREDIENTS

750ml/1¼ pints/3 cups chicken stock
4 boneless, skinless chicken breasts
50g/2oz/¼ cup butter
2 onions, chopped
115g/4oz piece rindless smoked
  streaky (fatty) bacon, chopped
25g/1oz/¼ cup plain
  (all-purpose) flour
4 cobs of corn
300ml/½ pint/1¼ cups milk
400g/14oz can butter (lima)
  beans, drained
45ml/3 tbsp chopped fresh parsley
salt and ground black pepper

6 Cut the chicken into bite-size pieces and stir into the soup. Stir in the butter beans and the remaining milk. Bring to the boil and cook for 5 minutes, then season well and stir in the parsley.

1 Bring the chicken stock to the boil in a large pan. Add the chicken breasts and bring back to the boil. Reduce the heat and cook for 12–15 minutes, until cooked through and tender. Use a slotted spoon to remove the chicken from the pan and leave to cool. Reserve the stock.

2 Melt the butter in a pan. Add the onions and cook for 4–5 minutes, until softened but not brown.

3 Add the bacon and cook for 5–6 minutes, until beginning to brown. Sprinkle in the flour and cook for 1 minute, stirring continuously.

4 Gradually stir in the hot stock and bring to the boil, stirring until thickened. Remove from the heat.

5 Using a sharp knife, remove the kernels from the corn cobs. Stir the kernels into the pan with half the milk. Return to the heat and cook, stirring occasionally, for 12–15 minutes, until the corn is tender.

VARIATION
Canned corn can be used instead of fresh corn.

Energy 539Kcal/2267kJ; Protein 51.8g; Carbohydrate 37.4g, of which sugars 11.5g; Fat 21.4g, of which saturates 10.3g; Cholesterol 155mg; Calcium 155mg; Fibre 6.4g; Sodium 1120mg.

CHICKEN SOUP <u>WITH</u> KNAIDLACH

A BOWL OF CHICKEN SOUP CAN HEAL THE SOUL AS WELL AS THE BODY, AS ANYONE WHO HAS EVER SUFFERED FROM FLU AND BEEN COMFORTED, OR SUFFERED GRIEF AND BEEN CONSOLED, WILL KNOW. THIS SOUP IS SERVED WITH KNAIDLACH — DUMPLINGS MADE OF MATZO, EGGS AND CHICKEN FAT.

SERVES 6–8

INGREDIENTS

1–1.5kg/2¼–3¼lb chicken, cut
   into portions
2–3 onions
3–4 litres/5–7 pints/12–16 cups water
3–5 carrots, thickly sliced
3–5 celery sticks, thickly sliced
1 small parsnip, cut in half
30–45ml/2–3 tbsp roughly chopped
   fresh parsley
30–45ml/2–3 tbsp chopped fresh dill
1–2 pinches ground turmeric
2 chicken stock (bouillon) cubes
2 garlic cloves, finely chopped
   (optional)
salt and ground black pepper
For the knaidlach
175g/6oz/¾ cup medium matzo meal
2 eggs, lightly beaten
45ml/3 tbsp vegetable oil or rendered
   chicken fat
1 garlic clove, finely chopped (optional)
30ml/2 tbsp chopped fresh parsley,
   plus extra to garnish
½ onion, finely grated
1–2 pinches of chicken stock
   (bouillon) cube or powder (optional)
about 90ml/6 tbsp water
salt and ground black pepper

1 Put the chicken pieces in a very large pan. Keeping them whole, cut a large cross in the stem end of each onion and add to the pan with the water, carrots, celery, parsnip, parsley, half the fresh dill, the turmeric, and salt and black pepper.

2 Cover the pan and bring to the boil, then immediately lower the heat to a simmer. Skim and discard the scum that rises to the top. (Scum will continue to form but it is only the first scum that rises that will detract from the clarity and flavour of the soup.)

3 Add the crumbled stock cubes and simmer for 2–3 hours. When the soup is flavourful, skim off the fat. Alternatively, chill the soup and remove the layer of solid fat that forms.

4 To make the knaidlach, combine the matzo meal with the eggs, oil or fat, chopped garlic, if using, parsley, onion, salt and pepper in a large bowl. Add only a little chicken stock cube or powder, if using, as these are salty. Add the water and mix together until the mixture is of the consistency of a thick, soft paste.

5 Cover the matzo batter and chill for 30 minutes, during which time the mixture will become firm.

6 Bring a pan of water to the boil and have a bowl of water next to the stove. Dip two tablespoons into the water, then take a spoonful of the matzo batter. With wet hands, roll it into a ball, then slip it into the boiling water and reduce the heat so that the water simmers. Continue with the remaining matzo batter, working relatively quickly, then cover the pan and cook for 15–20 minutes.

7 Remove the knaidlach from the pan with a slotted spoon and transfer to a plate for about 20 minutes to firm up.

8 To serve, reheat the soup, adding the remaining dill and the garlic, if using. Put two or three knaidlach in each bowl, pour over the hot soup and garnish.

VARIATIONS
• Instead of knaidlach, the soup can be served over rice or noodles.
• To make lighter knaidlach, separate the eggs and add the yolks to the matzo mixture. Whisk the whites until stiff, then fold into the mixture.

Energy 455Kcal/1890kJ; Protein 26.9g; Carbohydrate 33.4g, of which sugars 10.1g; Fat 23.7g, of which saturates 5.4g; Cholesterol 173mg; Calcium 65mg; Fibre 3.9g; Sodium 136mg.

CHICKEN AND COCONUT SOUP

THIS RECIPE COMBINES THE ORIENTAL FLAVOURS OF THAILAND IN A SMOOTH EUROPEAN-STYLE SOUP, AND THE FINISHED DISH IS COMPLEMENTED BY A TOPPING OF CRISP SHALLOTS.

SERVES 6

INGREDIENTS
40g/1½oz/3 tbsp butter
1 onion, finely chopped
2 garlic cloves, chopped
2.5cm/1in piece fresh root ginger,
   finely chopped
10ml/2 tsp Thai green curry paste
2.5ml/½ tsp turmeric
400ml/14fl oz can coconut milk
475ml/16fl oz/2 cups
   chicken stock
2 lime leaves, shredded
1 lemon grass stalk, finely chopped
8 skinless, boneless chicken thighs
350g/12oz spinach, roughly chopped
10ml/2 tsp Thai fish sauce
30ml/2 tbsp lime juice
30ml/2 tbsp vegetable oil
2 shallots, thinly sliced
small handful of Thai purple
   basil leaves
salt and ground black pepper

1 Melt the butter in a large, heavy-based pan. Add the onion, garlic and ginger. Cook for 4–5 minutes, until soft.

2 Stir in the curry paste and turmeric, and cook for a further 2–3 minutes, stirring continuously.

3 Pour in two-thirds of the coconut milk; cook for 5 minutes. Add the stock, lime leaves, lemon grass and chicken. Heat until simmering; cook for 15 minutes or until the chicken is tender.

4 Use a slotted spoon to remove the chicken thighs. Set them aside to cool.

5 Add the spinach to the pan and cook for 3–4 minutes. Stir in the remaining coconut milk and seasoning, then process the soup in a food processor or blender until almost smooth. Return the soup to the rinsed-out pan. Cut the chicken thighs into bite-size pieces and stir these into the soup with the fish sauce and lime juice.

6 Reheat the soup gently until hot, but do not let it boil. Meanwhile, heat the oil in a frying pan and cook the shallots for 6–8 minutes, until crisp and golden, stirring occasionally. Drain on kitchen paper. Ladle the soup into bowls, then top with the basil leaves and fried shallots, and serve.

Energy 136Kcal/570kJ; Protein 14.1g; Carbohydrate 5.2g, of which sugars 4.9g; Fat 6.7g, of which saturates 3.8g; Cholesterol 49mg; Calcium 125mg; Fibre 1.4g; Sodium 344mg.

CHINESE CHICKEN AND CHILLI SOUP

GINGER AND LEMON GRASS ADD AN AROMATIC NOTE TO THIS TASTY, REFRESHING SOUP, WHICH CAN BE SERVED AS A LIGHT LUNCH OR APPETIZER.

SERVES 4

INGREDIENTS

150g/5oz boneless chicken breast
  portion, cut into thin strips
2.5cm/1in piece fresh root ginger,
  finely chopped
5cm/2in piece lemon grass stalk,
  finely chopped
1 red chilli, seeded and
  thinly sliced
8 baby corn cobs, halved lengthways
1 large carrot, cut into thin sticks
1 litre/1¾ pints/4 cups hot
  chicken stock
4 spring onions (scallions),
  thinly sliced
12 small shiitake mushrooms, sliced
115g/4oz/1 cup vermicelli
  rice noodles
30ml/2 tbsp soy sauce
salt and ground black pepper

2 Place the Chinese sand pot in an unheated oven. Set the temperature to 200°C/400°F/Gas 6 and cook the soup for 30–40 minutes, or until the stock is simmering and the chicken and vegetables are tender.

3 Add the spring onions and the mushrooms, cover and return the pot to the oven for 10 minutes.

4 Meanwhile place the noodles in a large bowl and cover with boiling water. Soak for the required time, following the packet instructions.

5 Stir the soy sauce into the soup, taste for seasoning and add salt and pepper as required.

6 Drain the noodles and divide them among four warmed serving bowls. Divide the soup between the bowls and serve immediately.

1 Place the chicken strips, chopped ginger, chopped lemon grass and sliced chilli in a Chinese sand pot. Add the halved baby corn and the carrot sticks. Pour over the hot chicken stock and cover the pot.

COOK'S TIP
Rice noodles are available in a variety of thicknesses and can be bought in straight lengths or in coils or loops. They are a creamy white colour and very brittle in texture. Rice noodles are pre-cooked so they only require a very short soaking time – check the packet for exact timings. Vermicelli rice noodles are very fine and will only need to be soaked for a few minutes.

Energy 165Kcal/693kJ; Protein 13.3g; Carbohydrate 26g, of which sugars 3.1g; Fat 0.9g, of which saturates 0.2g; Cholesterol 26mg; Calcium 23mg; Fibre 1.4g; Sodium 852mg.

CREAM OF DUCK SOUP WITH BLUEBERRY RELISH

THIS DELICIOUS, RICH SOUP IS IDEAL FOR SMART OCCASIONS. YOU CAN USE A WHOLE DUCK, BUT COOKING WITH DUCK BREASTS AND LEGS IS EASIER.

SERVES 4

INGREDIENTS
  2 duck breasts
  4 rindless streaky (fatty) bacon
    rashers, chopped
  1 onion, chopped
  1 garlic clove, chopped
  2 carrots, diced
  2 celery sticks, chopped
  4 large open mushrooms, chopped
  15ml/1 tbsp tomato purée (paste)
  2 duck legs
  15ml/1 tbsp plain (all-purpose) flour
  45ml/3 tbsp brandy
  150ml/¼ pint/⅔ cup port
  300ml/½ pint/1¼ cups red wine
  900ml/1½ pints/ 3¾ cups
    chicken stock
  1 bay leaf
  2 sprigs fresh thyme
  15ml/1 tbsp redcurrant jelly
  150ml/¼ pint/⅔ cup double
    (heavy) cream
  salt and ground black pepper
For the blueberry relish
  150g/5oz/1¼ cups blueberries
  15ml/1 tbsp caster (superfine) sugar
  grated rind and juice of 2 limes
  15ml/1 tbsp chopped fresh parsley
  15ml/1 tbsp balsamic vinegar

1 Use a sharp knife to score the skin and fat on the duck breasts.

2 Preheat a heavy-based pan. Place the duck breasts in the pan, skin sides down, and cook for 8–10 minutes, until golden. Turn and cook for a further 5–6 minutes.

3 Remove the duck from the pan and set aside. Drain off some of the fat, leaving about 45ml/3 tbsp in the pan.

4 Add the bacon, onion, garlic, carrots, celery and mushrooms to the pan and cook for 10 minutes, stirring occasionally. Stir in the tomato purée and cook for 2 minutes. Remove the skin and bones from the duck legs and chop the flesh. Add to the pan and cook for 5 minutes.

5 Stir in the flour and cook for 1 minute. Gradually stir in the brandy, port, wine and stock and bring to the boil, stirring. Add the bay leaf, thyme and redcurrant jelly, then stir until the jelly melts. Reduce the heat and simmer for 1 hour.

6 Meanwhile, make the relish. Put the blueberries, caster sugar, lime rind and juice, parsley and vinegar in a small bowl. Very lightly bruise the blueberries with a fork, leaving some of the berries whole. Set aside until required.

7 Strain the soup through a colander, then through a fine sieve (strainer) into a clean pan. Bring to the boil, reduce the heat and simmer for 10 minutes.

8 Meanwhile, remove and discard the skin and fat from the duck breasts and cut the meat into thin strips. Add the meat strips to the soup with the double cream and season well. Bring just to boiling point.

9 Ladle the soup into warmed bowls and top each serving with a dollop of the blueberry relish. Serve piping hot.

Energy 642Kcal/2673kJ; Protein 39.2g; Carbohydrate 14.2g, of which sugars 13.6g; Fat 35g, of which saturates 17.2g; Cholesterol 252mg; Calcium 83mg; Fibre 2.8g; Sodium 384mg.

DUCK BROTH <u>WITH</u> ORANGE SPICED DUMPLINGS

USING A DELICATE TOUCH WHEN BRINGING TOGETHER THE MIXTURE FOR THE DUMPLINGS WILL CREATE A LIGHT TEXTURE TO MATCH THEIR DELICIOUS FLAVOUR.

SERVES 4

INGREDIENTS
    1 duckling, about 1.75kg/4–4½lb,
      with liver
    1 large onion, halved
    2 carrots, thickly sliced
    ½ garlic bulb
    1 bouquet garni
    3 cloves
    30ml/2 tbsp chopped chives,
      to garnish
For the spiced dumplings
    2 thick slices white bread
    60ml/4 tbsp milk
    2 rashers (strips) rindless streaky
      (fatty) bacon
    1 shallot, finely chopped
    1 garlic clove, crushed
    1 egg yolk, beaten
    grated rind of 1 orange
    2.5ml/½ tsp paprika
    50g/2oz/½ cup plain
      (all-purpose) flour
    salt and ground black pepper

1 Set the duck liver aside. Using a sharp knife, cut off the breasts from the duckling and set them aside.

2 Put the carcass into a large, heavy-based pan and pour in enough water to cover the carcass. Bring to the boil and skim the scum off the surface.

3 Add the onion, carrots, garlic, bouquet garni and cloves. Reduce the heat and cover the pan, then simmer for 2 hours, skimming occasionally to remove scum.

4 Lift the carcass from the broth and leave to cool. Strain the broth, and skim it to remove any fat. Return the broth to the pan and simmer gently, uncovered, until reduced to 1.2 litres/2 pints/5 cups.

5 Remove all the meat from the duck carcass and shred it finely. Set aside.

6 For the dumplings, soak the bread in the milk for 5 minutes. Remove the skin and fat from the duck breasts. Mince (grind) the meat with the liver and bacon. Squeeze the milk from the bread, then add the bread to the meat with the shallot, garlic, egg yolk, orange rind, paprika, flour and seasoning, and mix.

7 Form a spoonful of the mixture into a ball, a little smaller than a walnut. Repeat with the remaining mixture to make 20 small dumplings.

8 Bring a large pan of lightly salted water to the boil and poach the dumplings for 4–5 minutes, until they are just tender.

9 Bring the duck broth back to the boil and add the dumplings.

10 Divide the shredded duck meat among four warmed bowls and ladle in the broth and dumplings. Garnish with chives.

Energy 289Kcal/1214kJ; Protein 29.9g; Carbohydrate 19g, of which sugars 2.8g; Fat 13g, of which saturates 3.1g; Cholesterol 196mg; Calcium 63mg; Fibre 1.3g; Sodium 373mg.

MEAT SOUPS

Nourishing meaty soups are just the thing for warming you up on cold winter days. This section includes soups from all around the world — Irish Kidney and Bacon Soup, Mediterranean Sausage and Pesto Soup, Russian Pea and Barley Soup, Chinese Pork and Rice Porridge, and Japanese Miso Soup with Pork and Vegetables. For special occasions, try one of the delicious traditional Jewish soups — Beef and Lamb Stew, or Fragrant Beetroot and Vegetable Soup with Spiced Lamb Kubbeh.

COCK-A-LEEKIE WITH PUY LENTILS AND THYME

THIS ANCIENT SCOTTISH SOUP IS MADE WITH BOTH BEEF AND CHICKEN TO FLAVOUR THE BROTH. THE ADDITION OF PUY LENTILS GIVES THIS VERSION EVEN MORE EARTHINESS.

SERVES 4

INGREDIENTS

2 leeks, cut into 5cm/2in julienne
115g/4oz/½ cup Puy lentils
1 bay leaf
a few sprigs of fresh thyme
115g/4oz minced (ground) beef
2 skinless, boneless chicken breasts
900ml/1½ pints/3¾ cups good
  home-made beef stock
8 ready-to-eat prunes, cut into strips
salt and ground black pepper
fresh thyme sprigs, to garnish

1 Bring a small pan of salted water to the boil and cook the julienne of leeks for 1–2 minutes. Drain and refresh under cold running water. Drain again and set aside.

COOK'S TIP
To cut fine and even julienne strips, cut the leek into 5cm/2in lengths. Cut each piece in half lengthways, then with the cut side down, cut the leek into thin strips.

2 Pick over the lentils to check for any small stones or grit. Put into a pan with the bay leaf and thyme and cover with cold water. Bring to the boil and cook for 25–30 minutes until tender. Drain and refresh under cold water.

3 Put the minced beef and chicken breasts in a pan and pour over enough stock to cover them. Bring to the boil and cook gently for 15–20 minutes, or until tender. Using a slotted spoon, remove the chicken from the stock and leave to cool.

4 When the chicken is cool enough to handle, cut it into strips. Return it to the stock in the pan and add the lentils and the remaining stock. Bring just to the boil and add seasoning to taste.

5 Divide the leeks and prunes among four warmed bowls. Ladle over the hot chicken and lentil broth. Garnish each portion with a few fresh thyme sprigs and serve immediately.

Energy 275Kcal/1160kJ; Protein 32.3g; Carbohydrate 23.5g, of which sugars 7.4g; Fat 6.4g, of which saturates 2.4g; Cholesterol 70mg; Calcium 47mg; Fibre 4.1g; Sodium 82mg.

CELERIAC SOUP WITH CABBAGE, BACON AND HERBS

VERSATILE, YET OFTEN OVERLOOKED, CELERIAC IS A WINTER VEGETABLE THAT MAKES EXCELLENT SOUP. IT TASTES WONDERFUL TOPPED WITH A COMPLEMENTARY SEASONAL VERSION OF A SALSA.

SERVES 4

INGREDIENTS
  50g/2oz butter
  2 onions, chopped
  675g/1½lb celeriac,
    roughly diced
  450g/1lb potatoes, roughly diced
  1.2 litres/2 pints/5 cups
    vegetable stock
  150ml/¼ pint/⅔ cup single
    (light) cream
  salt and ground black pepper
  sprigs of fresh thyme, to garnish
For the cabbage and bacon topping
  1 small savoy cabbage
  50g/2oz/¼ cup butter
  175g/6oz rindless streaky (fatty)
    bacon, roughly chopped
  15ml/1 tbsp chopped fresh thyme
  15ml/1 tbsp chopped fresh rosemary

1 Melt the butter in a pan. Add the onions and cook for 4–5 minutes, until softened. Add the celeriac. Cover the vegetables with a wetted piece of baking parchment, then put a lid on the pan and cook gently for 10 minutes.

2 Remove the paper. Stir in the potatoes and stock, bring to the boil, reduce the heat and simmer for 20 minutes. Leave to cool slightly. Using a slotted spoon, remove half the celeriac and potatoes from the soup and set them aside.

3 Purée the soup in a food processor or blender. Return the soup to the pan with the reserved celeriac and potatoes.

4 Prepare the cabbage and bacon mixture. Discard the tough outer leaves from the cabbage. Roughly tear the remaining leaves, discarding any hard stalks, and blanch them in boiling salted water for 2–3 minutes. Refresh under cold running water and drain.

5 Melt the butter in a large frying pan and cook the bacon for 3–4 minutes. Add the cabbage, thyme and rosemary, and stir-fry for 5–6 minutes, until tender. Season well.

6 Add the cream to the soup and season it well, then reheat gently until piping hot.

7 Ladle the soup into warmed bowls and pile the cabbage mixture in the centre of each portion. Garnish with sprigs of fresh thyme.

VARIATION
Savoy cabbage is used for the topping in this dish, but other greens, such as kale or spring greens, would also be suitable.

Energy 462Kcal/1919kJ; Protein 12.3g; Carbohydrate 24.3g, of which sugars 7.3g; Fat 35.7g, of which saturates 20.4g; Cholesterol 97mg; Calcium 144mg; Fibre 4.3g; Sodium 954mg.

IRISH BACON BROTH

A HEARTY MEAL IN A SOUP BOWL. THE BACON HOCK CONTRIBUTES FLAVOUR AND SOME MEAT TO THIS DISH, BUT IT MAY BE SALTY SO REMEMBER TO TASTE AND ADD EXTRA SALT ONLY IF REQUIRED.

SERVES 6–8

INGREDIENTS

1 bacon hock, about 900g/2lb
75g/3oz/⅓ cup pearl barley
75g/3oz/⅓ cup lentils
2 leeks, sliced, or onions, diced
4 carrots, diced
200g/7oz swede (rutabaga), diced
3 potatoes, diced
small bunch of herbs (thyme, parsley,
    bay leaf)
1 small cabbage, trimmed and
    quartered or sliced
salt and ground black pepper
chopped fresh parsley, to garnish
brown bread, to serve

COOK'S TIP
Traditionally, the cabbage is simply trimmed and quartered, although it may be sliced if you prefer.

1 Soak the bacon in cold water overnight. Next morning, drain, put into a large pan and cover with cold water. Bring to the boil and skim off any scum. Add the barley and lentils. Bring back to the boil and simmer for 15 minutes.

2 Add the vegetables, some black pepper and the herbs. Bring back to the boil, reduce the heat and simmer gently for 1½ hours, or until the meat is tender.

3 Lift the bacon hock from the pan with a slotted spoon. Remove the skin, then take the meat off the bones and break it into bitesize pieces. Return to the pan with the cabbage. Discard the herbs and cook for a little longer until the cabbage is cooked to your liking.

4 Adjust the seasoning and ladle into serving bowls, garnish with parsley and serve with freshly baked brown bread.

Energy 276Kcal/1166kJ; Protein 26.6g; Carbohydrate 33.6g, of which sugars 8.4g; Fat 4.8g, of which saturates 1.6g; Cholesterol 13mg; Calcium 87mg; Fibre 4.8g; Sodium 765mg.

IRISH KIDNEY AND BACON SOUP

ALTHOUGH THERE IS A MODERN TWIST IN THE SEASONINGS, THE TWO MAIN INGREDIENTS OF THIS MEATY SOUP ARE STILL VERY TRADITIONALLY IRISH.

SERVES 4–6

INGREDIENTS

225g/8oz ox (beef) kidney
15ml/1 tbsp vegetable oil
4 streaky (fatty) bacon rashers
  (strips), chopped
1 large onion, chopped
2 garlic cloves, finely chopped
15ml/1 tbsp plain (all-purpose) flour
1.5 litres/2½ pints/6¼ cups water
a good dash of Worcestershire sauce
a good dash of soy sauce
15ml/1 tbsp chopped fresh thyme,
  or 5ml/1 tsp dried
75g/3oz/¾ cup grated cheese
4–6 slices French bread, toasted
salt and ground black pepper

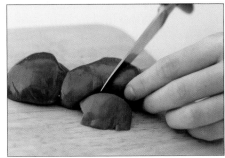

1 Wash the kidney in cold, salted water. Drain, dry well on kitchen paper and chop into small pieces.

COOK'S TIP
Ox kidneys are tougher than veal or lamb, so they need to be cooked more slowly.

2 Heat the vegetable oil in a large pan over a medium heat. Add the chopped streaky bacon and sauté for a few minutes. Add the prepared kidney and continue cooking until nicely browned. Stir in the chopped onion and chopped garlic, and cook until the onion is just soft but not browned.

3 Add the flour and cook for 2 minutes. Gradually add the water, stirring constantly. Add the sauces, thyme and seasoning to taste. Reduce the heat and simmer gently for 30–35 minutes.

4 Sprinkle the cheese on to the toast and grill until it is bubbling. Pour the soup into bowls, and top with the bread.

Energy 379Kcal/1592kJ; Protein 23.7g; Carbohydrate 34g, of which sugars 3.2g; Fat 17g, of which saturates 7.1g; Cholesterol 184mg; Calcium 225mg; Fibre 1.6g; Sodium 1167mg.

RUSSIAN PEA AND BARLEY SOUP

THIS THICK AND WARMING SOUP, GROCHOWKA, MAKES A SUBSTANTIAL APPETIZER, OR IT MAY BE SERVED AS A MEAL IN ITS OWN RIGHT, EATEN WITH HOT CRUSTY BREAD.

3 Dry fry the bacon cubes in a frying pan for 5 minutes, or until well browned and crispy. Remove from the pan with a slotted spoon, leaving the fat behind, and set aside.

4 Add the butter to the frying pan, add the onion and garlic and cook gently for 5 minutes. Add the celeriac and cook for a further 5 minutes, or until the onion is just starting to colour.

SERVES 6

INGREDIENTS
    225g/8oz/1¼ cups yellow split peas, rinsed in cold water
    25g/1oz/¼ cup pearl barley, rinsed in cold water
    1.75 litres/3 pints/7½ cups vegetable or ham stock
    50g/2oz smoked streaky (fatty) bacon, cubed
    25g/1oz/2 tbsp butter
    1 onion, finely chopped
    2 garlic cloves, crushed
    225g/8oz celeriac, cubed
    15ml/1 tbsp roughly chopped fresh marjoram
    salt and freshly ground black pepper
    bread, to serve

1 Put the peas and barley in a bowl, cover with plenty of water and leave to soak overnight.

2 The next day, drain and rinse the peas and barley. Put them in a large pan, pour in the stock and bring to the boil. Turn down the heat and simmer gently for 40 minutes.

5 Add the softened vegetables and bacon to the pan of stock, peas and barley. Season lightly with salt and pepper, then cover and simmer for 20 minutes, or until the soup is thick. Stir in the marjoram, add extra black pepper to taste and serve with bread.

Energy 189Kcal/799kJ; Protein 11g; Carbohydrate 25.8g, of which sugars 1.8g; Fat 5.5g, of which saturates 2.8g; Cholesterol 13mg; Calcium 39mg; Fibre 2.4g; Sodium 190mg.

BACON AND CHICKPEA SOUP WITH TORTILLA CHIPS

THIS SILKY-SMOOTH NUTTY SOUP IS ABSOLUTELY DELICIOUS AND SO EASY TO MAKE. TAKE IT TO THE SOFA WITH A BOWL OF WARM AND SPICY TORTILLA CHIPS AND DIP, CRUNCH AND SLURP YOUR WAY THROUGH YOUR FAVOURITE TELEVISION FIX.

SERVES 4–6

INGREDIENTS
    400g/14oz/2 cups dried chickpeas,
        soaked overnight in cold water
    115g/4oz/½ cup butter
    150g/5oz pancetta or streaky (fatty)
        bacon, roughly chopped
    2 onions, finely chopped
    1 carrot, chopped
    1 celery stick, chopped
    15ml/1 tbsp chopped fresh rosemary
    2 fresh bay leaves
    2 garlic cloves, halved
For the tortilla chips
    75g/3oz/6 tbsp butter
    2.5ml/½ tsp sweet paprika
    1.5ml/¼ tsp ground cumin
    175g/6oz plain tortilla chips
    salt and ground black pepper

1 Drain the chickpeas, put them in a large pan and cover with plenty of cold water. Bring to the boil and simmer for about 20 minutes. Strain and set aside.

2 Melt the butter in a large pan and add the pancetta or bacon. Fry over a medium heat until just beginning to turn golden. Add the chopped vegetables and cook for 5–10 minutes until soft.

COOK'S TIP
Packets of diced bacon are available in most supermarkets, and these are ideal for adding to soups.

3 Add the chickpeas to the pan with the rosemary, bay leaves, garlic cloves and enough water to cover completely. Bring to the boil, half cover, turn down the heat and simmer for 45–60 minutes, stirring occasionally. (The chickpeas should start to disintegrate and will thicken the soup.)

4 Allow the soup to cool slightly, then pour it into a blender or food processor and process until smooth. Return the soup to the rinsed-out pan, taste and season with salt and plenty of black pepper. Reheat gently.

5 To make the tortilla chips, preheat the oven to 180°C/350°F/Gas 4. Melt the butter with the paprika and cumin in a pan, then lightly brush the mixture over the tortilla chips. Reserve any leftover spiced butter.

6 Spread the chips out on a baking sheet and warm through in the oven for 5 minutes.

7 Ladle the soup into bowls, pour some of the reserved spiced butter over each and sprinkle with a little paprika. Serve with the warm tortilla chips.

Energy 996Kcal/4154kJ; Protein 31.4g; Carbohydrate 80.1g, of which sugars 6.6g; Fat 63.3g, of which saturates 30.1g; Cholesterol 126mg; Calcium 252mg; Fibre 14.3g; Sodium 1186mg.

MISO SOUP WITH PORK AND VEGETABLES

THIS IS QUITE A RICH AND FILLING SOUP. ITS JAPANESE NAME, TANUKI JIRU, MEANS RACCOON SOUP FOR HUNTERS, BUT AS RACCOONS ARE NOT EATEN NOWADAYS, PORK IS USED INSTEAD.

SERVES 4

INGREDIENTS
    200g/7oz lean boneless pork
    15cm/6in piece gobo or 1 parsnip
    50g/2oz mooli (daikon)
    4 fresh shiitake mushrooms
    ½ konnyaku or 125g/4½oz tofu
    a little sesame oil, for stir-frying
    600ml/1 pint/2½ cups second dashi
        stock, or the same amount of water
        and 10ml/2 tsp dashi-no-moto
    70ml/4½ tbsp miso
    2 spring onions (scallions), chopped
    5ml/1 tsp sesame seeds

1 Press the meat down on a chopping board using the palm of your hand and slice horizontally into very thin long strips, then cut the strips crossways into stamp-size pieces. Set the pork aside.

2 Peel the gobo using a potato peeler, then cut diagonally into 1cm/½in thick slices. Quickly plunge the slices into a bowl of cold water to stop them discolouring. If you are using parsnip, peel, cut it in half lengthways, then cut it into 1cm/½in thick half-moon-shaped slices.

3 Peel and slice the mooli into 1.5cm/⅔in thick discs. Cut the discs into 1.5cm/⅔in cubes. Remove the shiitake stalks and cut the caps into quarters.

4 Place the konnyaku, if using, in a pan of boiling water and cook for 1 minute. Drain and cool. Cut in quarters lengthways, then crossways into 3mm/⅛in thick pieces.

5 Heat a little sesame oil in a heavy cast-iron or enamelled pan until purple smoke rises. Stir-fry the pork, then add the konnyaku or tofu and all the vegetables except for the spring onions. When the colour of the meat has changed, add the stock.

6 Bring to the boil over a medium heat, and skim off the foam until the soup looks fairly clear. Reduce the heat, cover and simmer for 15 minutes.

7 Put the miso in a small bowl and mix with 60ml/4 tbsp hot stock to make a smooth paste. Stir one-third of the miso into the soup; taste and add more if required. Add the spring onion and remove from the heat. Serve very hot in individual soup bowls, sprinkled with sesame seeds.

COOK'S TIPS
• Gobo is burdock root, and can be substituted with parsnip in this recipe.
• Mooli, also known as daikon, is a long, white vegetable which is a member of the radish family.
• Konnyaku is a gelatinous cake made from a relative of the sweet potato.

Energy 110Kcal/459kJ; Protein 16g; Carbohydrate 1.3g, of which sugars 0.9g; Fat 4.5g, of which saturates 1g; Cholesterol 32mg; Calcium 295mg; Fibre 0.4g; Sodium 573mg.

SWEET AND SOUR PORK SOUP

THIS VERY QUICK, SHARP AND TANGY SOUP IS PERFECT FOR AN INFORMAL SUPPER. IT CAN ALSO BE MADE WITH SHREDDED CHICKEN BREAST INSTEAD OF PORK.

SERVES 6–8

INGREDIENTS
900g/2lb pork fillet, trimmed
1 unripe papaya, halved, seeded,
  peeled and shredded
3 shallots, chopped
5 garlic cloves, chopped
5ml/1 tsp crushed black peppercorns
15ml/1 tbsp shrimp paste
30ml/2 tbsp vegetable oil
1.5 litres/2½ pints/6¼ cups
  chicken stock
2.5cm/1in piece fresh root
  ginger, grated
120ml/4fl oz/½ cup tamarind water
15ml/1 tbsp honey
juice of 1 lime
2 small red chillies, seeded
  and sliced
4 spring onions (scallions), sliced
salt and ground black pepper

1 Cut the pork into very fine strips, 5cm/2in long. Mix with the papaya and set aside. Process the shallots, garlic, peppercorns and shrimp paste in a food processor or blender to form a paste.

2 Heat the oil in a heavy-based pan and fry the paste for 1–2 minutes. Add the stock and bring to the boil. Reduce the heat. Add the pork and papaya, ginger and tamarind water.

3 Simmer the soup for 7–8 minutes, until the pork is tender.

4 Stir in the honey, lime juice, and most of the sliced chillies and spring onions. Season to taste with salt and ground black pepper.

5 Ladle the soup into bowls and serve immediately, garnished with the remaining chillies and onions.

Energy 229Kcal/963kJ; Protein 32.8g; Carbohydrate 11.1g, of which sugars 10.9g; Fat 6.2g, of which saturates 2.1g; Cholesterol 95mg; Calcium 37mg; Fibre 2.3g; Sodium 111mg.

PORK AND RICE PORRIDGE

Energy 375Kcal/1574kJ; Protein 26.8g; Carbohydrate 31.1g, of which sugars 0.2g; Fat 16.8g, of which saturates 4g; Cholesterol 71mg; Calcium 32mg; Fibre 0.3g; Sodium 89mg.

ORIGINATING IN CHINA, THIS DISH HAS NOW SPREAD THROUGHOUT THE WHOLE OF SOUTH-EAST ASIA AND IS LOVED FOR ITS COMFORTING BLANDNESS. IT IS INVARIABLY SERVED WITH A FEW STRONGLY FLAVOURED ACCOMPANIMENTS.

2 Pour the stock into a large pan. Bring to the boil and add the rice. Season the minced pork. Add it by taking small teaspoons and tapping the spoon on the side of the pan so that the meat falls into the soup in small lumps.

3 Stir in the fish sauce and pickled garlic and simmer for 10 minutes, until the pork is cooked. Stir in the celery.

4 Serve the rice porridge in individual warmed bowls. Sprinkle the prepared garlic and shallots on top and season with plenty of ground pepper.

COOK'S TIP
Pickled garlic has a distinctive flavour and is available from Asian food stores.

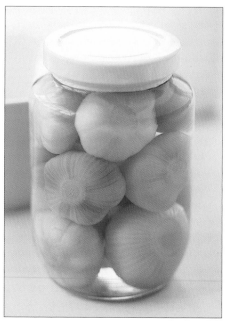

SERVES 2

INGREDIENTS
 900ml/1½ pints/3¾ cups
  vegetable stock
 200g/7oz/1¾ cups cooked rice
 225g/8oz minced (ground) pork
 15ml/1 tbsp Thai fish sauce
 2 heads pickled garlic,
  finely chopped
 1 celery stick, finely diced
 salt and ground black pepper
To garnish
 30ml/2 tbsp groundnut (peanut) oil
 4 garlic cloves, thinly sliced
 4 small red shallots, finely sliced

1 Make the garnishes by heating the groundnut oil in a frying pan and cooking the garlic and shallots over a low heat until brown. Drain on kitchen paper and reserve.

GOLDEN CHORIZO AND CHICKPEA SOUP

THIS HEARTY SPANISH SOUP IS SUBSTANTIAL ENOUGH TO MAKE A COMPLETE MEAL. SMALL UNCOOKED CHORIZO SAUSAGES ARE AVAILABLE FROM SPANISH DELICATESSENS, BUT READY-TO-EAT CHORIZO CAN BE CUT INTO CHUNKS AND USED INSTEAD.

SERVES 4

INGREDIENTS
115g/4oz/⅔ cup dried chickpeas
pinch of saffron strands
45ml/3 tbsp olive oil
450g/1lb uncooked mini chorizo
  sausages
5ml/1 tsp dried chilli flakes
6 garlic cloves, finely chopped
450g/1lb tomatoes, roughly chopped
350g/12oz new potatoes, quartered
2 bay leaves
450ml/¾ pint/scant 2 cups water
60ml/4 tbsp chopped fresh parsley
salt and ground black pepper
30ml/2 tbsp extra virgin olive oil,
  to garnish
crusty bread, to serve

1 Put the chickpeas in a large bowl, cover with plenty of cold water and leave to soak overnight.

2 Next day, drain and place in a large pan. Cover with plenty of fresh water and bring to the boil, skimming off any scum as it forms. Cover and simmer for 2–3 hours, until tender. Add more boiling water, if necessary, to keep the chickpeas well covered during cooking. Drain, reserving the cooking liquid.

3 Heat the oil in a large, deep frying pan. Add the chorizo sausages and fry over a medium heat for 5 minutes, until a lot of oil has seeped out of the sausages and they are pale golden brown. Drain and set aside.

4 Soak the saffron strands in a little warm water.

5 Add the chilli flakes and garlic to the fat in the frying pan and cook for a few seconds. Stir in the saffron with its soaking water, the chopped tomatoes, chickpeas, potatoes, chorizo sausages and bay leaves. Pour in 450ml/¾ pint/ scant 2 cups of the chickpea cooking liquor and the water, and stir in salt and pepper to taste.

6 Bring to the boil, then reduce the heat and simmer for 45–50 minutes, stirring gently occasionally, until the potatoes are tender and the soup has thickened slightly.

7 Add the chopped parsley to the soup and adjust the seasoning. Ladle the soup into four large, warmed soup plates and drizzle a little extra virgin olive oil over each portion. Serve with crusty bread.

Energy 642Kcal/2674kJ; Protein 21.7g; Carbohydrate 42.3g, of which sugars 8.1g; Fat 44g, of which saturates 12.5g; Cholesterol 68mg; Calcium 174mg; Fibre 6.1g; Sodium 997mg.

KALE, CHORIZO AND POTATO SOUP

This hearty winter soup has a spicy kick to it, which comes from the chorizo sausage. The soup becomes more potent if chilled overnight. It is worth buying the best possible chorizo sausage to improve the flavour.

SERVES 6–8

INGREDIENTS

225g/8oz kale, stems removed
225g/8oz chorizo sausage
675g/1½lb red potatoes
1.75 litres/3 pints/7½ cups
  vegetable stock
5ml/1 tsp ground black pepper
pinch cayenne pepper (optional)
12 slices French bread, grilled
salt and ground black pepper

1 Place the kale in a food processor and process for a few seconds to chop it finely.

2 Prick the sausages and place in a pan with enough water to cover. Simmer for 15 minutes. Drain and cut into thin slices.

3 Cook the potatoes in lightly salted boiling water for about 15 minutes or until tender. Drain and place in a bowl, then mash, adding a little of the cooking liquid to form a thick paste.

COOK'S TIP
Chorizo sausage is usually sold whole or cut into lengths or rounds.

4 Bring the vegetable stock to the boil and add the kale. Add the chorizo and simmer for 5 minutes. Add the paste gradually, and simmer for 20 minutes. Season with black pepper and cayenne.

5 Place bread slices in each bowl, and pour over the soup. Serve, generously sprinkled with pepper.

Energy 411Kcal/1740kJ; Protein 13.2g; Carbohydrate 69.3g, of which sugars 6.2g; Fat 11g, of which saturates 4.1g; Cholesterol 15mg; Calcium 140mg; Fibre 4g; Sodium 812mg.

MEDITERRANEAN SAUSAGE AND PESTO SOUP

*THIS DELICIOUS SOUP MAKES A SATISFYING ONE-POT MEAL THAT BRINGS THE SUMMERY FLAVOUR OF
BASIL TO MIDWINTER MEALS. THE LENTILS ENHANCE THE FLAVOUR OF THE SMOKED SAUSAGE. THICK
SLICES OF WARM CRUSTY BREAD MAKE THE PERFECT ACCOMPANIMENT.*

SERVES 4

INGREDIENTS
  15ml/1 tbsp olive oil, plus extra
    for frying
  1 red onion, chopped
  450g/1lb smoked pork sausages
  225g/8oz/1 cup red lentils
  400g/14oz can chopped tomatoes
  1 litre/1¾ pints/4 cups water
  oil, for deep-frying
  salt and ground black pepper
  60ml/4 tbsp pesto and fresh basil
    sprigs, to garnish

1 Heat the oil in a large pan and cook
the onion until softened. Coarsely chop
all but one of the sausages and add
them to the pan. Cook for 5 minutes,
stirring, or until the sausages are cooked.

2 Stir in the lentils, tomatoes and water,
and bring to the boil. Reduce the heat,
cover and simmer for about 20 minutes.
Cool the soup slightly before puréeing
it in a blender. Return the soup to the
rinsed pan.

3 Cook the remaining sausage in a little
oil in a small frying pan, turning it often,
for 10 minutes, or until lightly browned
and firm. Transfer to a chopping board
or plate and leave to cool slightly, then
slice thinly.

4 Heat the oil for deep-frying to
190ºC/375ºF or until a cube of day-old
bread browns in about 60 seconds.
Deep-fry the sausage slices and basil
briefly until the sausages are brown
and the basil leaves are crisp.

5 Lift them out using a slotted spoon
and drain on kitchen paper.

6 Reheat the soup, add seasoning to
taste, then ladle into warmed individual
soup bowls. Sprinkle with the deep-fried
sausage slices and basil and swirl a
little pesto through each portion. Serve
with warm crusty bread.

Energy 656Kcal/2741kJ; Protein 30.9g; Carbohydrate 46.7g, of which sugars 8.2g; Fat 39.7g, of which saturates 13.1g; Cholesterol 75mg; Calcium 250mg; Fibre 4.8g; Sodium 1109mg.

SOUP OF TOULOUSE SAUSAGE WITH BORLOTTI BEANS AND BREADCRUMBS

A BIG-FILLER SOUP, THIS RECIPE IS BASED LOOSELY ON CASSOULET. FRENCH SAUSAGES AND ITALIAN BEANS CONTRIBUTE FLAVOUR AND SUBSTANCE, AND THE SOUP IS TOPPED WITH GOLDEN BREADCRUMBS.

SERVES 6

INGREDIENTS

  250g/9oz/generous 1¼ cups
    borlotti beans
  115g/4oz piece pancetta,
    finely chopped
  6 Toulouse sausages, thickly sliced
  1 large onion, finely chopped
  2 garlic cloves, chopped
  2 carrots, finely diced
  2 leeks, finely chopped
  6 tomatoes, peeled, seeded
    and chopped
  30ml/2 tbsp tomato purée (paste)
  1.27 litres/2¼ pints/5⅔ cups
    vegetable stock
  175g/6oz spring greens, roughly
    shredded
  25g/1oz/2 tbsp butter
  115g/4oz/2 cups fresh white
    breadcrumbs
  50g/2oz/⅔ cup freshly grated
    Parmesan cheese
  salt and ground black pepper

1 Put the borlotti beans in a large bowl, cover with plenty of cold water and leave to soak overnight.

2 Next day, place the beans in a pan, cover with plenty of cold water and bring to the boil, then boil for 10 minutes. Drain well.

3 Heat a large pan and dry fry the pancetta until browned and the fat runs. Add the sausages and cook for 4–5 minutes, stirring occasionally, until beginning to brown.

4 Add the onion and garlic and cook for 3–4 minutes until softened. Add the beans, carrots, leeks, tomatoes and tomato purée, then add the stock. Stir, bring to the boil and cover. Simmer for about 1¼ hours or until the beans are tender, then stir in the spring greens and cook for 12–15 minutes more. Season well.

5 Meanwhile, melt the butter in a frying pan and fry the breadcrumbs, stirring, for 4–5 minutes, until golden, then stir in the Parmesan.

6 Ladle the soup into six warmed bowls. Sprinkle the fried breadcrumb mixture over each portion. Serve with some warm crusty bread.

VARIATION
Toulouse sausage, which is flavoured with garlic, can be substituted with Polish kielbasa or Italian sweet sausage.

Energy 574Kcal/2405kJ; Protein 29g; Carbohydrate 47.7g, of which sugars 10.2g; Fat 31g, of which saturates 12.5g; Cholesterol 75mg; Calcium 284mg; Fibre 10.7g; Sodium 1179mg.

BEEF AND BARLEY SOUP

THIS TRADITIONAL IRISH FARMHOUSE SOUP MAKES A WONDERFULLY RESTORATIVE DISH ON A COLD DAY. THE FLAVOURS DEVELOP PARTICULARLY WELL IF IT IS MADE IN ADVANCE AND REHEATED.

SERVES 6–8

INGREDIENTS

450–675g/1–1½lb rib steak, or
  other stewing beef on the bone
2 large onions
50g/2oz/¼ cup pearl barley
50g/2oz/¼ cup green split peas
3 large carrots, chopped
2 white turnips, peeled and chopped
  into dice
3 celery stalks, chopped
1 large or 2 medium leeks, thinly
  sliced and thoroughly washed in
  cold water
sea salt and ground black pepper
chopped fresh parsley, to serve

1 Bone the meat and put the bones and half an onion, roughly sliced, into a large pan. Cover with cold water, season and bring to the boil. Skim if necessary, then simmer until needed.

2 Meanwhile, trim any fat or gristle from the meat and cut into small pieces. Chop the remaining onions finely. Drain the stock from the bones, make it up with water to 2 litres/3½ pints/9 cups, and return to the rinsed pan with the meat, onions, barley and split peas.

3 Season, bring to the boil, and skim if necessary. Reduce the heat, cover and simmer for about 30 minutes.

4 Add the rest of the vegetables and simmer for 1 hour, or until the meat is tender. Check the seasoning.

5 Serve in large warmed bowls, generously sprinkled with parsley.

Energy 167Kcal/705kJ; Protein 16g; Carbohydrate 21.4g, of which sugars 7.8g; Fat 2.6g, of which saturates 0.8g; Cholesterol 34mg; Calcium 54mg; Fibre 3.6g; Sodium 58mg.

MEXICAN BEEF CHILLI <u>WITH</u> MONTEREY JACK NACHOS

STEAMING BOWLS OF BEEF CHILLI SOUP, PACKED WITH BEANS, ARE DELICIOUS TOPPED WITH CRUSHED TORTILLAS AND CHEESE. POP THE BOWLS UNDER THE GRILL TO MELT THE CHEESE, IF YOU WISH.

SERVES 4

INGREDIENTS
   45ml/3 tbsp olive oil
   350g/12oz rump steak, cut into
      small pieces
   2 onions, chopped
   2 garlic cloves, crushed
   2 green chillies, seeded and
      finely chopped
   30ml/2 tbsp mild chilli powder
   5ml/1 tsp ground cumin
   2 bay leaves
   30ml/2 tbsp tomato purée (paste)
   900ml/1½ pints/3¾ cups beef stock
   2 x 400g/14oz cans mixed beans,
      drained and rinsed
   45ml/3 tbsp chopped fresh coriander
      (cilantro) leaves
   salt and ground black pepper
For the topping
   bag of plain tortilla chips,
      lightly crushed
   225g/8oz/2 cups Monterey Jack
      cheese, grated

1 Heat the oil in a large pan over a high heat and cook the meat all over until golden. Use a slotted spoon to remove it from the pan.

2 Reduce the heat and add the onions, garlic and chillies, then cook for 4–5 minutes, until softened.

VARIATION
Use Cheddar cheese instead of Monterey Jack if you prefer.

3 Add the chilli powder and ground cumin, and cook for a further 2 minutes. Return the meat to the pan, then stir in the bay leaves, tomato purée and beef stock. Bring to the boil.

4 Reduce the heat, cover the pan and simmer for about 45 minutes, or until the meat is tender.

5 Put a quarter of the beans into a bowl and mash with a potato masher. Stir these into the soup to thicken it slightly. Add the remaining beans and simmer for about 5 minutes. Season and stir in the chopped coriander. Ladle the soup into warmed bowls and spoon tortilla chips on top. Pile grated cheese over the tortilla chips and serve.

Energy 749Kcal/3135kJ; Protein 50g; Carbohydrate 54.1g, of which sugars 10.3g; Fat 37.2g, of which saturates 16.1g; Cholesterol 106mg; Calcium 609mg; Fibre 14.5g; Sodium 1473mg.

BRAISED CABBAGE SOUP WITH BEEF AND HORSERADISH CREAM

THIS BRILLIANT WINTER SOUP REALLY IS A COMPLETE MAIN COURSE IN A BOWL. THE JOINT OF BEEF CAN BE COOKED AS RARE OR AS WELL DONE AS YOU LIKE.

SERVES 6

INGREDIENTS

  900g/2lb red cabbage, hard core
    discarded and leaves shredded
  2 onions, finely sliced
  1 large cooking apple, peeled, cored
    and chopped
  45ml/3 tbsp soft light brown sugar
  2 garlic cloves, crushed
  1.5ml/¼ tsp grated nutmeg
  2.5ml/½ tsp caraway seeds
  45ml/3 tbsp red wine vinegar
  1 litre/1¾ pints/4 cups beef stock
  675kg/1½lb sirloin joint
  30ml/2 tbsp olive oil
  salt and ground black pepper
  watercress, to garnish
For the horseradish cream
  15–30ml/1–2 tbsp fresh horseradish
  10ml/2 tsp wine vinegar
  2.5ml/½ tsp Dijon mustard
  150ml/¼ pint/⅔ cup double
    (heavy) cream

1 Preheat the oven to 150°C/300°F/ Gas 2. Mix together the first eight ingredients and 45ml/3 tbsp of the stock. Add plenty of seasoning, then put into a large buttered casserole and cover with a tight-fitting lid.

2 Bake for 2½ hours, checking every 30 minutes or so to ensure that the cabbage is not becoming too dry. If necessary, add a few more tablespoons of the stock. Remove the casserole from the oven and set aside. Increase the oven temperature to 230°C/450°F/ Gas 8.

3 Trim off most of the fat from the sirloin, leaving a thin layer. Tie the joint with string. Heat the oil in a heavy frying pan until smoking. Add the beef and cook until well browned all over.

4 Transfer to a roasting tin and roast for about 15–20 minutes for medium-rare or 25–30 minutes for well-done beef.

5 For the horseradish cream, grate the horseradish and mix with the wine vinegar, mustard and seasoning into 45ml/3 tbsp of the cream. Lightly whip the remaining cream and fold in the horseradish mixture. Chill until required.

6 Spoon the braised cabbage into a saucepan and pour in the remaining stock. Bring just to boiling point.

7 Remove the beef from the oven and leave to rest for 5 minutes, then remove the string and carve into slices.

8 Ladle the soup into bowls and divide the beef among them, resting on the cabbage. Spoon a little horseradish cream on to each serving of beef, and garnish with small bunches of watercress. Serve at once.

Energy 395Kcal/1645kJ; Protein 29.4g; Carbohydrate 19.4g, of which sugars 18.5g; Fat 22.5g, of which saturates 11.1g; Cholesterol 92mg; Calcium 104mg; Fibre 3.8g; Sodium 97mg.

IRISH COUNTRY SOUP

*TRADITIONALLY, BUTTERED CHUNKS OF BROWN BREAD, OR IRISH SODA BREAD, WOULD BE SERVED WITH
THIS HEARTY ONE-POT MEAL WHICH IS BASED ON THE CLASSIC IRISH STEW.*

SERVES 4

INGREDIENTS
    15ml/1 tbsp vegetable oil
    675g/1½lb boneless lamb chump
      chops, trimmed and cut into
      small cubes
    2 small onions, quartered
    2 leeks, thickly sliced
    1 litre/1¾ pints/4 cups water
    2 large potatoes, cut into chunks
    2 carrots, thickly sliced
    sprig of fresh thyme, plus extra
      to garnish
    15g/½oz/1 tbsp butter
    30ml/2 tbsp chopped fresh parsley
    salt and ground black pepper
    brown or Irish soda bread, to serve

VARIATION
The vegetables can be varied according
to the season. Swede (rutabaga), turnip,
celeriac and even cabbage could be
added in place of some of those listed.

1 Heat the oil in a large pan, add
the lamb in batches and fry, turning
occasionally, until well browned all over.
Use a slotted spoon to remove the lamb
from the pan and set aside.

2 When all the lamb has been browned,
add the onions to the pan and cook
for 4–5 minutes, until the onions are
browned. Return the meat to the pan
and add the leeks. Pour in the water,
then bring to the boil. Reduce the heat,
then cover and simmer for about 1 hour.

3 Add the potatoes, carrots and fresh
thyme, and cook for 40 minutes, until
the lamb is tender. Remove from the
heat and leave to stand for 5 minutes,
then skim off the fat.

4 Pour off the stock into a clean pan
and whisk the butter into it. Stir in the
parsley and season well, then pour the
liquid back over the soup ingredients.

5 Ladle the soup into warmed bowls
and garnish with sprigs of fresh thyme.

Energy 453Kcal/1893kJ; Protein 36.5g; Carbohydrate 20.5g, of which sugars 6.2g; Fat 25.6g, of which saturates 11.3g; Cholesterol 136mg; Calcium 53mg; Fibre 3.7g; Sodium 185mg.

ROAST LAMB SHANKS IN BARLEY BROTH

SUCCULENT ROASTED LAMB SHANKS STUDDED WITH GARLIC AND ROSEMARY MAKE A FABULOUS MEAL WHEN SERVED IN A HEARTY VEGETABLE, BARLEY AND TOMATO BROTH.

SERVES 4

INGREDIENTS

    4 small lamb shanks
    4 garlic cloves, cut into slivers
    handful of fresh rosemary sprigs
    30ml/2 tbsp olive oil
    2 carrots, diced
    2 celery sticks, diced
    1 large onion, chopped
    1 bay leaf
    few sprigs of fresh thyme
    1.2 litres/2 pints/5 cups
      lamb stock
    50g/2oz pearl barley
    450g/1lb tomatoes, peeled and
      roughly chopped
    grated rind of 1 large lemon
    30ml/2 tbsp chopped fresh parsley
    salt and ground black pepper

1 Preheat the oven to 150°C/300°F/ Gas 2. Make small cuts all over the lamb and insert slivers of garlic and sprigs of rosemary into them.

2 Heat the oil in a flameproof casserole and brown the shanks two at a time. Remove and set aside. Add the carrots, celery and onion in batches and cook until lightly browned. Put all the vegetables in the casserole with the bay leaf and thyme. Pour in stock to cover, place the lamb shanks on top and roast for 2 hours.

3 Meanwhile, pour the remaining stock into a large saucepan. Add the pearl barley, then bring to the boil. Reduce the heat, cover and simmer for 1 hour, or until the barley is tender.

4 Remove the lamb shanks from the casserole using a slotted spoon.

5 Skim the fat from the surface of the roasted vegetables, then add them to the broth. Stir in the tomatoes, lemon rind and parsley.

6 Bring the soup back to the boil. Reduce the heat and simmer for 5 minutes. Add the lamb shanks and heat through, then season. Put a lamb shank into each of four large bowls, then ladle the barley broth over the meat and serve at once.

Energy 287Kcal/1199kJ; Protein 22.5g; Carbohydrate 19.5g, of which sugars 7.6g; Fat 13.7g, of which saturates 0.9g; Cholesterol 0mg; Calcium 35mg; Fibre 2.3g; Sodium 24mg.

LAMB AND VEGETABLE BROTH

*THIS IS A GOOD MODERN ADAPTATION OF THE TRADITIONAL RECIPE FOR IRISH MUTTON BROTH,
KNOWN LOCALLY AS BRACHÁN CAOIREOLA, AND IS DELICIOUS SERVED WITH WHOLEMEAL BREAD
TO MAKE A FILLING LUNCH DISH ON A COLD WINTER'S DAY.*

SERVES 6

INGREDIENTS

   675g/1½lb best end of neck of lamb
     on the bone (cross rib)
   1 large onion
   2 bay leaves
   3 carrots, chopped
   ½ white turnip, diced
   ½ small white cabbage, shredded
   2 large leeks, thinly sliced
   15ml/1 tbsp tomato purée (paste)
   30ml/2 tbsp chopped fresh parsley
   salt and ground black pepper

COOK'S TIP

Best end of neck (cross rib) is the rib
joint between the middle neck and loin.
It is the best cut to use for this soup.

1 Trim any excess fat from the meat.
Chop the onion, and put the lamb
and bay leaves in a large pan. Add
1.5 litres/2½ pints/6¼ cups water and
bring to the boil. Skim the surface
and then simmer for about 1½–2 hours.
Remove the lamb on to a board and
leave to cool until ready to handle.

2 Remove the meat from the bones
and cut into small pieces. Discard the
bones and return the meat to the broth.
Add the vegetables, tomato purée and
parsley, and season well. Simmer for
another 30 minutes, until the vegetables
are just tender. Ladle into warmed soup
bowls and serve piping hot.

Energy 167Kcal/696kJ; Protein 14.6g; Carbohydrate 10.5g, of which sugars 9g; Fat 7.6g, of which saturates 3.4g; Cholesterol 48mg; Calcium 58mg; Fibre 3.7g; Sodium 81mg.

BEEF AND LAMB STEW

THIS TRADITIONAL JEWISH CHAMIM IS MADE WITH SAVOURY MEATS AND CHICKPEAS, BAKED IN A VERY LOW OVEN FOR SEVERAL HOURS. A PARCEL OF RICE IS OFTEN ADDED TO THE BROTH PART WAY THROUGH COOKING, WHICH PRODUCES A LIGHTLY PRESSED RICE WITH A SLIGHTLY CHEWY TEXTURE.

SERVES 8

INGREDIENTS

250g/9oz/1 cup chickpeas,
  soaked overnight
45ml/3 tbsp olive oil
1 onion, chopped
10 garlic cloves, chopped
1 parsnip, sliced
3 carrots, sliced
5–10ml/1–2 tsp ground cumin
2.5ml/½ tsp ground turmeric
15ml/1 tbsp chopped fresh root ginger
2 litres/3½ pints/8 cups beef stock
1 potato, peeled and cut into chunks
½ marrow (large zucchini), sliced or
  cut into chunks
400g/14oz fresh or canned
  tomatoes, diced
45–60ml/3–4 tbsp brown or
  green lentils
2 bay leaves
250g/9oz salted meat such as
  salt beef (or double the quantity
  of lamb)
250g/9oz piece of lamb
½ large bunch fresh coriander
  (cilantro), chopped
200g/7oz/1 cup long grain rice
1 lemon, cut into wedges, and a
  spicy sauce such as fresh chillies,
  finely chopped, to serve

1 Preheat the oven to 120°C/250°F/ Gas ½. Drain the chickpeas.

2 Heat the oil in a large flameproof casserole, add the onion, garlic, parsnip, carrots, cumin, turmeric and ginger and cook for 2–3 minutes. Add the chickpeas, stock, potato, marrow, tomatoes, lentils, bay leaves, salted meat, lamb and coriander. Cover and cook in the oven for about 3 hours.

COOK'S TIP
Add 1–2 pinches of bicarbonate of soda (baking soda) to the soaking chickpeas to make them tender, but do not add too much as it can make them mushy.

3 Put the rice on a double thickness of muslin (cheesecloth) and tie together at the corners, allowing enough room for the rice to expand while it is cooking.

4 Two hours before the end of cooking, remove the casserole from the oven. Place the rice parcel in the casserole, anchoring the edge of the muslin parcel under the lid so that the parcel is held above the soup and allowed to steam. Return the casserole to the oven and continue cooking for a further 2 hours.

5 Carefully remove the lid and the rice. Skim any fat off the top of the soup and ladle the soup into bowls with a scoop of the rice and one or two pieces of meat. Serve with lemon wedges and a spoonful of hot sauce or chopped fresh chillies.

Energy 385Kcal/1621kJ; Protein 25.6g; Carbohydrate 48.6g, of which sugars 5.3g; Fat 10.8g, of which saturates 2.7g; Cholesterol 24mg; Calcium 116mg; Fibre 5.4g; Sodium 54mg.

FRAGRANT BEETROOT AND VEGETABLE SOUP WITH SPICED LAMB KUBBEH

THE JEWISH COMMUNITY FROM COCHIN IN INDIA IS SCATTERED NOW BUT IS STILL FAMOUS FOR ITS CUISINE. THIS TANGY SOUP IS SERVED WITH DUMPLINGS MADE OF BRIGHT YELLOW PASTA WRAPPED AROUND A SPICY LAMB FILLING, AND A DOLLOP OF FRAGRANT GREEN HERB PASTE.

SERVES 6–8

INGREDIENTS
   15ml/1 tbsp vegetable oil
   ½ onion, finely chopped
   6 garlic cloves
   1 carrot, diced
   1 courgette (zucchini), diced
   ½ celery stick, diced (optional)
   4–5 cardamom pods
   2.5ml/½ tsp curry powder
   4 vacuum-packed beetroot (beets)
      (cooked not pickled), finely diced
      and juice reserved
   1 litre/1¾ pints/4 cups
      vegetable stock
   400g/14oz can chopped tomatoes
   45–60ml/3–4 tbsp chopped fresh
      coriander (cilantro) leaves
   2 bay leaves
   15ml/1 tbsp sugar
   salt and ground black pepper
   15–30ml/1–2 tbsp white wine
      vinegar, to serve
For the kubbeh
   2 large pinches of saffron threads
   15ml/1 tbsp hot water
   15ml/1 tbsp vegetable oil
   1 large onion, chopped
   250g/9oz lean minced (ground) lamb
   5ml/1 tsp vinegar
   ½ bunch fresh mint, chopped
   115g/4oz/1 cup plain (all-purpose) flour
   2–3 pinches of salt
   2.5–5ml/½–1 tsp ground turmeric
   45–60ml/3–4 tbsp cold water
For the ginger and coriander paste
   4 garlic cloves, chopped
   15–25ml/1–1½ tbsp chopped
      fresh root ginger
   ½–4 fresh mild chillies
   ½ large bunch fresh coriander
      (cilantro)
   30ml/2 tbsp white wine vinegar
   extra virgin olive oil

COOK'S TIP
Serve any leftover paste with meatballs
or spread on sandwiches.

1 For the paste, process the garlic, ginger and chillies in a food processor. Add the coriander, vinegar, oil and salt and process to a purée. Set aside.

2 To make the kubbeh filling, place the saffron and hot water in a small bowl and leave to infuse (steep). Meanwhile, heat the oil in a pan and fry the onion until softened. Put the onion and saffron water in a food processor and blend. Add the lamb, season and blend. Add the vinegar and mint, then chill.

3 To make the kubbeh dough, put the flour, salt and ground turmeric in a food processor, then gradually add the water, processing until it forms a sticky dough. Knead on a floured surface for 5 minutes, wrap in a plastic bag and leave to stand for 30 minutes.

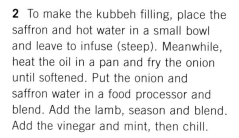

4 Divide the dough into 10–15 pieces. Roll each into a ball, then, using a pasta machine, roll into very thin rounds.

5 Lay the rounds on a well-floured surface. Place a spoonful of filling in the middle of each. Dampen the edges of the dough, then bring them together and seal. Set aside on a floured surface.

6 To make the soup, heat the oil in a pan, add the onion and fry for about 10 minutes, or until softened but not browned. Add half the garlic, the carrot, courgette, celery (if using), cardamom pods and curry powder, and cook for 2–3 minutes.

7 Add three of the diced beetroot, the stock, tomatoes, coriander, bay leaves and sugar to the pan. Bring to the boil, then reduce the heat and simmer for about 20 minutes.

8 Add the remaining beetroot, beetroot juice and garlic to the soup. Season with salt and pepper to taste and set aside until ready to serve.

9 To serve, reheat the soup and poach the dumplings in a large pan of salted boiling water for about 4 minutes. Using a slotted spoon, remove the dumplings from the water as they are cooked and place on a plate to keep warm.

10 Ladle the soup into bowls, adding a dash of vinegar to each bowl, then add two or three dumplings and a small spoonful of the ginger and coriander paste to each. Serve immediately.

Energy 210Kcal/881kJ; Protein 11.6g; Carbohydrate 22.1g, of which sugars 6.8g; Fat 9g, of which saturates 2.7g; Cholesterol 32mg; Calcium 55mg; Fibre 2.5g; Sodium 74mg.

INDIAN LAMB SOUP WITH RICE AND COCONUT

THIS MEATY SOUP THICKENED WITH LONG GRAIN RICE AND FLAVOURED WITH CUMIN AND CORIANDER SEEDS IS BASED ON THE CLASSIC INDIAN MULLIGATAWNY SOUP.

SERVES 6

INGREDIENTS

   2 onions, chopped
   6 garlic cloves, crushed
   5cm/2in piece fresh root
     ginger, grated
   90ml/6 tbsp olive oil
   30ml/2 tbsp black poppy seeds
   5ml/1 tsp cumin seeds
   5ml/1 tsp coriander seeds
   2.5ml/½ tsp ground turmeric
   450g/1lb boneless lamb chump
     chops, trimmed and cut into
     bite-size pieces
   1.5ml/¼ tsp cayenne pepper
   1.2 litres/2 pints/5 cups
     lamb stock
   50g/2oz/generous ⅓ cup long
     grain rice
   30ml/2 tbsp lemon juice
   60ml/4 tbsp coconut milk
   salt and ground black pepper
   fresh coriander (cilantro) sprigs and
     toasted flaked coconut, to garnish

1 Process the onions, garlic, ginger and 15ml/1 tbsp of the oil in a food processor or blender to form a paste. Set aside.

2 Heat a small, heavy-based frying pan. Add the poppy, cumin and coriander seeds and toast for a few seconds, shaking the pan, until they begin to release their aroma.

3 Transfer the toasted seeds to a mortar and grind them to a powder with a pestle. Stir in the ground turmeric. Set aside.

4 Heat the rest of the oil in a heavy-based pan. Fry the lamb in batches over a high heat for about 4–5 minutes until browned all over. Remove the lamb and set aside.

5 Add the onion, garlic and ginger paste to the pan and cook for 1–2 minutes, stirring continuously. Stir in the ground spices and cook for 1 minute. Return the meat to the pan with any meat juices that have seeped out while it has been standing. Add the cayenne, stock and seasoning.

6 Bring to the boil, cover and simmer for 30–35 minutes or until the lamb is tender.

7 Stir in the rice, then cover and cook for a further 15 minutes.

8 Add the lemon juice and coconut milk and simmer for a further 2 minutes.

9 Ladle the soup into six warmed bowls and garnish with sprigs of coriander and lightly toasted flaked coconut. Serve piping hot.

Energy 249Kcal/1036kJ; Protein 15.8g; Carbohydrate 7.5g, of which sugars 0.8g; Fat 17.3g, of which saturates 4.5g; Cholesterol 56mg; Calcium 14mg; Fibre 0.2g; Sodium 64mg.

MOROCCAN HARIRA

THIS IS A HEARTY MAIN-COURSE MEAT AND VEGETABLE SOUP, EATEN DURING THE MONTH OF RAMADAN, WHEN THE MUSLIM POPULATION FASTS BETWEEN SUNRISE AND SUNSET.

SERVES 4

INGREDIENTS
    450g/1lb well-flavoured tomatoes
    225g/8oz lamb, cut into pieces
    2.5ml/½ tsp ground turmeric
    2.5ml/½ tsp ground cinnamon
    25g/1oz/2 tbsp butter
    60ml/4 tbsp chopped fresh
      coriander (cilantro)
    30ml/2 tbsp chopped fresh
      parsley
    1 onion, chopped
    50g/2oz/¼ cup split red lentils
    75g/3oz/½ cup dried chickpeas,
      soaked overnight in cold water
    600ml/1 pint/2½ cups water
    4 baby (pearl) onions or shallots
    25g/1oz/¼ cup fine noodles
    salt and ground black pepper
    fresh coriander, lemon slices
      and ground cinnamon, to garnish

COOK'S TIPS
• Most of the vitamins in fruits and
vegetables are just under the skin. So,
if you wish to improve the nutritional
content, or simply save some time, the
skins of the tomatoes can be left on.
• For maximum cinnamon flavour,
grind a broken cinnamon stick in a
spice grinder or a coffee grinder kept
especially for spices.

1 Plunge the tomatoes into boiling
water for 30 seconds, then refresh in
cold water. Peel off the skins. Cut into
quarters and remove the seeds. Chop
the flesh roughly.

2 Put the pieces of lamb, ground
turmeric, cinnamon, butter, fresh
coriander, parsley and onion into a
large pan, and cook over a medium
heat, stirring, for 5 minutes.

3 Add the chopped tomatoes and
continue to cook for 10 minutes, stirring
the mixture frequently.

4 Rinse the lentils under running water
and drain them well. Stir them into the
contents of the pan, with the drained
chickpeas and the measured water.
Season with salt and pepper. Bring
to the boil, lower the heat, cover, and
simmer gently for 1½ hours.

5 Add the onions or shallots. Cook for
25 minutes. Add the noodles and cook
for 5 minutes more. Spoon into bowls
and garnish with the coriander, lemon
slices and cinnamon.

Energy 294Kcal/1234kJ; Protein 19.7g; Carbohydrate 25.2g, of which sugars 4.9g; Fat 13.5g, of which saturates 6.6g; Cholesterol 58mg; Calcium 55mg; Fibre 4g; Sodium 119mg.

FISH SOUPS

Fish soups are always delicious and can be eaten either as a first course or as an entire meal. Chunky soups such as Matelote, Bouillabaisse and Fish Soup with Tomatoes and Mushrooms are perfect for winter and so hearty that they can be eaten as a meal in themselves. Sophisticated soups such as Pad Thai Red Monkfish Soup, Bourride of Red Mullet and Fennel and Soup Niçoise with Seared Tuna are great for entertaining and sure to impress guests.

FISH SOUP <u>WITH</u> TOMATOES <u>AND</u> MUSHROOMS

Energy 132Kcal/556kJ; Protein 15.6g; Carbohydrate 8g, of which sugars 4.5g; Fat 4.4g, of which saturates 2.4g; Cholesterol 40mg; Calcium 29mg; Fibre 1.6g; Sodium 341mg.

WITH SOME FRESH CRUSTY HOME-MADE BROWN BREAD OR GARLIC BREAD, THIS QUICK-AND-EASY SOUP CAN BE SERVED LIKE A STEW AND WILL MAKE A DELICIOUS FIRST COURSE OR SUPPER.

SERVES 6

INGREDIENTS

25g/1oz/2 tbsp butter
1 onion, finely chopped
1 garlic clove, crushed
1 small red (bell) pepper, chopped
salt and ground black pepper
2.5ml/½ tsp sugar
a dash of Tabasco sauce
25g/1oz/¼ cup plain
   (all-purpose) flour
600ml/1 pint/2½ cups fish stock
400g/14oz can chopped tomatoes
115g/4oz/1½ cups mushrooms,
   chopped
about 300ml/½ pint/1¼ cups milk
225g/8oz white fish, cut into cubes
115g/4oz smoked haddock or cod,
   skinned, and cut into bitesize cubes
12–18 mussels, cleaned (optional)
chopped fresh parsley, to garnish

1 Melt the butter in a large heavy pan and cook the chopped onion and crushed garlic gently in it until softened but not browned.

2 Add the chopped red pepper. Season with salt and pepper, the sugar and Tabasco sauce.

3 Sprinkle the flour over and cook gently for 2 minutes, stirring.

4 Gradually stir in the stock and add the canned tomatoes, with their juices and the mushrooms.

5 Bring to the boil over medium heat, stir well, then reduce the heat and simmer gently until the vegetables are soft. Add the milk and bring back to the boil. Add the fish to the pan and simmer for 3 minutes.

6 Add the mussels, if using, and cook for another 3–4 minutes, or until the fish is just tender but not breaking up. Discard any mussels that remain closed. Adjust the consistency with a little extra fish stock or milk, if necessary. Check the seasoning.

7 Ladle the soup into six warmed bowls and serve piping hot, garnished with chopped parsley.

FISH SOUP WITH ROUILLE

MAKING THIS SOUP IS SIMPLICITY ITSELF, YET THE FLAVOUR SUGGESTS IT IS THE PRODUCT OF PAINSTAKING PREPARATION AND COOKING.

SERVES 6

INGREDIENTS

1kg/2¼lb mixed fish
30ml/2 tbsp olive oil
1 onion, chopped
1 carrot, chopped
1 leek, chopped
2 large ripe tomatoes, chopped
1 red (bell) pepper, seeded
    and chopped
2 garlic cloves, peeled
150g/5oz/⅔ cup tomato
    purée (paste)
1 large fresh bouquet garni
300ml/½ pint/1¼ cups dry
    white wine
salt and ground black pepper
For the rouille
2 garlic cloves, roughly chopped
5ml/1 tsp coarse salt
1 thick slice of white bread, crust
    removed, soaked in water and
    squeezed dry
1 fresh red chilli, seeded and
    roughly chopped
45ml/3 tbsp olive oil
salt and cayenne pepper
For the garnish
12 slices of baguette, toasted in
    the oven
50g/2oz Gruyère cheese,
    finely grated

1 Cut the fish into 7.5cm/3in chunks, removing any obvious bones. Heat the oil in a large pan, then add the fish and chopped vegetables. Stir until these begin to colour.

2 Add all the other soup ingredients, then pour in just enough cold water to cover the mixture. Season well and bring to just below boiling point, then lower the heat to a bare simmer, cover and cook for 1 hour.

3 Meanwhile, make the rouille. Put the garlic and coarse salt in a mortar and crush to a paste with a pestle. Add the soaked bread and chilli and pound until smooth, or purée in a food processor. Whisk in the olive oil, a drop at a time, to make a smooth, shiny sauce that resembles mayonnaise. Season with salt and add a pinch of cayenne if you like a fiery taste. Set the rouille aside.

4 Lift out and discard the bouquet garni from the soup. Purée the soup in batches in a food processor, then strain through a fine sieve (strainer) placed over a clean pan, pushing the solids through with the back of a ladle.

5 Reheat the soup without letting it boil. Check the seasoning and ladle into individual bowls. Top each serving with two slices of toasted baguette, a spoonful of rouille and some grated Gruyère.

COOK'S TIP
Any firm fish can be used for this recipe. If you use whole fish, include the heads, which enhance the flavour of the soup.

Energy 518Kcal/2179kJ; Protein 41.5g; Carbohydrate 49g, of which sugars 10.8g; Fat 14.9g, of which saturates 3.6g; Cholesterol 85mg; Calcium 193mg; Fibre 4.3g; Sodium 665mg.

SPANISH FISH SOUP
WITH ORANGE

THE SPANISH NAME FOR THIS SOUP IS SOPA CACHORREÑA *— SEVILLE ORANGE SOUP — AND IT IS GOOD SERVED POST-CHRISTMAS, WHEN BITTER SEVILLE ORANGES ARE IN SEASON.*

2 Heat the oil in a large flameproof casserole over a high heat. Smash the garlic cloves with the flat of a knife and fry until they are well-coloured. Discard them and turn down the heat. Fry the onion gently until it is softened, adding the tomato halfway through.

3 Strain in the hot fish stock (adding the orange spiral if you wish) and bring back to the boil. Add the potatoes to the pan and cook them for about 5 minutes.

4 Add the fish pieces to the soup, a few at a time, without letting it go off the boil. Cook for about 15 minutes. Add the squeezed orange juice and lemon juice, if using, and the paprika, with salt and pepper to taste. Serve in bowls, garnished with a little parsley.

SERVES 6

INGREDIENTS
   1kg/2¼lb small hake or whiting, whole but cleaned
   1.2 litres/2 pints/5 cups water
   4 bitter oranges or 4 sweet oranges and 2 lemons
   30ml/2 tbsp olive oil
   5 garlic cloves, unpeeled
   1 large onion, finely chopped
   1 tomato, peeled, seeded and chopped
   4 small potatoes, cut into rounds
   5ml/1 tsp paprika
   salt and ground black pepper
   15–30ml/1–2 tbsp finely chopped fresh parsley, to garnish

1 Fillet the fish and cut each fillet into three, reserving all the trimmings. Put the fillets on a plate, salt lightly and chill. Put the trimmings in a pan, add the water and a spiral of orange rind. Bring to a simmer, skim, then cover and cook gently for 30 minutes.

Energy 175Kcal/738kJ; Protein 20.2g; Carbohydrate 18.8g, of which sugars 8.7g; Fat 2.6g, of which saturates 0.4g; Cholesterol 23mg; Calcium 59mg; Fibre 2.3g; Sodium 113mg.

MEDITERRANEAN LEEK <u>AND</u> FISH SOUP
<u>WITH</u> TOMATOES

THIS CHUNKY SOUP, WHICH IS ALMOST A STEW, MAKES A ROBUST AND WONDERFULLY AROMATIC MEAL IN A BOWL. SERVE IT WITH CRISP-BAKED CROÛTES SPREAD WITH A TASTY GARLIC MAYONNAISE.

SERVES 4

INGREDIENTS

2 large thick leeks
30ml/2 tbsp olive oil
5ml/1 tsp crushed coriander seeds
a good pinch of dried red chilli flakes
300g/11oz small salad potatoes,
  peeled and thickly sliced
400g/14oz can chopped tomatoes
600ml/1 pint/2½ cups fish stock
150ml/¼ pint/⅔ cup white wine
1 fresh bay leaf
1 star anise
strip of pared orange rind
good pinch of saffron threads
450g/1lb white fish fillets, such as
  monkfish, sea bass, cod or haddock
450g/1lb small squid, cleaned
250g/9oz raw peeled prawns (shrimp)
30–45ml/2–3 tbsp chopped flat
  leaf parsley
salt and ground black pepper
To serve
1 short French loaf, sliced and toasted
garlic mayonnaise

3 Add the potatoes and tomatoes, and pour in the stock and wine. Add the bay leaf, star anise, orange rind and saffron. Bring to the boil, lower the heat and partially cover the pan. Simmer for 20 minutes or until the potatoes are tender. Taste and adjust the seasoning.

4 Cut the white fish fillets into chunks. Cut the squid sacs into rectangles and score a criss-cross pattern into them without cutting right through.

5 Add the fish to the soup and cook gently for 4 minutes. Add the prawns and cook for 1 minute. Add the squid and the sliced white part of the leek and cook, stirring occasionally, for a further 2 minutes.

6 Finally, stir in the chopped parsley and serve immediately, ladling the soup into warmed bowls. Offer the toasted French bread and garlic mayonnaise with the soup.

1 Slice the leeks, keeping the green tops separate from the white bottom pieces. Wash the leek slices thoroughly in a colander and drain them well. Set the white slices aside for later.

2 Heat the oil in a heavy pan over a low heat, then add the green leek slices, the crushed coriander seeds and the dried red chilli flakes. Cook, stirring occasionally, for 5 minutes.

Energy 340Kcal/1437kJ; Protein 51.8g; Carbohydrate 7.2g, of which sugars 5.3g; Fat 9.2g, of which saturates 1.6g; Cholesterol 416mg; Calcium 111mg; Fibre 2.9g; Sodium 330mg.

MATELOTE

This fishermen's chunky soup is traditionally made from freshwater fish, including eel. Any firm fish can be used, but try to include at least some eel, and use a robust dry white or red wine for extra flavour.

SERVES 6

INGREDIENTS

1kg/2¼ lb mixed fish, including
  450g/1lb conger eel if possible
50g/2oz/¼ cup butter
1 onion, thickly sliced
2 celery sticks, thickly sliced
2 carrots, thickly sliced
1 bottle dry white or red wine
1 fresh bouquet garni containing
  parsley, bay leaf and chervil
2 cloves
6 black peppercorns
beurre manié for thickening, see
  Cook's Tip
salt and cayenne pepper
For the garnish
  25g/1oz/2 tbsp butter
  12 baby onions, peeled
  12 button (white) mushrooms
  chopped flat leaf parsley

1 Cut all the fish into thick slices, removing any obvious bones. Melt the butter in a large pan, put in the fish and sliced vegetables and stir over a medium heat until lightly browned. Pour in the wine and enough cold water to cover. Add the bouquet garni and spices and season. Bring to the boil, lower the heat and simmer gently for 20–30 minutes, until the fish is tender, skimming the surface occasionally.

2 Meanwhile, prepare the garnish. Heat the butter in a deep frying pan and sauté the baby onions until golden and tender. Add the mushrooms and fry until golden. Season and keep hot.

3 Strain the soup through a large sieve (strainer) into a clean pan. Discard the herbs and spices in the sieve, then divide the fish among deep soup plates (you can skin the fish if you wish, but this is not essential) and keep hot.

4 Reheat the soup until it boils. Lower the heat and whisk in the *beurre manié* little by little until the soup thickens. Season it and pour over the fish. Garnish each portion with the fried baby onions and mushrooms and sprinkle with chopped parsley.

COOK'S TIP
To make the *beurre manié* for thickening, mix 15g/½oz/1 tbsp softened butter with 15ml/1 tbsp plain (all-purpose) flour. Add to the boiling soup a pinch at a time, whisking all the time.

Energy 323Kcal/1346kJ; Protein 31.4g; Carbohydrate 2.3g, of which sugars 1.9g; Fat 11.6g, of which saturates 6.7g; Cholesterol 103mg; Calcium 35mg; Fibre 0.8g; Sodium 192mg.

BOUILLABAISSE

AUTHENTIC BOUILLABAISSE COMES FROM THE SOUTH OF FRANCE AND INCLUDES RASCASSE (SCORPION FISH) AS A CHARACTERISTIC INGREDIENT. IT IS, HOWEVER, PERFECTLY POSSIBLE TO MAKE THIS WONDERFUL MAIN-COURSE SOUP WITHOUT IT. USE AS LARGE A VARIETY OF FISH AS YOU CAN.

SERVES 4

INGREDIENTS
   45ml/3 tbsp olive oil
   2 onions, chopped
   2 leeks, white parts only, cleaned
      and chopped
   4 garlic cloves, chopped
   450g/1lb ripe tomatoes, peeled
      and chopped
   3 litres/5 pints/12 cups boiling fish
      stock or water
   15ml/1 tbsp tomato purée (paste)
   large pinch of saffron threads
   1 fresh bouquet garni, containing
      2 thyme sprigs, 2 bay leaves and
      2 fennel sprigs
   3kg/6½lb mixed fish, cleaned and
      cut into large chunks
   4 potatoes, peeled and thickly sliced
   salt, pepper and cayenne pepper
   rouille and aioli (see Cook's Tip),
      to serve
For the garnish
   16 slices of French bread, toasted
      and rubbed with garlic
   30ml/2 tbsp chopped parsley

1 Heat the oil in a large pan. Add the onions, leeks, garlic and tomatoes. Cook until slightly softened. Stir in the stock or water, tomato purée and saffron. Add the bouquet garni and boil until the oil is amalgamated. Lower the heat; add the fish and potatoes.

COOK'S TIP
For aioli, mix together 600ml/1 pint/ 2½ cups mayonnaise with 2 crushed garlic cloves and cayenne pepper.

2 Simmer the soup for 5–8 minutes, removing each type of fish as it becomes cooked. Continue to cook until the potatoes are very tender. Season well with salt, pepper and cayenne.

3 Divide the fish and potatoes among individual soup plates. Strain the soup and ladle it over the fish. Garnish with toasted French bread and parsley, and serve with rouille and aioli.

Energy 888Kcal/3748kJ; Protein 105.5g; Carbohydrate 88g, of which sugars 14g; Fat 14.8g, of which saturates 2.3g; Cholesterol 230mg; Calcium 217mg; Fibre 7.3g; Sodium 953mg.

THAI FISH BROTH

LEMON GRASS, CHILLIES AND GALANGAL ARE AMONG THE FLAVOURINGS USED IN THIS FRAGRANT SOUP.

SERVES 2–3

INGREDIENTS
    1 litre/1¾ pints/4 cups fish or
        light chicken stock
    4 lemon grass stalks
    3 limes
    2 small fresh hot red chillies,
        seeded and thinly sliced
    2cm/¾ in piece fresh galangal,
        peeled and thinly sliced
    6 coriander (cilantro) stalks and leaves
    2 kaffir lime leaves, coarsely
        chopped (optional)
    350g/12oz monkfish fillet, skinned
        and cut into 2.5cm/1in pieces
    15ml/1 tbsp rice vinegar
    45ml/3 tbsp Thai fish sauce
    30ml/2 tbsp chopped coriander
        leaves, to garnish

1 Pour the stock into a pan and bring it to the boil. Meanwhile, slice the bulb end of each lemon grass stalk diagonally into pieces about 3mm/⅛in thick. Peel off four wide strips of lime rind with a potato peeler, taking care to avoid the white pith underneath which would make the soup bitter. Squeeze the limes and reserve the juice.

2 Add the sliced lemon grass, lime rind, chillies, galangal and coriander stalks to the stock, with the kaffir lime leaves, if using. Simmer for 1–2 minutes.

VARIATIONS
Prawns (shrimp), scallops, squid or sole can be substituted for the monkfish. If you use kaffir lime leaves, you will need the juice of only 2 limes.

3 Add the monkfish, rice vinegar and fish sauce, with half the reserved lime juice. Simmer for about 3 minutes, until the fish is just cooked. Lift out and discard the coriander stalks, taste the broth and add more lime juice if necessary; the soup should taste quite sour. Sprinkle with the coriander leaves and serve very hot.

PAD THAI RED MONKFISH SOUP

THIS LIGHT COCONUT SOUP IS BASED ON THAILAND'S CLASSIC STIR-FRIED NOODLE DISH.

SERVES 4

INGREDIENTS
175g/6oz flat rice noodles
30ml/2 tbsp vegetable oil
2 garlic cloves, chopped
15ml/1 tbsp red curry paste
450g/1lb monkfish tail, cut into
  bite-size pieces
300ml/½ pint/1¼ cups
  coconut cream
750ml/1¼ pints/3 cups hot
  chicken stock
45ml/3 tbsp Thai fish sauce
15ml/1 tbsp palm sugar
60ml/4 tbsp roughly chopped
  roasted peanuts
4 spring onions (scallions),
  shredded lengthways
50g/2oz beansprouts
large handful of fresh Thai
  basil leaves
salt and ground black pepper
1 red chilli, seeded and cut
  lengthways into slivers,
  to garnish

1 Soak the noodles in boiling water for 10 minutes, or according to the packet instructions. Drain.

2 Heat the oil in a wok or saucepan over a high heat. Add the garlic and cook for 2 minutes. Stir in the curry paste and cook for 1 minute.

COOK'S TIP
Thai fish sauce (nam pla) is made from salted, fermented fish. The colour of the sauce can vary considerably. Look for a light-coloured sauce, as it is considered better than the darker version.

3 Add the monkfish and stir-fry over a high heat for 4–5 minutes, until just tender. Pour in the coconut cream and stock. Stir in the fish sauce and sugar, and bring just to the boil. Add the drained noodles and cook for 1–2 minutes, until tender.

4 Stir in half the peanuts, half the spring onions, half the beansprouts, the basil and seasoning. Ladle the soup into deep bowls and scatter over the remaining peanuts. Garnish with the rest of the spring onions and beansprouts, and the red chilli.

Energy 379Kcal/1589kJ; Protein 25.5g; Carbohydrate 41.2g, of which sugars 4.7g; Fat 12g, of which saturates 2g; Cholesterol 18mg; Calcium 49mg; Fibre 0.9g; Sodium 111mg.

BOURRIDE OF RED MULLET AND FENNEL

THIS FISH SOUP FROM PROVENCE IN FRANCE IS MADE WITH FRESH MAYONNAISE. THE SECRET OF
SUCCESS IS TO COOK THE SOUP GENTLY.

SERVES 4

INGREDIENTS
    25ml/1½ tbsp olive oil
    1 onion, chopped
    3 garlic cloves, chopped
    2 fennel bulbs, halved, cored and
        thinly sliced
    4 tomatoes, chopped
    1 bay leaf
    1 fresh thyme sprig
    1.2 litres/2 pints/5 cups fish stock
    675g/1½ lb red mullet or snapper
    8 slices baguette
    1 garlic clove
    30ml/2 tbsp sun-dried tomato paste
    12 black olives, stoned and quartered
    salt and ground black pepper
    fresh fennel fronds, to garnish
For the mayonnaise
    2 egg yolks
    10ml/2 tsp white wine vinegar
    300ml/½ pint/1¼ cups extra virgin
        olive oil

1 Heat the olive oil in a large, heavy-based pan. Add the onion and garlic and cook for 5 minutes, until softened. Add the fennel and cook for a further 2–3 minutes. Stir in the tomatoes, bay leaf, thyme and fish stock. Bring the mixture to the boil, then reduce the heat and simmer for 30 minutes.

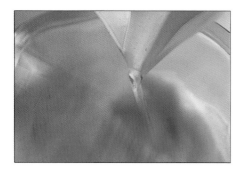

2 Meanwhile, make the mayonnaise. Put the egg yolks and vinegar in a bowl. Season and whisk well. Whisk in the oil, a little at a time, increasing the speed from a few drops at a time to a slow trickle. Transfer to a bowl and set aside.

3 Scale and fillet the mullet. Cut each fillet into two or three pieces, then add them to the soup and cook gently for 5 minutes. Use a slotted spoon to remove the mullet, and set aside.

4 Strain the cooking liquid through a fine sieve (strainer), pressing the vegetables with a ladle to extract as much of the flavour as possible.

5 Whisk about a ladleful of the soup into the mayonnaise, then whisk in the remaining soup in one go.

6 Return the soup to a clean pan and cook very gently, whisking continuously, until the mixture is slightly thickened. Add the fish to the soup and set aside.

7 Toast the baguette slices on both sides. Rub each slice with the clove of garlic and spread with sun-dried tomato paste. Divide the olives among the toasted bread slices.

8 Reheat the soup, but do not allow it to boil. Ladle it into bowls and top each with two toasts. Garnish with fennel.

Energy 322Kcal/1354kJ; Protein 35.3g; Carbohydrate 17.5g, of which sugars 6.4g; Fat 12.9g, of which saturates 1g; Cholesterol 0mg; Calcium 173mg; Fibre 4.4g; Sodium 299mg.

SOUP NIÇOISE <u>WITH</u> SEARED TUNA

INGREDIENTS FOR THE FAMOUS SALAD FROM NICE IN THE SOUTH OF FRANCE ARE TRANSFORMED INTO A SIMPLE, YET ELEGANT, SOUP BY ADDING A HOT GARLIC-INFUSED STOCK.

SERVES 4

INGREDIENTS

12 bottled anchovy fillets, drained
30ml/2 tbsp milk
115g/4oz green beans, halved
4 plum tomatoes
16 black olives, stoned
1 litre/1¾ pints/4 cups good
  vegetable stock
3 garlic cloves, crushed
30ml/2 tbsp lemon juice
15ml/1 tbsp olive oil
4 tuna steaks, about 75g/3oz each
small bunch of spring onions
  (scallions), shredded lengthways
handful of fresh basil leaves,
  finely shredded
salt and ground black pepper
fresh crusty bread, to serve

1 Soak the anchovies in the milk for 10 minutes. Drain well and dry on kitchen paper.

2 Cook the green beans in boiling salted water for 2–3 minutes. Drain, refresh under cold running water and drain. Split any thick beans diagonally lengthways. Wash the olives to remove any oil, then cut into quarters.

3 Peel, halve and seed the tomatoes, then cut into wedges. Set all the prepared ingredients aside.

4 Bring the stock to the boil in a large, heavy-based pan. Add the garlic, reduce the heat and simmer for 10 minutes. Season the stock well and add the lemon juice.

5 Meanwhile, brush a griddle pan or frying pan with the oil and heat until very hot. Season the tuna and cook for about 2 minutes on each side. Do not overcook the tuna or it will become dry.

6 Gently toss together the green beans, tomatoes, spring onions, anchovies, black olives and shredded basil leaves.

7 Put the seared tuna steaks into four bowls and pile the vegetable mixture on top. Carefully ladle the hot garlic stock around the ingredients. Serve at once, with crusty bread.

COOK'S TIP
Buy anchovy fillets that have been bottled in extra virgin olive oil if you can, as they have a far superior flavour to the smaller anchovy fillets.

Energy 217Kcal/909kJ; Protein 27.4g; Carbohydrate 3g, of which sugars 2.7g; Fat 10.7g, of which saturates 2.2g; Cholesterol 34mg; Calcium 76mg; Fibre 2g; Sodium 829mg.

SALMON SOUP <u>WITH</u> SALSA <u>AND</u> ROUILLE

THIS SMART FISH SOUP IS THE PERFECT CHOICE FOR SUMMER ENTERTAINING. SORREL IS A GOOD
PARTNER FOR SALMON, BUT DILL OR FENNEL ARE EQUALLY DELICIOUS ALTERNATIVES.

<u>SERVES 4</u>

INGREDIENTS
   90ml/6 tbsp olive oil
   1 onion, chopped
   1 leek, chopped
   1 celery stick, chopped
   1 fennel bulb, roughly chopped
   1 red (bell) pepper, seeded
    and sliced
   3 garlic cloves, chopped
   grated rind and juice of 2 oranges
   1 bay leaf
   400g/14oz can chopped tomatoes
   1.2 litres/2 pints/5 cups fish stock
   pinch of cayenne pepper
   800g/1¾lb salmon fillet, skinned
   300ml/½ pint/1¼ cups double
    (heavy) cream
   salt and ground black pepper
   4 thin slices baguette, to serve

For the ruby salsa
   2 tomatoes, peeled, seeded
    and diced
   ½ small red onion, very
    finely chopped
   15ml/1 tbsp cod's roe
   15ml/1 tbsp chopped fresh sorrel

For the rouille
   120ml/4fl oz/½ cup mayonnaise
   1 garlic clove, crushed
   5ml/1 tsp sun-dried tomato paste

1 Heat the oil in a large pan and add the chopped onion, leek, celery, fennel, pepper and garlic. Cover the pan and cook gently for 20 minutes or until all the vegetables have softened. Do not allow the onion and garlic to brown.

2 Add the orange rind and juice, bay leaf and tomatoes. Cover and cook for 4–5 minutes, stirring occasionally. Add the stock and cayenne, cover the pan and simmer for 30 minutes.

3 Add the salmon and cook gently for 8–10 minutes, until just cooked. Using a slotted spoon, remove the salmon and place it on a large plate.

4 Flake the salmon into large pieces, and remove any bones that were missed when the fish was originally filleted. Put the flaked salmon in a dish and set it aside.

COOK'S TIP
For a smart presentation, choose wide, shallow soup plates, so that there is plenty of room for the rouille-topped toast on top of the flaked salmon. The ruby salsa adds the finishing touch.

5 Meanwhile, make the salsa. Put the tomatoes in a bowl and add the finely chopped red onion. Stir in the cod's roe and the chopped fresh sorrel. Transfer the mixture to a serving dish and set it aside.

6 To make the rouille to top the toast, mix the mayonnaise with the crushed garlic and the sun-dried tomato paste in a bowl.

7 Leave the soup to cool slightly, then remove and discard the bay leaf. Purée the soup in a food processor or blender until smooth, then press it through a fine sieve (strainer) into the rinsed pan.

8 Stir in the cream and season well, then add the flaked salmon. Toast the baguette slices under a hot grill (broiler) on both sides and set aside.

9 Reheat the soup gently without letting it boil. Ladle it into bowls and float the toasted baguette slices on top. Add a spoonful of rouille to each slice of baguette and spoon some ruby salsa on top. Serve immediately.

Energy 1153Kcal/4772kJ; Protein 44.9g; Carbohydrate 13.7g, of which sugars 12.5g; Fat 102.5g, of which saturates 34.9g; Cholesterol 225mg; Calcium 127mg; Fibre 4.7g; Sodium 268mg.

SALMON CHOWDER

DILL IS THE PERFECT PARTNER FOR SALMON IN THIS CREAMY SOUP FROM THE USA. IT TAKES ITS INSPIRATION FROM THE SATISFYING SOUPS THAT ARE TYPICAL OF THE EASTERN SEABOARD OF THE COUNTRY, AND IS BEST SERVED IMMEDIATELY AFTER COOKING, WHEN THE SALMON IS JUST TENDER.

SERVES 4

INGREDIENTS

20g/¾oz/1½ tbsp butter
1 onion, finely chopped
1 leek, finely chopped
1 small fennel bulb, finely chopped
25g/1oz/¼ cup plain
 (all-purpose) flour
1.75 litres/3 pints/7 cups fish stock
2 medium potatoes, cut into
 1cm/½in cubes
450g/1lb salmon fillet, skinned and
 cut into 2cm/¾in cubes
175ml/6fl oz/¾ cup milk
120ml/4fl oz/½ cup whipping cream
30ml/2 tbsp chopped fresh dill
salt and ground black pepper

1 Melt the butter in a large pan. Add the onion, leek and chopped fennel and cook for 6 minutes until softened.

2 Stir in the flour. Reduce the heat to low and cook for 3 minutes, stirring occasionally with a wooden spoon.

3 Add the fish stock and potatoes to the mixture in the pan. Season with a little salt and ground black pepper. Bring to the boil, then reduce the heat, cover and simmer gently for about 20 minutes or until the potatoes are tender when tested with a fork.

4 Add the cubed salmon fillet and simmer gently for 3–5 minutes until it is just cooked.

5 Stir the milk, cream and chopped dill into the contents of the pan. Cook until just warmed through, stirring occasionally, but do not allow to boil. Adjust the seasoning to taste, then ladle into warmed soup bowls to serve.

Energy 464Kcal/1934kJ; Protein 27.9g; Carbohydrate 22.1g, of which sugars 6.5g; Fat 30g, of which saturates 12.9g; Cholesterol 101mg; Calcium 131mg; Fibre 3.1g; Sodium 122mg.

CURRIED SALMON SOUP

A HINT OF MILD CURRY PASTE REALLY ENHANCES THE FLAVOUR OF THIS SOUP, WITHOUT MAKING IT TOO SPICY. GRATED CREAMED COCONUT ADDS A LUXURY TOUCH, WHILE HELPING TO AMALGAMATE THE FLAVOURS. SERVED WITH CHUNKS OF WARM BREAD, THIS MAKES A SUBSTANTIAL APPETIZER.

SERVES 4

INGREDIENTS

50g/2oz/¼ cup butter
2 onions, roughly chopped
10ml/2 tsp mild curry paste
475ml/16fl oz/2 cups water
150ml/¼ pint/⅔ cup white wine
300ml/½ pint/1¼ cups double
 (heavy) cream
50g/2oz/½ cup creamed coconut,
 grated, or 120ml/4fl oz/½ cup
 coconut cream
2 potatoes, about 350g/12oz, cubed
450g/1lb salmon fillet, skinned
 and cut into bitesize pieces
60ml/4 tbsp chopped fresh
 flat leaf parsley
salt and ground black pepper

1 Melt the butter in a large pan, add the onions and cook for 3–4 minutes, until beginning to soften. Stir in the curry paste. Cook for 1 minute more.

2 Add the water, wine, cream and creamed coconut or coconut cream, with seasoning. Bring to the boil, stirring until the coconut has dissolved.

3 Add the potatoes to the pan. Simmer, covered, for about 15 minutes or until they are almost tender. Do not allow them to break down into the mixture.

4 Add the fish gently so as not to break it up. Simmer for 2–3 minutes until just cooked. Add the parsley and adjust the seasoning. Serve immediately.

Energy 837Kcal/3466kJ; Protein 26.3g; Carbohydrate 16.6g, of which sugars 3.6g; Fat 71.8g, of which saturates 41.2g; Cholesterol 186mg; Calcium 74mg; Fibre 0.9g; Sodium 158mg.

SMOKED HADDOCK AND POTATO SOUP

*"Cullen Skink" is a classic Scottish dish using one of the country's tastiest fish.
The result is a thick, creamy soup with a rich, smoky fish flavour.*

SERVES 6

INGREDIENTS

350g/12oz smoked haddock fillet
1 onion, chopped
bouquet garni
900ml/1½ pints/3¾ cups water
500g/1¼lb floury potatoes,
  quartered
600ml/1 pint/2½ cups milk
40g/1½oz/3 tbsp butter
salt and ground black pepper
chopped chives, to garnish
crusty bread, to serve

1 Put the haddock, onion, bouquet garni and water into a large heavy-based pan and bring to the boil. Skim the scum from the surface, then cover, reduce the heat and poach gently for 10–15 minutes, until the haddock flakes easily.

2 Lift the haddock from the pan, cool slightly, then remove the skin and bones. Flake the flesh and put to one side. Return the skin and bones to the pan and simmer for 30 minutes.

3 Strain the fish stock and return to the pan, then add the potatoes and simmer for about 25 minutes. Remove the potatoes from the pan. Add the milk to the pan and bring to the boil.

4 Mash the potatoes with the butter, then whisk into the soup. Add the flaked fish to the pan and heat through. Season. Ladle into soup bowls, sprinkle with chives and serve with crusty bread.

Energy 205Kcal/864kJ; Protein 16.1g; Carbohydrate 19g, of which sugars 6.4g; Fat 7.8g, of which saturates 4.7g; Cholesterol 41mg; Calcium 142mg; Fibre 1g; Sodium 536mg.

SMOKED HADDOCK CHOWDER

BASED ON A TRADITIONAL SCOTTISH RECIPE, THIS SOUP HAS AMERICAN-STYLE SWEETNESS FROM THE SWEET POTATOES AND BUTTERNUT SQUASH, AND IS FLAVOURED WITH A HINT OF THAI BASIL.

SERVES 6

INGREDIENTS
400g/14oz sweet potatoes
  (pink-fleshed variety)
225g/8oz butternut squash
50g/2oz/¼ cup butter
1 onion, chopped
450g/1lb smoked haddock fillets
300ml/½ pint/1¼ cups water
600ml/1 pint/2½ cups milk
small handful of Thai basil leaves
60ml/4 tbsp double (heavy) cream
salt and ground black pepper

3 Use a sharp knife to skin the smoked haddock fillets.

4 Add the fillets and water to the pan. Bring to the boil, reduce the heat and simmer for 10 minutes, until the fish is cooked. Use a slotted spoon to lift the fish out of the pan, and leave to cool. Set the cooking liquid aside.

5 When cool enough to handle, carefully break the flesh into large flakes, discarding the skin and bones. Set the fish aside.

6 Press the sweet potatoes through a sieve (strainer) and beat in the remaining butter with seasoning to taste. Strain the reserved fish cooking liquid and return it to the rinsed pan, then whisk in the sweet potato. Stir in the milk and bring to the boil. Simmer for about 2–3 minutes.

7 Stir in the butternut squash, fish, Thai basil leaves and cream. Season the soup to taste and heat through without boiling. Ladle the soup into six warmed soup bowls and serve immediately.

1 Peel the sweet potatoes and butternut squash and cut into small, bitesize pieces. Cook them separately in boiling salted water for 15 minutes or until just tender. Drain both well.

2 Melt half the butter in a large, heavy-based pan. Add the onion and cook for 4–5 minutes, until soft.

COOK'S TIP
The best type of smoked fish to use in this recipe is Finnan haddock, but other types of smoked haddock can be used with equal success.

Energy 285Kcal/1196kJ; Protein 19.1g; Carbohydrate 20.7g, of which sugars 9.9g; Fat 14.7g, of which saturates 8.9g; Cholesterol 64mg; Calcium 166mg; Fibre 2.1g; Sodium 173mg.

SMOKED MACKEREL AND TOMATO SOUP

ALL THE INGREDIENTS FOR THIS UNUSUAL SOUP ARE COOKED IN A SINGLE PAN, SO IT IS NOT ONLY QUICK AND EASY TO PREPARE, BUT REDUCES THE CLEARING UP. SMOKED MACKEREL GIVES THE SOUP A ROBUST FLAVOUR, BUT THIS IS TEMPERED BY THE CITRUS TONES IN THE LEMON GRASS AND TAMARIND.

SERVES 4

INGREDIENTS
200g/7oz smoked mackerel fillets
4 tomatoes
1 litre/1¾ pints/4 cups
    vegetable stock
1 lemon grass stalk, finely chopped
5cm/2in piece fresh galangal,
    finely diced
4 shallots, finely chopped
2 garlic cloves, finely chopped
2.5ml/½ tsp dried chilli flakes
15ml/1 tbsp Thai fish sauce
5ml/1 tsp palm sugar or light
    muscovado (brown) sugar
45ml/3 tbsp thick tamarind juice,
    made by mixing tamarind paste
    with warm water
small bunch of fresh chives or spring
    onions (scallions), to garnish

1 Prepare the smoked mackerel fillets. Remove and discard the skin, if necessary, then chop the flesh into large pieces. Remove any stray bones with your fingers or a pair of tweezers.

2 Cut the tomatoes in half, squeeze out most of the seeds with your fingers, then finely dice the flesh with a sharp knife. Set aside.

3 Pour the stock into a large pan and add the lemon grass, galangal, shallots and garlic. Bring to the boil, reduce the heat and simmer for 15 minutes.

4 Add the fish, tomatoes, chilli flakes, fish sauce, sugar and tamarind juice. Simmer for 4–5 minutes, until the fish and tomatoes are heated through. Serve garnished with chives or spring onions.

Energy 203Kcal/845kJ; Protein 10.3g; Carbohydrate 5.3g, of which sugars 5g; Fat 15.8g, of which saturates 3.3g; Cholesterol 53mg; Calcium 21mg; Fibre 1.2g; Sodium 385mg.

COD, BROAD BEAN AND SPINACH CHOWDER

FRESH COD AND VEGETABLES ARE ABUNDANT IN THIS THICK AND CREAMY SOUP, WHICH IS FINISHED WITH CRISP GRANARY CROÛTONS TO SOAK UP THE DELICIOUS LIQUID. MAKE IT EARLY IN THE SUMMER TO TAKE ADVANTAGE OF THE YOUNGEST, SWEETEST FRESH BEANS.

SERVES 6

INGREDIENTS
    1 litre/1¾ pints/4 cups milk
    150ml/¼ pint/⅔ cup double
      (heavy) cream
    675g/1½lb cod fillet, skinned
      and boned
    45ml/3 tbsp olive oil
    1 onion, sliced
    2 garlic cloves, finely chopped
    450g/1lb potatoes, thickly sliced
    450g/1lb fresh broad (fava)
      beans, podded
    225g/8oz baby spinach leaves
    pinch of grated nutmeg
    30ml/2 tbsp chopped fresh
      chives
    salt and ground black pepper
    fresh chives, to garnish

For the croûtons
    60ml/4 tbsp olive oil
    6 slices Granary (whole-wheat)
      bread, crusts removed, cut into
      large cubes

1 Pour the milk and cream into a large pan and bring to the boil. Add the cod and bring back to the boil. Reduce the heat and simmer for 2–3 minutes, then remove from the heat and leave to stand for about 6 minutes, until the fish is just cooked. Use a slotted spoon to remove the fish from the cooking liquid.

2 Using a fork, flake the cooked cod into chunky pieces, removing any bones or skin, then cover and set aside.

3 Heat the olive oil in a large pan and add the onion and garlic. Cook for about 5 minutes, until softened, stirring occasionally. Add the potatoes, stir in the milk mixture and bring to the boil. Reduce the heat and cover the pan. Cook for 10 minutes. Add the broad beans; cook for 10 minutes more or until the beans are tender and the potatoes just begin to break up.

4 Meanwhile, to make the croûtons, heat the oil in a frying pan and add the bread cubes. Cook over a medium heat, stirring often, until golden all over. Remove using a slotted spoon and leave to drain on kitchen paper.

5 Add the cod to the soup and heat through gently. Just before serving, add the spinach and stir for 1–2 minutes, until wilted. Season the soup well and stir in the nutmeg and chives.

6 Ladle the soup into six warmed soup bowls and pile the croûtons on top. Garnish with fresh chives and serve immediately.

COOK'S TIP
When fresh broad (fava) beans are out of season, frozen beans are acceptable as an alternative. Make sure that you cook them for the time recommended on the packet.

Energy 603Kcal/2525kJ; Protein 37.9g; Carbohydrate 44.7g, of which sugars 12.2g; Fat 31.6g, of which saturates 12.4g; Cholesterol 96mg; Calcium 398mg; Fibre 7.6g; Sodium 375mg.

CARIBBEAN SALT COD <u>AND</u> OKRA SOUP

INSPIRED BY INGREDIENTS POPULARLY USED IN CARIBBEAN COOKING, THIS COLOURFUL, CHUNKY SOUP IS SERVED IN DEEP BOWLS AROUND A CHIVE-FLAVOURED SWEET YAM MASH. OKRA GIVES THE DISH A FLAVOUR THAT IS A CROSS BETWEEN ASPARAGUS AND AUBERGINE.

2 Heat the oil in a heavy-based pan. Add the garlic, onion and chilli, and cook for 4–5 minutes until softened.

3 Add the salt cod and cook for 3–4 minutes, until it begins to colour. Stir in the tomatoes, wine and bay leaves and bring to the boil. Pour in the water, bring to the boil, reduce the heat and simmer for 10 minutes.

4 Meanwhile, trim the stalk ends off the okra and cut the pods into chunks. Add to the soup and cook for 10 minutes. Stir in the callaloo or spinach and cook for 5 minutes, until the okra is tender.

5 Meanwhile, prepare the creamed yam. Peel the yam and cut it into large dice, then place in a saucepan with the lemon juice and add cold water to cover. Bring to the boil and cook for 15–20 minutes, until tender. Drain well, then return the yam to the pan and dry it out over the heat for a few seconds. Mash with the butter and cream, and season well. Stir in the chives.

6 Season the soup and stir in the chopped parsley. Spoon portions of creamed yam into the centres of six soup bowls and ladle the soup around it. Serve immediately.

SERVES 6

INGREDIENTS
200g/7oz salt cod, soaked for
  24 hours, changing the water
  several times
15ml/1 tbsp olive oil
1 garlic clove, chopped
1 onion, chopped
1 green chilli, seeded and chopped
6 plum tomatoes, peeled and
  chopped
250ml/8fl oz/1 cup white wine
2 bay leaves
900ml/1½ pints/3¾ cups water
225g/8oz okra

225g/8oz callaloo or spinach
30ml/2 tbsp chopped fresh parsley
salt and ground black pepper

For the creamed yam
  675g/1½lb yam
  juice of 1 lemon
  50g/2oz/¼ cup butter
  30ml/2 tbsp double (heavy) cream
  15ml/1 tbsp chopped fresh
    chives

1 Drain and skin the salt cod, then rinse it under cold running water. Cut the flesh into bite-size pieces, removing any bones, and set aside.

Energy 322Kcal/1352kJ; Protein 10.7g; Carbohydrate 36.7g, of which sugars 5.3g; Fat 12.8g, of which saturates 6.6g; Cholesterol 40mg; Calcium 159mg; Fibre 4.6g; Sodium 137mg.

JAMAICAN RICE AND BEAN SOUP WITH SALT COD

BASED ON THE CLASSIC CARIBBEAN DISH OF RICE AND PEAS, THIS RECIPE IS MADE WITH BLACK-EYED BEANS, BUT KIDNEY BEANS OR, MORE TRADITIONALLY, PIGEON PEAS CAN BE USED INSTEAD. THIS IS A VERY HEARTY SOUP THAT CAN BE SERVED AS A COMPLETE MEAL.

SERVES 6

INGREDIENTS
15ml/1 tbsp sunflower oil
75g/3oz/6 tbsp butter
115g/4oz thick rindless bacon
  rashers, cut into lardons
1 onion, chopped
2 garlic cloves, chopped
1 red chilli, seeded and chopped
225g/8oz/generous 1 cup long
  grain rice
2 fresh thyme sprigs
1 cinnamon stick
400g/14oz can black-eyed beans,
  drained and rinsed
900ml/1½ pints/3¾ cups water
350g/12oz salt cod, soaked for
  24 hours, changing the water
  several times
plain (all-purpose) flour, for dusting
400g/14oz can coconut milk
175g/6oz baby spinach leaves
30ml/2 tbsp chopped fresh parsley
salt and ground black pepper

1 Heat the oil and 25g/1oz/2 tbsp of the butter in a large, heavy-based pan. Add the bacon strips and cook for 3–4 minutes, until golden. Stir in the onion, garlic and chilli and cook for a further 4–5 minutes.

2 Stir in the rice. Cook for 1–2 minutes, until the grains are translucent. Stir in the thyme, cinnamon stick and black-eyed beans and cook for 1–2 minutes. Pour in the water and bring to the boil. Reduce the heat to low and cook for 25–30 minutes.

3 Meanwhile, wash the soaked salt cod under cold running water. Pat dry with kitchen paper and remove the skin. Cut into large bite-size pieces and toss in the flour until evenly coated. Shake off the excess flour.

4 Melt the remaining butter in a large, heavy-based frying pan. Add the cod, in batches if necessary, and cook for 4–5 minutes until tender and golden. Remove the cod and set aside.

5 Stir the coconut milk into the cooked rice and beans. Remove the cinnamon stick and cook for 2–3 minutes. Stir in the spinach and cook for a further 2–3 minutes. Add the cod and chopped parsley, season and heat through. Ladle the soup into bowls and serve.

COOK'S TIP
Lardons are thicker and slightly longer than matchsticks. Cut them from thick bacon or a joint of gammon.

Energy 443Kcal/1852kJ; Protein 30g; Carbohydrate 43.2g, of which sugars 5.1g; Fat 16.8g, of which saturates 8.3g; Cholesterol 71mg; Calcium 105mg; Fibre 3.8g; Sodium 999mg.

SHELLFISH SOUPS

If you like shellfish, you will find some of the most delicious and luxurious soups in this section. Malaysian Laksa Lemak is a marvellous party dish with which to impress your guests. Or you could try Spanish Seafood Soup, a hearty dish that has all the colours and flavours of the Mediterranean. From Japan there is a delicate Clear Soup with Seafood Sticks, often eaten with sushi, and from China there is Wonton and Prawn Tail Soup, or Crab and Corn Soup.

CLEAR SOUP WITH SEAFOOD STICKS

THIS DELICATE JAPANESE SOUP, WHICH IS OFTEN EATEN WITH SUSHI, IS VERY QUICK TO MAKE IF YOU PREPARE THE FIRST DASHI BEFOREHAND OR IF YOU USE FREEZE-DRIED DASHI-NO-MOTO.

SERVES 4

INGREDIENTS
4 mitsuba sprigs or 4 chives
  and a few sprigs of mustard and
  cress
4 seafood sticks
400ml/14fl oz/1⅔ cups first dashi
  stock, or the same amount of water
  and 5ml/1 tsp dashi-no-moto
15ml/1 tbsp Japanese soy
  sauce (shoyu)
7.5ml/1½ tsp salt
grated rind of yuzu (optional),
  to garnish

1 Mitsuba leaves are normally sold with the stems and roots on to retain freshness. Cut off the root, then cut 5cm/2in from the top, retaining both the long straw-like stem and the leaf.

2 Blanch the stems in hot water from the kettle. If you use chives, choose them at least 10cm/4in in length and blanch them, too.

3 Take a seafood stick and carefully tie around the middle with a mitsuba stem or chive, holding it in place with a knot. Do not pull too tightly, as the bow will easily break. Repeat the process to make four tied seafood sticks.

4 Hold one seafood stick in your hand. With your finger, carefully loosen both ends to make it look like a tassel.

5 Place one seafood stick in each soup bowl, then put the four mitsuba leaves or mustard and cress on top.

6 Heat the stock in a pan and bring to the boil. Add shoyu and salt to taste. Pour the stock gently over the mitsuba and seafood stick. Sprinkle with grated yuzu rind, if using.

COOK'S TIPS
• Mitsuba is a member of the parsley family and is available from Asian stores.
• Dashi stock can be bought as instant dashi-no-moto, or you can make your own.
• Yuzu is a popular Japanese citrus fruit, about the same size as a clementine, with a firm, thick, yellow skin.

Energy 9Kcal/36kJ; Protein 1.1g; Carbohydrate 1g, of which sugars 0.3g; Fat 0.1g, of which saturates 0g; Cholesterol 4mg; Calcium 2mg; Fibre 0g; Sodium 1025mg.

PRAWN AND EGG-KNOT SOUP

OMELETTES AND PANCAKES ARE OFTEN USED TO ADD PROTEIN TO LIGHT ORIENTAL SOUPS. IN THIS RECIPE, THIN OMELETTES ARE TWISTED INTO LITTLE KNOTS AND ADDED AT THE LAST MINUTE.

SERVES 4

INGREDIENTS

   1 spring onion (scallion), shredded
   800ml/1⅓ pints/3½ cups well-
      flavoured stock or instant dashi
   5ml/1 tsp soy sauce
   dash of sake or dry white wine
   pinch of salt
For the prawn (shrimp) balls
   200g/7oz/generous 1 cup raw large
      prawns, shelled, thawed if frozen
   65g/2½oz cod fillet, skinned
   5ml/1 tsp egg white
   5ml/1 tsp sake or dry white wine,
      plus a dash extra
   22.5ml/4½ tsp cornflour (cornstarch)
      or potato flour
   2–3 drops soy sauce
   pinch of salt
For the omelette
   1 egg, beaten
   dash of mirin
   pinch of salt
   oil, for cooking

1 To make the prawn balls, use a pin to remove the black vein running down the back of each prawn. Place the prawns, cod, egg white, sake or dry white wine, cornflour or potato flour, soy sauce and a pinch of salt in a food processor or blender and process to a thick, sticky paste. Shape the mixture into 4 balls, place in a steaming basket and steam over a pan of vigorously boiling water for about 10 minutes.

2 To make the garnish, soak the spring onion shreds in iced water for about 5 minutes, until they curl, then drain.

3 To make the omelette, mix the egg with the mirin and salt. Heat a little oil in a frying pan and pour in the egg mixture, coating the pan evenly. When the omelette has set, turn it over and cook for 30 seconds. Leave to cool.

4 Cut the omelette into strips and tie each in a knot. Heat the stock or dashi, then add the soy sauce, sake or wine and salt. Divide the prawn balls and egg-knots among 4 bowls and add the soup. Garnish with the spring onion.

Energy 98Kcal/412kJ; Protein 13.6g; Carbohydrate 7.1g, of which sugars 0.2g; Fat 1.9g, of which saturates 0.5g; Cholesterol 153mg; Calcium 51mg; Fibre 0.1g; Sodium 218mg.

WONTON AND PRAWN TAIL SOUP

A WELL-FLAVOURED CHICKEN STOCK OR BROTH IS A MUST FOR THIS CLASSIC CHINESE SNACK, WHICH IS POPULAR ON FAST-FOOD STALLS IN TOWNS AND CITIES THROUGHOUT SOUTHERN CHINA. SERVE IT AS AN APPETIZER OR PART OF A MAIN MEAL.

SERVES 4

INGREDIENTS
200g/7oz minced (ground) pork
200g/7oz cooked, peeled prawns
  (shrimp), thawed if frozen
10ml/2 tsp rice wine or dry sherry
10ml/2 tsp light soy sauce
5ml/1 tsp sesame oil
24 thin wonton wrappers
1.2 litres/2 pints/5 cups
  chicken stock
12 tiger prawns, shelled, with
  tails still on
350g/12oz pak choi (bok choy),
  coarsely shredded
salt and ground black pepper
4 spring onions (scallions),
  sliced, and 1cm/½in piece fresh
  root ginger, finely shredded,
  to garnish

1 Put the pork, prawns, rice wine or sherry, soy sauce and sesame oil in a large bowl. Add plenty of seasoning and mix the ingredients.

2 Put about 10ml/2 tsp of pork mixture in the centre of each wonton wrapper. Bring up the sides of the wrapper and pinch them together to seal the filling in a small bundle.

3 Bring a large pan of water to the boil. Add the wontons and cook for 3 minutes, then drain well and set aside.

4 Pour the stock into a pan and bring to the boil. Season to taste. Add the tiger prawns and cook for 2–3 minutes, until just tender. Add the wontons and pak choi and cook for 1–2 minutes. Garnish with spring onions and ginger to serve.

Energy 208Kcal/874kJ; Protein 26.8g; Carbohydrate 11.8g, of which sugars 2.2g; Fat 6.2g, of which saturates 2g; Cholesterol 179mg; Calcium 234mg; Fibre 2.4g; Sodium 655mg.

COCONUT AND SEAFOOD SOUP

THE LONG LIST OF INGREDIENTS COULD MISLEAD YOU INTO THINKING THAT THIS THAI SOUP IS COMPLICATED AND VERY TIME-CONSUMING TO PREPARE. IN FACT, IT IS EXTREMELY EASY TO PUT TOGETHER AND THE MARRIAGE OF FLAVOURS WORKS BEAUTIFULLY.

SERVES 4

INGREDIENTS

600ml/1 pint/2½ cups fish stock
5 thin slices fresh galangal or fresh
   root ginger
2 lemon grass stalks, chopped
3 kaffir lime leaves, shredded
bunch garlic chives, about 25g/1oz
small bunch fresh coriander
   (cilantro), about 15g/½oz
15ml/1 tbsp vegetable oil
4 shallots, chopped
400ml/14fl oz can coconut milk
30–45ml/2–3 tbsp Thai fish sauce
45–60ml/3–4 tbsp Thai green
   curry paste
450g/1lb raw large prawns (shrimp),
   peeled and deveined
450g/1lb prepared squid
a little fresh lime juice (optional)
salt and ground black pepper
60ml/4 tbsp crisp fried shallot
   slices, to serve

1 Pour the fish stock into a large pan and add the slices of galangal or ginger, the lemon grass and half the shredded kaffir lime leaves.

VARIATIONS
• Instead of squid, you could add 400g/14oz firm white fish, such as monkfish, cut into small pieces.
• You could also replace the squid with mussels. Steam 675g/1½lb live mussels in a tightly covered pan for 3–4 minutes, or until they have opened. Discard any that remain shut, then remove them from their shells and add to the soup.

2 Reserve a few garlic chives for the garnish, then chop the remainder. Add half the chopped garlic chives to the pan. Strip the coriander leaves from the stalks and set the leaves aside. Add the stalks to the pan. Bring to the boil, reduce the heat to low and cover the pan, then simmer gently for 20 minutes. Strain the stock into a bowl.

3 Rinse and dry the pan. Add the oil and shallots. Cook over a medium heat for 5–10 minutes, until the shallots are just beginning to brown.

4 Stir in the strained stock, coconut milk, the remaining kaffir lime leaves and 30ml/2 tbsp of the fish sauce. Heat gently until simmering and cook over a low heat for 5–10 minutes.

5 Stir in the curry paste and prawns, then cook for 3 minutes. Add the squid and cook for a further 2 minutes. Add the lime juice, if using, and season, adding more fish sauce to taste. Stir in the remaining chives and the reserved coriander leaves. Serve in bowls and sprinkle each portion with fried shallots and whole garlic chives.

Energy 205Kcal/871kJ; Protein 37.7g; Carbohydrate 7.5g, of which sugars 5.8g; Fat 3g, of which saturates 0.8g; Cholesterol 473mg; Calcium 144mg; Fibre 0.4g; Sodium 449mg.

THAI PUMPKIN, PRAWN <u>AND</u> COCONUT SOUP

THE NATURAL SWEETNESS OF THE PUMPKIN IS HEIGHTENED BY THE ADDITION OF A LITTLE SUGAR IN THIS ATTRACTIVE SOUP, BUT THIS IS BALANCED BY THE CHILLIES, SHRIMP PASTE AND DRIED SHRIMP. COCONUT CREAM BLURS THE BOUNDARIES BEAUTIFULLY.

SERVES 4–6

INGREDIENTS
    450g/1lb pumpkin
    2 garlic cloves, crushed
    4 shallots, finely chopped
    2.5ml/½ tsp shrimp paste
    1 lemon grass stalk, chopped
    2 fresh green chillies, seeded
    15ml/1 tbsp dried shrimp, soaked
        for 10 minutes in warm water
        to cover
    600ml/1 pint/2½ cups
        chicken stock
    600ml/1 pint/2½ cups
        coconut cream
    30ml/2 tbsp Thai fish sauce
    5ml/1 tsp granulated sugar
    115g/4oz small cooked shelled
        prawns (shrimp)
    salt and ground black pepper
To garnish
    2 fresh red chillies, seeded and
        thinly sliced
    10–12 fresh basil leaves

1 Peel the pumpkin and cut it into quarters with a sharp knife. Scoop out the seeds with a teaspoon and discard. Cut the flesh into chunks about 2cm/¾in thick and set aside.

2 Put the garlic, shallots, shrimp paste, lemon grass, green chillies and salt to taste in a mortar. Drain the dried shrimp, discarding the soaking liquid, and add them, then use a pestle to grind the mixture into a paste. Alternatively, place all the ingredients in a food processor and process to a paste.

3 Bring the chicken stock to the boil in a large pan. Add the ground paste and stir well to dissolve.

4 Add the pumpkin chunks and bring to a simmer. Simmer for 10–15 minutes, or until the pumpkin is tender.

5 Stir in the coconut cream, then bring the soup back to simmering point. Do not let it boil. Add the fish sauce, sugar and ground black pepper to taste.

6 Add the prawns and cook for a further 2–3 minutes, until they are heated through. Serve in warmed soup bowls, garnished with chillies and basil leaves.

COOK'S TIP
Shrimp paste is made from ground shrimp fermented in brine.

Energy 73Kcal/310kJ; Protein 6.5g; Carbohydrate 10.4g, of which sugars 9.8g; Fat 0.9g, of which saturates 0.5g; Cholesterol 56mg; Calcium 102mg; Fibre 1.3g; Sodium 399mg.

THAI PRAWN AND SQUASH SOUP

THIS SQUASH SOUP COMES FROM NORTHERN THAILAND. IT IS QUITE HEARTY, SOMETHING OF A CROSS BETWEEN A SOUP AND A STEW. THE BANANA FLOWER ISN'T ESSENTIAL — YOU MAY FIND IT DIFFICULT TO OBTAIN — BUT IT DOES ADD A UNIQUE AND AUTHENTIC FLAVOUR.

SERVES 4

INGREDIENTS
  1 butternut squash, about 300g/11oz
  1 litre/1¾ pints/4 cups
    vegetable stock
  90g/3½oz/scant 1 cup green beans,
    cut into 2.5cm/1in pieces
  45g/1¾oz dried banana
    flower (optional)
  15ml/1 tbsp Thai fish sauce
  225g/8oz raw prawns (shrimp)
  small bunch fresh basil
  cooked rice, to serve
For the chilli paste
  115g/4oz shallots, sliced
  10 drained bottled green peppercorns
  1 small fresh green chilli, seeded
    and finely chopped
  2.5ml/½ tsp shrimp paste

1 Peel the butternut squash and cut it in half. Scoop out the seeds with a teaspoon and discard, then cut the flesh into neat cubes. Set aside.

2 Make the chilli paste by pounding the shallots, peppercorns, chilli and shrimp paste together using a mortar and pestle or puréeing them in a spice blender.

3 Heat the stock gently in a large pan, then stir in the chilli paste. Add the squash, beans and banana flower, if using. Bring to the boil and cook for 15 minutes.

4 Add the fish sauce, prawns and basil. Bring to simmering point, then simmer for 3 minutes. Serve in warmed bowls, accompanied by rice.

Energy 64Kcal/271kJ; Protein 11.3g; Carbohydrate 3.4g, of which sugars 2.8g; Fat 0.7g, of which saturates 0.2g; Cholesterol 110mg; Calcium 82mg; Fibre 1.7g; Sodium 199mg.

SEAFOOD CHOWDER

CHOWDER TAKES ITS NAME FROM THE FRENCH WORD FOR CAULDRON — CHAUDIÈRE — THE TYPE OF POT TRADITIONALLY USED FOR SOUPS AND STEWS. LIKE MOST CHOWDERS, THIS IS A SUBSTANTIAL DISH, WHICH COULD EASILY BE SERVED WITH CRUSTY BREAD FOR A LUNCH OR SUPPER.

SERVES 4–6

INGREDIENTS

200g/7oz/generous 1 cup drained, canned corn kernels
600ml/1 pint/2½ cups milk
15g/½oz/1 tbsp butter
1 small leek, sliced
1 small garlic clove, crushed
2 rindless smoked streaky (fatty) bacon rashers (strips), chopped
1 small green (bell) pepper, seeded and diced
1 celery stalk, chopped
115g/4oz/generous ½ cup white long grain rice
5ml/1 tsp plain (all-purpose) flour
about 450ml/¾ pint/scant 2 cups hot chicken or vegetable stock
4 large scallops, preferably with corals
115g/4oz white fish fillet, such as monkfish or plaice
15ml/1 tbsp finely chopped fresh parsley
good pinch of cayenne pepper
30–45ml/2–3 tbsp single (light) cream (optional)
salt and freshly ground black pepper

1 Place half the corn kernels in a food processor or blender. Add a little of the milk and process until thick and creamy.

VARIATION
Instead of monkfish or plaice, try this chowder with haddock or cod, which go well with cream, if using.

2 Melt the butter in a large pan and gently fry the leek, garlic and bacon for 4–5 minutes until the leek has softened but not browned. Add the diced green pepper and chopped celery and sweat over a very gentle heat for 3–4 minutes more, stirring frequently.

3 Stir in the rice and cook for a few minutes until the grains begin to swell. Sprinkle over the flour. Cook, stirring occasionally, for about 1 minute, then gradually stir in the remaining milk and the stock.

4 Bring the mixture to the boil over a medium heat, then lower the heat and stir in the creamed corn mixture, with the whole corn kernels. Season well.

5 Cover the pan and simmer the chowder very gently for 20 minutes or until the rice is tender, stirring occasionally, and adding a little more chicken stock or water if the mixture thickens too quickly or the rice begins to stick to the bottom of the pan.

6 Pull the corals away from the scallops and slice the white flesh into 5mm/¼in pieces. Cut the fish fillet into bite-size chunks.

7 Stir the scallops and fish into the chowder, cook for 4 minutes, then stir in the corals, parsley and cayenne. Cook for a few minutes to heat through, then stir in the cream, if using. Adjust the seasoning and serve.

Energy 361Kcal/1520kJ; Protein 21.9g; Carbohydrate 47.1g, of which sugars 13.6g; Fat 10.1g, of which saturates 4.9g; Cholesterol 41mg; Calcium 213mg; Fibre 2.1g; Sodium 437mg.

MEDITERRANEAN SEAFOOD SOUP
WITH SAFFRON ROUILLE

VARY THE FISH CONTENT OF THIS SOUP ACCORDING TO THE FRESHEST AVAILABLE, BUT CHOOSE FIRM VARIETIES THAT WILL NOT FLAKE AND FALL APART EASILY DURING COOKING.

SERVES 4

INGREDIENTS

450g/1lb fresh clams, scrubbed
120ml/4fl oz/½ cup white wine
15ml/1 tbsp olive oil
4 garlic cloves, crushed
5ml/1 tsp fennel seeds
pinch of dried chilli flakes
1 fennel bulb, cored and sliced
1 red (bell) pepper, seeded
  and sliced
8 plum tomatoes, halved
1 onion, cut into thin wedges
225g/8oz small waxy potatoes, sliced
1 bay leaf
1 fresh thyme sprig
600ml/1 pint/2½ cups fish stock
1 mini French stick
225g/8oz monkfish fillet, sliced
350g/12oz red mullet or snapper,
  scaled, filleted and cut into strips
45ml/3 tbsp Pernod
salt and ground black pepper
fennel fronds, to garnish
For the rouille
  a few saffron strands
  150ml/¼ pint/⅔ cup mayonnaise
  dash of Tabasco sauce

1 Discard any open clams that do not shut when tapped sharply. Place the rest in a large pan with the wine. Cover and cook over a high heat for 4 minutes, until the shells have opened.

COOK'S TIP
Always use clams and other shellfish within one day of purchase.

2 Drain the clams, strain their cooking liquid and set it aside. Discard any unopened shells and reserve 8 clams in their shells. Remove the remaining clams from their shells and set aside.

3 Heat the oil in a pan. Add the garlic, fennel seeds and chilli flakes and cook for about 2 minutes, until softened.

4 Add the fennel, pepper, tomatoes, onion and cooking liquid. Cover and cook for 10 minutes, stirring occasionally.

5 Stir in the potatoes, bay leaf and thyme, then pour in the fish stock. Cover and cook for 15–20 minutes, until the vegetables are tender.

6 Meanwhile, make the saffron rouille. Pound the saffron strands to a powder in a mortar, then beat it into the mayonnaise with the Tabasco sauce. Cut the French stick into eight thin slices and toast them on both sides. Set aside.

7 Add the monkfish, red mullet and Pernod to the soup and cook for 3–4 minutes, until tender. Add all the clams (with and without shells) and heat through for 30 seconds. Remove the bay leaf and thyme sprigs, and season the soup well. Spoon the rouille on to the toasts. Ladle the soup into bowls, garnish each bowl with a frond of fennel and serve with the toasts.

Energy 728Kcal/3048kJ; Protein 50.2g; Carbohydrate 40g, of which sugars 10.9g; Fat 37.1g, of which saturates 5.4g; Cholesterol 111mg; Calcium 238mg; Fibre 4.7g; Sodium 1940mg.

VERMOUTH SOUP WITH SEARED SCALLOPS, ROCKET OIL AND CAVIAR

SEARED SCALLOPS FORM AN ELEGANT TOWER IN THE CENTRE OF THIS CRÈME DE LA CRÈME OF FINE SOUPS. THE CAVIAR GARNISH LOOKS — AND TASTES — SUPERB.

SERVES 4

INGREDIENTS
    25g/1oz/2 tbsp butter
    5 shallots, sliced
    300ml/½ pint/1¼ cups dry
      white wine
    300ml/½ pint/1¼ cups vermouth
    900ml/1½ pints/3¾ cups fish stock
    300ml/½ pint/1¼ cups double
      (heavy) cream
    300ml/½ pint/1¼ cups single
      (light) cream
    15ml/1 tbsp olive oil
    12 large scallops
    salt and ground black pepper
    15ml/1 tbsp caviar and chopped
      chives, to garnish
For the rocket oil
    115g/4oz rocket leaves
    120ml/4fl oz/½ cup olive oil

1 Prepare the rocket oil first. Process the rocket leaves and olive oil in a food processor or blender for 1–2 minutes to give a green paste. Line a small bowl with a piece of muslin (cheesecloth) and scrape the paste into it. Gather up the muslin and squeeze it well to extract the green, rocket-flavoured oil from the paste. Set aside.

2 Melt the butter in a large pan. Add the shallots and cook over a gentle heat for 8–10 minutes, until soft but not browned. Add the wine and vermouth and boil for 8–10 minutes, until the liquid is reduced to about a quarter of the volume.

3 Add the stock and bring back to the boil. Boil until reduced by half. Pour in the double and single creams, and return to the boil. Reduce the heat and simmer gently for 12–15 minutes, until just thick enough to coat the back of a spoon.

4 Strain through a fine sieve (strainer) into the rinsed pan, and set aside.

5 Heat a ridged griddle or frying pan. Brush the scallops with oil, add them to the pan and sear for 1–2 minutes on each side, until just cooked, when they will be white and tender.

6 Reheat the soup gently, then check and adjust the seasoning to taste.

7 Arrange three scallops, one on top of the other, in the centre of each of four warmed, shallow soup plates. Ladle the hot soup around the scallops and top them with a little of the caviar. Drizzle some rocket oil over the surface of the soup, then sprinkle with chopped chives.

Energy 557Kcal/2303kJ; Protein 13.1g; Carbohydrate 4.7g, of which sugars 2.6g; Fat 48.9g, of which saturates 28.9g; Cholesterol 140mg; Calcium 63mg; Fibre 0.2g; Sodium 148mg.

SCALLOP AND JERUSALEM ARTICHOKE SOUP

THE SUBTLE SWEETNESS OF SCALLOPS COMBINES WELL WITH THE FLAVOUR OF JERUSALEM ARTICHOKES IN THIS ATTRACTIVE AND SATISFYING GOLDEN SOUP.

SERVES 6

INGREDIENTS

  1kg/2¼lb Jerusalem artichokes
  juice of ½ lemon
  115g/4oz/½ cup butter
  1 onion, finely chopped
  600ml/1 pint/2½ cups fish stock
  300ml/½ pint/1¼ cups milk
  generous pinch of saffron threads
  6 large or 12 small scallops, with
    their corals
  150ml/¼ pint/⅔ cup
    whipping cream
  salt and ground white pepper
  45ml/3 tbsp flaked almonds and
    15ml/1 tbsp finely chopped
    fresh chervil, to garnish

1 Working quickly, scrub and peel the Jerusalem artichokes, cut them into 2cm/¾in chunks and drop them into a bowl of cold water which has been acidulated with the lemon juice. This will prevent the prepared artichokes from discolouring.

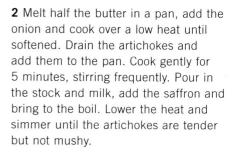

2 Melt half the butter in a pan, add the onion and cook over a low heat until softened. Drain the artichokes and add them to the pan. Cook gently for 5 minutes, stirring frequently. Pour in the stock and milk, add the saffron and bring to the boil. Lower the heat and simmer until the artichokes are tender but not mushy.

3 Meanwhile, carefully separate the scallop corals from the white flesh. Prick the corals and slice each scallop in half horizontally. Heat half the remaining butter in a frying pan, add the scallops and corals and cook very briefly (for about 1 minute) on each side. Dice the scallops and corals, keeping them separate, and set them aside until needed.

4 When the artichokes are cooked, tip the contents of the pan into a blender or food processor. Add half the white scallop meat and purée until very smooth. Return the soup to the clean pan, season with salt and white pepper and keep hot over a low heat while you prepare the garnish.

5 Heat the remaining butter in a frying pan, add the almonds and toss over a medium heat until golden brown. Add the diced corals and cook for about 30 seconds.

6 Stir the cream into the soup and add the remaining diced white scallop meat. Ladle the soup into individual bowls and garnish each serving with the almonds, scallop corals and a sprinkling of chervil.

Energy 408Kcal/1691kJ; Protein 12.8g; Carbohydrate 18.8g, of which sugars 16.4g; Fat 31.9g, of which saturates 17.5g; Cholesterol 86mg; Calcium 150mg; Fibre 4.7g; Sodium 247mg.

LOBSTER BISQUE

BISQUE IS A LUXURIOUS, VELVETY SOUP WHICH CAN BE MADE WITH ANY CRUSTACEANS, SUCH AS CRAB OR SHRIMP. IF LOBSTER IS YOUR FAVOURITE SHELLFISH, THIS VERSION IS FOR YOU.

SERVES 6

INGREDIENTS

500g/1¼lb fresh lobster
75g/3oz/6 tbsp butter
1 onion, chopped
1 carrot, diced
1 celery stick, diced
45ml/3 tbsp brandy
250ml/8fl oz/1 cup dry white wine
1 litre/1¾ pints/4 cups fish stock
15ml/1 tbsp tomato purée (paste)
75g/3oz/scant ½ cup long grain rice
1 fresh bouquet garni
150ml/¼ pint/⅔ cup double (heavy)
  cream, plus extra to garnish
salt, ground white pepper and
  cayenne pepper

1 Cut the lobster into pieces. Melt half the butter in a large pan, add the vegetables and cook over a low heat until soft. Put in the lobster and stir gently until the shells turn red.

2 Pour over the brandy and set it alight. When the flames die down, add the wine and boil until reduced by half. Pour in the fish stock and simmer for 2–3 minutes. Remove the lobster.

3 Stir in the tomato purée and rice, add the bouquet garni and cook until the rice is tender, about 15 minutes. Meanwhile, remove the lobster meat from the shell and return the shells to the pan. Dice the meat and set it aside.

COOK'S TIP
It is best to buy a live lobster, chilling it in the freezer until it is comatose and then killing it just before cooking. If you can't face the procedure, use a cooked lobster; take care not to over-cook the flesh. Stir for only 30–60 seconds.

4 When the rice is cooked, discard all the larger bits of shell. Tip the mixture into a blender or food processor and whizz to a purée. Press the purée through a fine sieve (strainer) over the clean pan. Stir the mixture, then heat until almost boiling. Season with salt, pepper and cayenne, then lower the heat and stir in the cream. Dice the remaining butter and whisk it into the bisque. Add the diced lobster meat and serve at once. If you like, pour a small spoonful of brandy into each soup bowl and swirl in a little extra cream.

Energy 347Kcal/1438kJ; Protein 8.5g; Carbohydrate 12.9g, of which sugars 2.6g; Fat 24.3g, of which saturates 15g; Cholesterol 94mg; Calcium 48mg; Fibre 0.6g; Sodium 195mg.

CLAM CHOWDER

IF FRESH CLAMS ARE HARD TO FIND, USE FROZEN OR CANNED CLAMS FOR THIS CLASSIC RECIPE FROM NEW ENGLAND. LARGE CLAMS SHOULD BE CUT INTO CHUNKY PIECES. RESERVE A FEW CLAMS IN THEIR SHELLS TO GARNISH, IF YOU LIKE. TRADITIONALLY, THE SOUP IS SERVED WITH SAVOURY BISCUITS CALLED SALTINE CRACKERS. YOU SHOULD BE ABLE TO FIND THESE IN ANY GOOD DELICATESSEN.

SERVES 4

INGREDIENTS
  100g/3¾oz salt pork or thinly sliced
    unsmoked bacon, diced
  1 large onion, chopped
  2 potatoes, peeled and cut into cubes
  1 bay leaf
  1 fresh thyme sprig
  300ml/½ pint/1¼ cups milk
  400g/14oz cooked clams, cooking
    liquid reserved
  150ml/¼ pint/⅔ cup double
    (heavy) cream
  salt, ground white pepper and
    cayenne pepper
  finely chopped fresh parsley, to garnish

1 Put the salt pork or unsmoked bacon in a pan, and heat gently, stirring frequently, until the fat runs and the meat is starting to brown. Add the chopped onion and fry over a low heat until softened but not browned.

2 Add the cubed potatoes, the bay leaf and thyme sprig, stir well to coat with fat, then pour in the milk and reserved clam liquid and bring to the boil. Lower the heat and simmer for about 10 minutes, until the potatoes are tender but still firm. Lift out the bay leaf and thyme sprig and discard.

3 Remove the shells from most of the clams. Add all the clams to the pan and season to taste with salt, pepper and cayenne. Simmer gently for 5 minutes more, then stir in the cream. Heat until the soup is very hot, but do not allow it to boil. Pour into a tureen, garnish with the chopped parsley and serve.

CHINESE CRAB AND CORN SOUP

FROZEN WHITE CRAB MEAT WORKS AS WELL AS FRESH IN THIS DELICATELY FLAVOURED SOUP.

SERVES 4

INGREDIENTS
  600ml/1 pint/2½ cups fish or
    chicken stock
  2.5cm/1in piece fresh root ginger,
    peeled and very finely sliced
  400g/14oz can creamed corn
  150g/5oz cooked white crab meat
  15ml/1 tbsp arrowroot or
    cornflour (cornstarch)
  15ml/1 tbsp rice wine or dry sherry
  15–30ml/1–2 tbsp light soy sauce
  1 egg white
  salt and ground white pepper
  shredded spring onions (scallions),
    to garnish

1 Put the stock and ginger in a large pan and bring to the boil. Stir in the creamed corn and bring back to the boil.

2 Switch off the heat and add the crab meat. Put the arrowroot or cornflour in a cup and stir in the rice wine or sherry to make a smooth paste; stir this into the soup. Cook over a low heat for about 3 minutes until the soup has thickened and is slightly glutinous in consistency. Add light soy sauce, salt and white pepper to taste.

3 In a bowl, whisk the egg white to a stiff foam. Gradually fold it into the soup. Ladle the soup into heated bowls, garnish each portion with spring onions and serve.

COOK'S TIP
This soup can be made with whole kernel corn, but creamed corn gives a better texture. If you can't find it in a can, use thawed frozen creamed corn instead; the result will be just as good.

VARIATION
To make prawn (shrimp) and corn soup, substitute 150g/5oz cooked peeled prawns for the crab meat. Chop the peeled prawns roughly and add to the soup at the beginning of step 2.

Top: Energy 392Kcal/1631kJ; Protein 24.3g; Carbohydrate 15.3g, of which sugars 5.7g; Fat 26.3g, of which saturates 15.1g; Cholesterol 136mg; Calcium 191mg; Fibre 0.7g; Sodium 1632mg.
Bottom: Energy 184Kcal/779kJ; Protein 10.6g; Carbohydrate 33.8g, of which sugars 9.9g; Fat 1.6g, of which saturates 0.3g; Cholesterol 27mg; Calcium 51mg; Fibre 1.4g; Sodium 762mg.

CRAB, COCONUT AND CORIANDER SOUP

QUICK AND EASY TO PREPARE, THIS SOUP HAS ALL THE FLAVOURS ASSOCIATED WITH THE BAHIA REGION OF BRAZIL: CREAMY COCONUT, PALM OIL, FRAGRANT CORIANDER AND CHILLI.

SERVES 4

INGREDIENTS
  30ml/2 tbsp olive oil
  1 onion, finely chopped
  1 celery stick, finely chopped
  2 garlic cloves, crushed
  1 fresh red chilli, seeded and
    chopped
  1 large tomato, peeled and chopped
  45ml/3 tbsp chopped fresh
    coriander (cilantro)
  1 litre/1¾ pints/4 cups fresh crab
    or fish stock
  500g/1¼lb crab meat
  250ml/8fl oz/1 cup coconut milk
  30ml/2 tbsp palm oil
  juice of 1 lime
  salt
  hot chilli oil and lime wedges,
    to serve

1 Heat the olive oil in a pan over a low heat. Stir in the onion and celery, and sauté gently for 5 minutes, until softened and translucent. Stir in the garlic and chilli and cook for a further 2 minutes.

2 Add the tomato and half the coriander and increase the heat. Cook, stirring, for 3 minutes, then add the stock. Bring to the boil, then simmer for 5 minutes.

3 Stir the crab, coconut milk and palm oil into the pan and simmer over a very low heat for a further 5 minutes. The consistency should be thick, but not stew-like, so add some water if needed.

4 Stir in the lime juice and remaining coriander, then season with salt to taste. Serve in heated bowls with the chilli oil and lime wedges on the side.

Energy 228Kcal/951kJ; Protein 23.6g; Carbohydrate 5.4g, of which sugars 5g; Fat 12.6g, of which saturates 3.7g; Cholesterol 90mg; Calcium 199mg; Fibre 1.1g; Sodium 767mg.

CHILLI CLAM BROTH

THIS SOUP OF SUCCULENT CLAMS IN A TASTY STOCK COULD NOT BE EASIER TO PREPARE. POPULAR IN COASTAL AREAS OF COLOMBIA, IT MAKES THE PERFECT LUNCH ON A HOT SUMMER'S DAY.

SERVES 6

INGREDIENTS
   30ml/2 tbsp olive oil
   1 onion, finely chopped
   3 garlic cloves, crushed
   2 fresh red chillies, seeded and
      finely chopped
   250ml/8fl oz/1 cup dry white wine
   400ml/14fl oz can plum
      tomatoes, drained
   1 large potato, about 250g/9oz,
      peeled and diced
   400ml/14fl oz/1⅔ cups fish stock
   1.3kg/3lb fresh clams
   15ml/1 tbsp chopped fresh
      coriander (cilantro)
   15ml/1 tbsp chopped fresh flat
      leaf parsley
   salt
   lime wedges, to garnish

1 Heat the oil in a pan. Add the onion and sauté for 5 minutes over a low heat. Stir in the garlic and chillies and cook for a further 2 minutes. Pour in the wine and bring to the boil, then simmer for 2 minutes.

2 Add the tomatoes, diced potato and stock. Bring to the boil, cover and lower the heat so that the soup simmers.

3 Season with salt and cook for 15 minutes, until the potatoes are beginning to break up and the tomatoes have made a rich sauce.

4 Meanwhile, wash the clams thoroughly under cold running water. Gently tap any that are open, and discard them if they do not close.

5 Add the clams to the soup, cover the pan and cook for about 3–4 minutes, or until the clams have opened, then stir in the chopped herbs. Season with salt to taste.

6 Check over the clams and throw away any that have failed to open. Ladle the soup into warmed bowls. Offer the lime wedges separately, to be squeezed over the soup just before eating.

Energy 290Kcal/1217kJ; Protein 36.2g; Carbohydrate 14.1g, of which sugars 3.5g; Fat 7.2g, of which saturates 1.3g; Cholesterol 145mg; Calcium 184mg; Fibre 1.5g; Sodium 2614mg.

LOUISIANA SEAFOOD GUMBO

GUMBO IS A SOUP, BUT IS SERVED OVER RICE AS A MAIN COURSE. IN LOUISIANA, OYSTERS ARE CHEAP AND PROLIFIC, AND WOULD BE USED HERE INSTEAD OF MUSSELS.

SERVES 6

INGREDIENTS
  450g/1lb fresh mussels
  450g/1lb prawns (shrimp), in the shell
  1 cooked crab, about 1kg/2¼lb
  small bunch of parsley, leaves
    chopped and stalks reserved
  150ml/¼ pint/⅔ cup vegetable oil
  115g/4oz/1 cup plain flour
  1 green (bell) pepper, chopped
  1 large onion, chopped
  2 celery sticks, sliced
  3 garlic cloves, finely chopped
  75g/3oz smoked spiced sausage,
    skinned and sliced
  275g/10oz/1½ cups white long
    grain rice
  6 spring onions (scallions), shredded
  cayenne pepper, to taste
  Tabasco sauce, to taste
  salt

1 Wash the mussels in several changes of cold water, pulling away the black "beards". Discard any mussels that are broken or do not close when you tap them firmly.

2 Bring 250ml/8fl oz/1 cup water to the boil in a deep pan. Add the mussels, cover tightly and cook over a high heat, shaking frequently, for 3 minutes. As the mussels open, lift them out with tongs into a sieve (strainer) set over a bowl. Discard any that fail to open. Shell the mussels, discarding the shells. Return the liquid from the bowl to the pan and make the quantity up to 2 litres/3½ pints/8 cups with water.

3 Peel the prawns and set them aside, reserving a few for the garnish. Put the shells and heads into the pan.

4 Remove all the meat from the crab, separating the brown and white meat. Add all the pieces of shell to the pan with 5ml/2 tsp salt.

5 Bring the shellfish stock to the boil, skimming it regularly. When there is no more froth on the surface, add the parsley stalks and simmer for 15 minutes. Cool the stock, then strain it into a measuring jug and make up to 2 litres/3½ pints/8 cups with water.

6 Heat the oil in a heavy-based pan and stir in the flour. Stir constantly over a medium heat with a wooden spoon or whisk until the roux reaches a golden-brown colour. Immediately add the pepper, onion, celery and garlic. Continue cooking for about 3 minutes until the onion is soft. Stir in the sausage. Reheat the stock.

7 Stir the brown crab meat into the roux, then ladle in the hot stock a little at a time, stirring constantly until it has all been smoothly incorporated. Bring to a low boil, partially cover the pan, then simmer the gumbo for 30 minutes.

8 Meanwhile, cook the rice in plenty of lightly salted boiling water until the grains are tender.

9 Add the prawns, mussels, white crab meat and spring onions to the gumbo. Return to the boil and season with salt if necessary, cayenne and a dash or two of Tabasco sauce. Simmer for a further minute, then add the chopped parsley leaves. Serve immediately, ladling the soup over the hot rice in soup plates.

COOK'S TIP
It is vital to stir constantly to darken the roux without burning. Should black specks appear at any stage of cooking, discard the roux and start again. Have the onion, green (bell) pepper and celery ready to add to the roux the minute it reaches the correct golden-brown stage, as this arrests its darkening.

Energy 518Kcal/2161kJ; Protein 23.6g; Carbohydrate 54.8g, of which sugars 2.1g; Fat 22.9g, of which saturates 3.7g; Cholesterol 55mg; Calcium 143mg; Fibre 1.5g; Sodium 728mg.

LEMON AND PUMPKIN MOULES MARINIÈRE

BASED ON THE CLASSIC FRENCH SHELLFISH DISH, THIS MUSSEL SOUP IS THICKENED WITH FRESH PUMPKIN AND FLAVOURED WITH DILL AND LEMON. THIS IS A VERY ELEGANT SOUP, IDEAL FOR SERVING AT A SPECIAL DINNER PARTY.

SERVES 4

INGREDIENTS

1kg/2¼lb fresh mussels
300ml/½ pint/1¼ cups dry
  white wine
1 large lemon
1 bay leaf
15ml/1 tbsp olive oil
1 onion, chopped
1 garlic clove, crushed
675g/1½lb pumpkin or squash
900ml/1½ pints/3¾ cups
  vegetable stock
30ml/2 tbsp chopped fresh dill
salt and ground black pepper
lemon wedges, to serve

1 Scrub the mussels in cold water and pull away the dark hairy beards protruding from the shells. Discard any open mussels that do not shut when tapped sharply, and put the rest into a large pan. Pour in the white wine.

2 Pare large pieces of rind from the lemon and squeeze the juice, then add both to the mussels with the bay leaf. Cover and bring to the boil, then cook for 4–5 minutes, shaking the pan, until all the mussels have opened.

3 Drain the mussels in a colander over a large bowl. Reserve the cooking liquid and the mussels.

4 Remove and discard the lemon rind and the bay leaf, and any mussels that have not opened.

5 When the mussels are cool enough to handle, set aside a few in their shells for the garnish. Remove the remaining mussels from their shells. Strain the reserved cooking liquid through a sieve (strainer) lined with muslin (cheesecloth) to remove any sand or grit.

6 Heat the oil in a large, clean pan. Add the onion and garlic and cook for 4–5 minutes, until softened.

7 Peel the pumpkin, remove the seeds and pith and roughly chop into chunks. Add the pumpkin flesh and the strained mussel cooking liquid to the pan. Bring to the boil and simmer, uncovered, for 5–6 minutes.

8 Pour in the vegetable stock and cook for a further 25–30 minutes, until the pumpkin has almost disintegrated.

9 Cool the soup slightly, then pour into a food processor or blender and process until smooth.

10 Return the soup to the rinsed pan and season well. Stir in the chopped dill and the shelled mussels, then bring just to the boil.

11 Ladle the soup into warmed soup plates and garnish with the reserved mussels in their shells. Serve lemon wedges with the soup.

Energy 161Kcal/678kJ; Protein 14.3g; Carbohydrate 4.2g, of which sugars 3.3g; Fat 4.6g, of which saturates 0.8g; Cholesterol 30mg; Calcium 203mg; Fibre 1.7g; Sodium 161mg.

PROVENÇAL FISH SOUP

THE ADDITION OF RICE MAKES THIS A SUBSTANTIAL MAIN-MEAL SOUP. BASMATI OR THAI RICE HAVE THE BEST FLAVOUR, BUT ANY LONG GRAIN RICE COULD BE USED. IF YOU PREFER A STRONGER TOMATO FLAVOUR, REPLACE THE WHITE WINE WITH EXTRA PASSATA.

SERVES 4–6

INGREDIENTS
    450g/1lb fresh mussels
    about 250ml/8fl oz/1 cup white wine
    675–900g/1½–2lb mixed white fish
        fillets such as monkfish, plaice,
        flounder, cod or haddock
    6 large scallops
    30ml/2 tbsp olive oil
    3 leeks, chopped
    1 garlic clove, crushed
    1 red (bell) pepper, seeded and cut
        into 2.5cm/1in pieces
    1 yellow (bell) pepper, seeded and
        cut into 2.5cm/1in pieces
    175g/6oz fennel bulb, cut into
        4cm/1½in pieces
    400g/14oz can chopped tomatoes
    150ml/¼ pint/⅔ cup passata
        (bottled strained tomatoes)
    about 1 litre/1¾ pints/4 cups
        well-flavoured fish stock
    generous pinch of saffron threads,
        soaked in 15ml/1 tbsp hot water
    175g/6oz/scant 1 cup basmati
        rice, soaked
    8 large raw prawns (shrimp), peeled
        and deveined
    salt and ground black pepper
    30–45ml/2–3 tbsp fresh dill, to garnish

1 Clean the mussels, discarding any that do not close when tapped with a knife. Place them in a heavy pan. Add 90ml/6 tbsp of the wine, cover, bring to the boil over a high heat and cook for about 3 minutes or until all the mussels have opened.

2 Strain, reserving the liquid. Discard any mussels that have not opened. Set aside half the mussels in their shells for the garnish; shell the rest and put them in a bowl.

3 Cut the fish into 2.5cm/1in cubes. Detach the corals from the scallops and slice the white flesh into three or four pieces. Add the scallops to the fish and the corals to the shelled mussels.

4 Heat the olive oil in a pan and fry the leeks and garlic for 3–4 minutes, until softened. Add the pepper chunks and fennel, and fry for 2 minutes more, until just softened.

COOK'S TIP
To make your own fish stock, place about 450g/1lb white fish trimmings – bones, heads, but not gills – in a large pan. Add a chopped onion, carrot, bay leaf, parsley sprig, 6 peppercorns and a piece of pared lemon rind. Pour in 1.2 litres/2 pints/5 cups water, bring to the boil, then simmer gently for 25–30 minutes. Strain through muslin (cheesecloth).

5 Add the tomatoes, passata, stock, saffron water, mussel liquid and wine. Season and cook for 5 minutes. Drain the rice, stir it into the mixture, cover and simmer for 10 minutes.

6 Carefully stir in the white fish and cook over a low heat for 5 minutes. Add the prawns, cook for 2 minutes, then add the scallop corals and shelled mussels and cook for 2–3 minutes more, until all the fish is tender. Add a little extra white wine or stock if needed. Spoon into warmed soup dishes, top with mussels in their shells and sprinkle with the dill. Serve immediately.

Energy 568Kcal/2385kJ; Protein 59.9g; Carbohydrate 50.5g, of which sugars 12.9g; Fat 9.7g, of which saturates 1.6g; Cholesterol 163mg; Calcium 182mg; Fibre 5.9g; Sodium 418mg.

SPANISH SEAFOOD SOUP

THIS HEARTY SOUP CONTAINS ALL THE COLOURS AND FLAVOURS OF THE MEDITERRANEAN. IT IS SUBSTANTIAL ENOUGH TO SERVE AS A MAIN COURSE, BUT CAN ALSO BE DILUTED WITH A LITTLE WHITE WINE AND WATER TO MAKE AN ELEGANT APPETIZER FOR SIX.

SERVES 4

INGREDIENTS

675g/1½lb raw prawns (shrimp),
  in the shell
900ml/1½ pints/3¾ cups cold water
1 onion, chopped
1 celery stick, chopped
1 bay leaf
45ml/3 tbsp olive oil
2 slices stale bread, crusts removed
1 small onion, finely chopped
1 large garlic clove, chopped
2 large tomatoes, halved
½ large green (bell) pepper,
  finely chopped
500g/1¼lb cockles (small clams)
  or mussels, cleaned
juice of 1 lemon
45ml/3 tbsp chopped fresh parsley
5ml/1 tsp paprika
salt and ground black pepper

COOK'S TIP
Good fish and shellfish dishes are normally based on proper fish stock (including the juices saved from opening mussels). This is equivalent to the French *court bouillon*, and takes 30 minutes' simmering. The method used here is one of the quickest, because the prawn heads come off neatly, and the rest of the shells are simply added as they are removed.

1 Pull the heads off the prawns and put them in a pan with the cold water. Add the onion, celery and bay leaf and simmer for 20–25 minutes.

2 Peel the prawns, adding the shells to the stock as you go along.

3 Heat the oil in a wide, deep flameproof casserole and fry the bread slices quickly, then reserve them. Fry the onion until it is soft, adding the garlic towards the end.

4 Scoop the seeds out of the tomatoes and discard. Chop the flesh and add to the casserole with the green pepper. Fry briefly, stirring occasionally.

5 Strain the stock into the casserole and bring to the boil. Check over the cockles or mussels, discarding any that are open or damaged.

6 Add half the cockles or mussels to the stock. When open, use a slotted spoon to transfer some of them out on to a plate. Remove the mussels or cockles from the shells and discard the shells. (You should end up having discarded about half of the shells.) Meanwhile, repeat the process to cook the remaining cockles or mussels.

7 Return the cockles or mussels to the soup and add the prawns. Add the bread, torn into little pieces, and the lemon juice and chopped parsley.

8 Season to taste with paprika, salt and pepper and stir gently to dissolve the bread. Serve at once in soup bowls, providing a plate for the empty shells.

Energy 234Kcal/978kJ; Protein 23.3g; Carbohydrate 11.3g, of which sugars 4.5g; Fat 10.9g, of which saturates 1.7g; Cholesterol 67mg; Calcium 216mg; Fibre 2g; Sodium 1193mg.

SAFFRON SEAFOOD SOUP

FILLING YET NOT TOO RICH, THIS GOLDEN SOUP WILL MAKE A DELICIOUS MEAL ON EARLY SUMMER EVENINGS, SERVED WITH LOTS OF HOT FRESH BREAD AND A GLASS OF FRUITY, DRY WHITE WINE. WHEN MUSSELS ARE NOT AVAILABLE USE PRAWNS (SHRIMP) IN THEIR SHELLS INSTEAD.

SERVES 4

INGREDIENTS

1 parsnip, quartered
2 carrots, quartered
1 onion, quartered
2 celery sticks, quartered
2 smoked bacon rashers (strips), rinds removed
juice of 1 lemon
pinch of saffron strands
450g/1lb fish heads
450g/1lb fresh mussels, scrubbed
1 leek, shredded
2 shallots, finely chopped
30ml/2 tbsp chopped dill, plus extra sprigs to garnish
450g/1lb haddock, skinned and boned
3 egg yolks
30ml/2 tbsp double (heavy) cream
salt and ground black pepper

1 Put the parsnip, carrots, onion, celery, bacon, lemon juice, saffron strands and fish heads in a large pan with 900ml/1½ pints/3¾ cups water and bring to the boil. Boil gently for about 20 minutes or until reduced by half.

COOK'S TIP
Fish stock freezes well and will keep for up to 6 months.

2 Discard any mussels that are open and don't close when tapped sharply. Add the rest to the pan of stock. Cook for about 4 minutes, until they have opened. Strain the soup and return the liquid to the pan. Discard any unopened mussels, then remove the remaining ones from their shells and set aside.

3 Add the leeks and shallots to the soup, bring to the boil and cook for 5 minutes. Add the dill and haddock, and simmer for a further 5 minutes until the fish is tender. Remove the haddock, using a slotted spoon, then flake it into a bowl, using a fork.

4 In another bowl, whisk together the eggs and double cream. Whisk in a little of the hot soup, then whisk the mixture back into the hot but not boiling liquid. Continue to whisk for several minutes as it heats through and thickens slightly, but do not let it boil.

5 Add the flaked haddock and mussels to the soup and check the seasoning. Garnish with tiny sprigs of dill and serve piping hot.

Energy 278Kcal/1167kJ; Protein 33.2g; Carbohydrate 9.8g, of which sugars 8.5g; Fat 12.1g, of which saturates 4.8g; Cholesterol 222mg; Calcium 147mg; Fibre 3.4g; Sodium 377mg.

SAFFRON-FLAVOURED MUSSEL SOUP

THERE'S A FRAGRANT TASTE OF THE SEA OFF THE SPANISH COAST IN THIS CREAMY SOUP FILLED WITH THE JET BLACK SHELLS OF PLUMP MUSSELS. SAFFRON GOES WELL WITH SHELLFISH, AND GIVES THE SOUP A LOVELY PALE YELLOW COLOUR.

SERVES 4

INGREDIENTS
  1.5kg/3–3½lb fresh mussels
  600ml/1 pint /2½ cups white wine
  a few fresh parsley stalks
  50g/2oz/¼ cup butter
  2 leeks, finely chopped
  2 celery sticks, finely chopped
  1 carrot, chopped
  2 garlic cloves, chopped
  large pinch of saffron strands
  600ml/1 pint/2½ cups double
    (heavy) cream
  3 tomatoes, peeled, seeded
    and chopped
  salt and ground black pepper
  30ml/2 tbsp chopped fresh chives,
    to garnish

1 Clean the mussels and pull away the beards. Put into a large pan with the wine and parsley stalks. Cover, bring to the boil and cook for 4–5 minutes, shaking the pan occasionally, until the mussels have opened. Discard the stalks and any unopened mussels.

2 Drain the mussels over a large bowl, reserving the cooking liquid. When cool enough to handle, remove about half of the cooked mussels from their shells. Set aside with the remaining mussels in their shells.

COOK'S TIP
The most efficient way to clean fresh mussels is to scrub them under cold running water, using a stiff brush to remove any sand or dirt.

3 Melt the butter in a large pan, add the leeks, celery, carrot and garlic, and cook for 5 minutes until softened. Strain the reserved mussel cooking liquid through a fine sieve (strainer) or muslin (cheesecloth). Add to the pan and cook over a high heat for 8–10 minutes to reduce the liquid slightly. Strain into a clean pan, add the saffron strands and cook for 1 minute.

4 Add the cream and bring back to the boil. Season well. Add all the mussels and the tomatoes and heat gently to warm through. Ladle the soup into four bowls, then scatter with the chopped chives and serve immediately.

Energy 1054Kcal/4359kJ; Protein 22.8g; Carbohydrate 7.5g, of which sugars 7.4g; Fat 93.4g, of which saturates 57.1g; Cholesterol 277mg; Calcium 327mg; Fibre 1.4g; Sodium 372mg.

LAKSA LEMAK

THIS SPICY MALAYSIAN SOUP IS NOT A DISH YOU CAN THROW TOGETHER IN 20 MINUTES, BUT IT IS MARVELLOUS PARTY FOOD. GUESTS SPOON NOODLES INTO WIDE SOUP BOWLS, ADD ACCOMPANIMENTS OF THEIR CHOICE, TOP UP WITH SOUP AND THEN TAKE A FEW PRAWN CRACKERS TO NIBBLE.

SERVES 6

INGREDIENTS

675g/1½lb small clams
2 × 400ml/14fl oz cans coconut milk
50g/2oz ikan bilis (dried anchovies)
900ml/1½ pints/3¾ cups water
115g/4oz shallots, finely chopped
4 garlic cloves, chopped
6 macadamia nuts or blanched
    almonds, chopped
3 lemon grass stalks, root trimmed
90ml/6 tbsp sunflower oil
1cm/½in cube shrimp paste
    (blachan)
25g/1oz/¼ cup mild curry powder
a few curry leaves
2–3 aubergines (eggplants), total
    weight about 675g/1¼lb, trimmed
675g/1½lb peeled prawns (shrimp)
10ml/2 tsp sugar
1 head Chinese leaves, thinly sliced
115g/4oz/2 cups beansprouts, rinsed
2 spring onions (scallions) chopped
50g/2oz crispy fried onions
115g/4oz fried tofu
675g/1½lb mixed noodles (laksa,
    mee and behoon) or one type only
prawn crackers, to serve

1 Scrub the clams and then put in a large pan with 1cm/½in water. Bring to the boil, cover and steam for 3–4 minutes until all the clams have opened. Drain. Make up the coconut milk to 1.2 litres/2 pints/5 cups with water. Put the ikan bilis in a pan and add the measured amount of water. Bring to the boil and simmer for 20 minutes.

2 Meanwhile, put the shallots, garlic and nuts into a mortar. Cut off the lower 5cm/2in of two of the lemon grass stalks, chop finely and add to the mortar. Pound the mixture to a paste.

3 Heat the oil in a large heavy pan, add the shallot paste and fry until the mixture gives off a rich aroma. Bruise the remaining lemon grass stalk and add to the pan. Toss over the heat to release its flavour. Mix the shrimp paste (blachan) and curry powder to a paste with a little of the coconut milk, add to the pan and toss the mixture over the heat for 1 minute, stirring all the time, and keeping the heat low. Stir in the remaining coconut milk. Add the curry leaves and allow the mixture to simmer while you prepare the accompaniments.

4 Strain the stock into a pan. Discard the ikan bilis, bring to the boil, then add the aubergines; cook for about 10 minutes or until tender and the skins can be peeled off easily. Lift out of the stock, peel and cut into thick strips.

5 Arrange the aubergines on a serving platter. Sprinkle the prawns with sugar, add to the stock and cook for 2–4 minutes, until they turn pink. Remove and place next to the aubergines. Add the Chinese leaves, beansprouts, spring onions and crispy fried onions to the platter, along with the clams.

6 Gradually stir the remaining ikan bilis stock into the pan of soup and bring to the boil. Rinse the fried tofu in boiling water, cool slightly and squeeze to remove excess oil. Cut each piece in half and add to the soup. Lower the heat to a very gentle simmer.

7 Cook the noodles according to the instructions on the packet, drain and pile in a dish. Remove the curry leaves and lemon grass from the soup. Place the noodles, soup and the platter of seafood and vegetables on the table, along with a bowl of prawn crackers. Guests can then help themselves.

VARIATION

You could substitute mussels for clams if you prefer. Scrub them thoroughly, removing any beards, and cook them in lightly salted water until they open. Like clams, discard any that remain closed.

COOK'S TIPS

• Ikan bilis are small fried fish tossed with chilli, vinegar and sugar.
• Dried shrimp or prawn paste, also called blachan, is sold in small blocks and is available from Asian stores.

INDEX